CHURCH-STATE ISSUES IN AMERICA TODAY

CHURCH-STATE ISSUES IN AMERICA TODAY

Volume 2: Religion, Family, and Education

Edited by
Ann W. Duncan and Steven L. Jones

PRAEGER PERSPECTIVES

Westport, Connecticut
London

Library of Congress Cataloging-in-Publication Data

Church-state issues in America today / edited by Ann W. Duncan and Steven L. Jones.
    p. cm.
    Includes bibliographical references and index.
    ISBN 978-0-275-99367-2 (set : alk. paper) — ISBN 978-0-275-99368-9 (vol. 1 : alk. paper) — ISBN 978-0-275-99369-6 (vol. 2 : alk. paper) — ISBN 978-0-275-99370-2 (vol. 3 : alk. paper)
    1. Church and state—United States. 2. United States—Church history. I. Duncan, Ann W., 1978–   II. Jones, Steven L., 1971–
BR516.C4925   2008
322'.10973—dc22   2007030692

British Library Cataloguing in Publication Data is available.

Copyright © 2008 by Ann W. Duncan and Steven L. Jones

All rights reserved. No portion of this book may be reproduced, by any process or technique, without the express written consent of the publisher.

Library of Congress Catalog Card Number: 2007030692
ISBN: 978-0-275-99367-2 (set)
      978-0-275-99368-9 (vol. 1)
      978-0-275-99369-6 (vol. 2)
      978-0-275-99370-2 (vol. 3)

First published in 2008

Praeger Publishers, 88 Post Road West, Westport, CT 06881
An imprint of Greenwood Publishing Group, Inc.
www.praeger.com

Printed in the United States of America

The paper used in this book complies with the Permanent Paper Standard issued by the National Information Standards Organization (Z39.48–1984).

10 9 8 7 6 5 4 3 2 1

Contents

	Preface Ann W. Duncan and Steven L. Jones	vii
1	The Family and Religion Gordon A. Babst	1
2	The Creation-Evolution Debate in the American Public School Classroom Jason R. Edwards	17
3	Freedom, Commitment, and the Challenges of Pledging of Allegiance in America's Public Schools Lee Canipe	47
4	Student Religious Expression within Public Schools William Lester	73
5	Free Speech and the Protection of Children Mark Edward Gammon	103
6	School Vouchers in America Michael Coulter	127
7	Religion and Higher Education J. David Holcomb	149
	Appendix: Selected Cases	179
	About the Editors and Contributors	189
	Index	193

Preface
Ann W. Duncan and Steven L. Jones

In 1925, the U.S. Supreme Court struck down an Oregon law requiring all children to attend public schools. The Court's decision in *Pierce v. Society of Sisters* guaranteed the rights of religious parents to send their children to a school that ratified their own faith commitments. Guaranteeing the right of a religious education did not, however, put an end to the conflicts between churches, families, and the state. Parents, the Court recognized, must prepare their children for what it famously called "additional obligations" beyond the basic literacy required for citizenship. Almost a century later, those additional obligations remain controversial. How does an institution charged with the moral and intellectual formation of the next generation balance the rights of parents and their children to adhere to a religious worldview while at the same time not endorsing any one worldview, religious or secular, at the expense of another? This second volume addresses those intersections of religion and government that concern parental rights, children, and the role of religion and religious observance in the schools. These chapters cover a variety of school settings and a variety of aspects of school life—from student expression to the use of religious language by the school and by private individuals and groups. All of the chapters point to children and education as key points of conflict in debates over the proper relationships between religion and government.

As Gordon Babst describes in his introductory chapter, the relationship between religion, family, and the law has evolved over time and reflects an American understanding of the family and school as the formative influences in the lives of children. The next three chapters address specific questions about the role of religion in public schools. Jason Edwards surveys the historical and current debate over creationism and evolutionism, highlighting the complex history of controversy over public school curriculum. Lee Canipe discusses the history of the Pledge of Allegiance and some of the issues underlying its current controversial nature—most notably the sometimes conflicting concerns of avoiding coercion in schools and promoting national unity and identity. In a chapter on student religious expression in public schools, William Lester discusses the challenge for school administrators to both maintain religious freedom and free speech and to avoid the establishment of religion in the public schools.

Discussing another free speech issue, Mark Gammon describes the growing concerns about the protection of children from untoward influence in the context of current technological innovations such as the Internet and the implications of these concerns for schools and public libraries. Moving to governmental support for parents choosing to put their children in non-public schools, Michael Coulter discusses the origins and history of the school choice movement in the context of school voucher programs, the use of tax credits, and the resulting challenges to the Establishment Clause. The final chapter by J. David Holcomb discusses many of the issues above in the context of higher education. Addressing both religious and non-religious public and private colleges and universities, Holcomb highlights court cases and controversies covering everything from governmental funding to curriculum to school funding of religious groups.

While each of these chapters highlight particular concerns and controversies, each issue and, indeed, each side of each issue—from an atheist opponent to the Pledge of Allegiance to an advocate of creationist curriculum in the public schools—reflect a passionate concern for the shaping of their children and a continued belief that the schools play a vital role in this formation. For this reason, debates over the role of religion in public schools will likely continue well into the future.

1

The Family and Religion
Gordon A. Babst

The family is an apparently universal historical social institution strongly associated with the household, parenting, lineage, inter-generationality, and personal identity. Often regarded as the central institution in any society, its construction and sustainability have been seen as pivotal to the enduring success of any society, and so what is meant by the family entails consulting the entire range of human inquiry, from anthropology to zoology. In this volume, attention is focused on the role of religion in the construction and maintenance of the family and our understanding of it. More specifically, this volume will examine the nexus of religion and the family in contemporary American society, with attention to the changing nature of the family as precipitated by changes in the individuals who are considered to make up a family, such as same-sex-headed households raising children. Here we provide some general historical background, discuss the functions of the family, and then approach the connections between the contemporary family and religion in the light of the individual interests and the social interest wrapped up in the family.

It will become clear that the family refers to either an actual family consisting of the persons related to each other (or said to be related to each other as family), or to a social construction involving religious elements that can be seen ideologically such that, seen in this way, some persons who relate to each other as family are not at all seen to be a genuine family and so may be disregarded, effaced, or stigmatized. It will also become clear that the family, once tradition-bound and socially-regulated, may evolve into a new site of individual freedom.

The freedom that is to be won, however, will emerge from the resolution of conflicts with supporters of a "traditional pro-family" agenda, a contest that must be engaged because traditional concepts of the family in the West, which have been informed in the main by religious sources, continue to underpin the law and so can be enforced on everyone, regardless of any particular family's fit with the law. In the law, then, is already ensconced a normative vision of the family such that to raise the issue of same-sex marriage, for example, is to engage in conversation with people of different views who have tradition and law on their side, and to implicate church/state issues as well. Likewise, issues such as providing parents with vouchers to use towards the education of their children in private schools, including sectarian ones, not only implicate church/state issues up front but may also intrude on many a family's personal choices that may not promote their or their children's liberty.

In this introductory chapter we will steer clear of specific legal arguments, and focus attention on the general relationship between religion, families, and the law, which subsequent chapters will fill-in with greater detail and analysis. The next section presents some significant perspectives from the history of the institution of the family in the West, focusing attention on understandings that are grounded in Hebrew and Christian biblical texts, Greek and Roman social norms, and modern practice in liberal-democratic societies such as the United States.

HISTORICAL BACKGROUND

The family is present in a number of places in the ancient Hebrew Bible, though it presents no consistent understanding of the family and its passages are far less explicit about the family than they are about sexual relations. While some contemporary commentators tend always to see in it specific, unequivocal meanings, even a literal reading presents a great variety of understandings about the family and its construction. For example, the Old Testament more than once seems to condone incest (e.g., Abraham and Sarah had the same father) and a married spouse having conjugal relations with an outside person for the purpose of conceiving a child, thereby revealing that the family is the site of childbearing, though not necessarily of exclusive monogamy irrespective of children. And for a man to take many wives also features favorably, as befits this definitively patriarchal society.[1]

Humankind is commanded to be fruitful and multiply and also to honor one's parents; hence, a relationship between succeeding generations is implicitly an aspect of the family in this tradition. One might even include the family of man as one understanding that is presented in the Old Testament, alongside understanding tribes as family, and heads of families understanding their extended families as tribes. One might also speculate that the Old Testament presents an alternative understanding of the family of man as split into different tribes based on the moral conduct of some of the descendents of Adam and Eve, an understanding that later contributed to the justification for the enslavement of native Africans in the American South, regarded as the descendants of Ham.[2]

Beyond ancient biblical sources, anthropologists indicate that ancient peoples most likely shared childrearing rather than leaving this in the hands of individuals or couples, and that lineage was determined matrilineally, at least for hunter-gatherer societies prior to the agricultural revolution that prompted people to settle into permanent villages and cities. Suffice it to say that a broader understanding of the family probably obtained among ancient peoples and was reified in their religious beliefs more than popular images or narrow readings of one or another ancient text may suggest. Nonetheless, written records tend to provide clearer descriptions of family life, or at least of the ideals of family life that may have been the prism through which the family was viewed.

The ancient Greek understanding of the family seems less based on religion than on social mores regarding gender roles and socioeconomic status. In Greek philosophical thought, intellectual or civic friendship was elevated above family. The wealthy Greek family in the classical age consisted of a man who lived most of his life in the company of other men, engaged in public affairs or in the military; a wife who had no public life outside of perhaps marketing, and certainly no political or social life outside of her circle of female friends; children; and slaves who did the household chores. The Greek pantheon does not suggest any preferred family structure, nor did its Roman successor. However, the classical Roman family with socioeconomic status considered itself more as part of a noble family dynasty than did the Greek.

Republican and then Imperial Rome was ruled more by male heirs in important families than through a male citizen's individual participation in collective decision-making, as was the case in old democratic Athens. The practice of exchanging wedding rings is said to have originated in Roman times, though then the ring was likely iron and was placed by the husband around the wife's neck, by which she was led from her birth family to her new family residence, a symbolic yet unambiguous indication of the husband's power over her. In Roman times the family meant everyone in the household or *familia*, whatsoever kin and servants happened to be included in the residence. This understanding continued into medieval Europe, though a winnowing of the extended family gradually occurred. Again, generalizations serve to illustrate but necessarily hide from view a great variety of understandings and practices associated with the family, especially at different levels in complex societies.

The advent of Christianity and the New Testament that chronicled its beginnings and counseled the early Christians was written in an intellectual culture that was Greek, in a region that was under Roman administration, and, of course, expressed continuity with a Jewish heritage even as it broke away from it. It was the view of the family articulated by several early Christian authors that has anchored the predominant tradition in the West ever since, a view that attempts to inscribe some explicit conformity between the practice of the family and religious beliefs in their writings.[3]

The New Testament presents the "Holy Family," consisting of a virgin woman, who is the mother of the Christ child, and her husband, who is not the father. Other women are presented who are presumably sexually active, childless, and husbandless, yet have the potential to be reborn in a new spirit that includes forgiveness for their past transgressions. The Christian New Testament generally is interpreted as establishing a new social order that stands in sharp contrast to its original context, as well as any context the early Christians found themselves in. For example, St. Paul wrote with ardour to persuade early Christians to turn away from their customary sexual behavior, because to break the connection between this most intimate, though often public, aspect of one's life and one's pagan religion was to effect a radical departure from the old and to make possible and facilitate an embrace of the new. Later, St. Augustine of Hippo, whose early life trajectory self-admittedly indulged his sexual appetite and youthful disdain for a more settled family life, upon conversion to Christianity became one of the staunchest advocates for the chaste life or, failing that, monogamy between one man and one woman. After all, the model for conception of a child occurred without sexual intimacy and did not involve the woman's husband, which may have as yet un-mined implications today for the religious acceptability of artificial insemination, surrogate motherhood, and other technological innovations that are transforming our understanding of the family.

While Augustine's restrictive prescriptions for marital bliss did not lend themselves to successful propagation of the species and maintaining an ongoing and expanding community, they nevertheless became central to the Christian vision of both sex and the family, a vision that has survived to this day. The form and nature of family life was connected to salvation, and thus issues of righteousness and transgressions assumed cosmic significance and were the concern of the entire society. The model family was not merely one man and one woman married to each other, but this pair in the image of the ideal union between Christ and the Church, reflecting a love that should be emulated by each individual and in which spirit the two persons are brought together in holy matrimony. Any fleshy desires between the married spouses were condemned, as the only purpose of carnal relations was to beget children, the sole and rightly desired outcome that redeemed the sex involved. Augustine's views were echoed by later Christian and non-Christian thinkers in the Western tradition, who had both this early Christian and the still earlier Greek and Roman gendered understandings of the family to consult. The family in the West has been tied to the template of a heterosexual monogamous union in which privilege resides in the husband, while the wife is bonded to domestic affairs, the realm of necessity, and not freedom, as the ancient Greek philosopher Aristotle would say.

The modern social contract tradition, which began in the seventeenth century, was conceived in and meant to apply to a society in which religion had a strong presence, even if conceived of as a civic religion. Arguably, the social contract theorists did not address injustice within the family, leaving it in an emerging zone of privacy and so shielded from the state, the better to carry on its functions. Status within the family continued to determine status and roles in civil society and to curtail the political rights of women, whether or not they were mothers or wives. Hence, women, for example, were expected to be subservient to their husbands, their voice covered by his in any public issue such as property rights and politics, and this was reflected in the law. The heterosexual family unit remained intact under social contract theory, and alternative familial arrangements were socially and legally taboo. Given the simultaneous emergence of the capitalist economy that was premised on independent, individual workers, the male member of the heterosexual family, the husband and father, became a wage earner, while the wife and mother became even more ensconced in the domestic sphere.[4]

Protestant theology supported this division of labor, and it articulated a vision of partnership between the spouses in the service of their community and of their God that sustained them through hard times and helped to explain the blessings of good times. Nonetheless, the division of labor within the family continued to undermine its capacity to promote the freedom of individuals and the authority of a secular sphere that could be free of religious influence. Matrimony's conjugal unity and common household have hidden distinct juridical personalities, an issue of secular inequality that has been less bothersome because of the imprimatur of religion, which, among other things, sanctified the free reproductive labor of women, making it central to their role in society.

It has been only in the last two centuries that individuals, utilizing and daring to expand the civil liberties available to them, have asserted a right to love whomever they please and to base the decision to marry, for example, on the basis of love, rather than on their or other persons' interests in property, family dynasty, or class. In the nineteenth century, several prominent civil libertarians attempted to raise public awareness of the intolerance of society towards persons whose sexuality, now an aspect of an individual's identity, was different from the norm, and to encourage the burgeoning social science research into human sexuality. These early writers and researchers hoped that in the face of the new, more scientific approach to understanding the social nature of human beings, the older understandings based in religion and popular morality would recede and fade from view.[5] These pioneers further hoped that reform in the law and in people's attitudes towards acceptable familial relations would change in the face of empirical research findings.

However, religious constraints continued to govern as regards the permissibility of whom to love or with whom it is acceptable to form a family unit, such that inter-religious families and mixed-race families remained off-limits, though these constraints slowly fell from favor while plural marriages and non-heterosexual relationships have remained widely censored by mainstream religion unto this day.[6] In the United States, it was not until after mobilization for World War II that many Americans encountered and got to know one another's differences as well as new points of commonality, breaking down the ignorance that racial bias, religious beliefs, and general unfamiliarity had long held in place in the face of individual desires to form bonds with each other across various, often legally-sanctioned, divides.

FUNCTIONS OF THE FAMILY

Given the cursory historical overview presented earlier, the family has been understood in many ways, both within the same general tradition and also in the light of different religious beliefs. One constant appears to be a concern for blood ties, which have been regarded as determinative of any or all of the following: personal identity, family relationships, property rights, socioeconomic status, and political privilege. Religion has served to sanctify and endorse an approach to blood ties that has vested familial power in the father and political decision-making in the male citizenry, thus assuring everyone of the legitimacy of blood ties as understood and administered in this legally sanctioned way. The stable family provided the institutional structure to raise children, and this ultimate function of the family was reflected in religious doctrine, practice, and belief. Yet as historical research has shown, the nurturing of children does not require the confines of the family and has occurred under the auspices of alternative arrangements.

The functions of the family closely resemble those of marriage, though it provides a larger vehicle in support of the social order and, in turn, a more convenient site for the administration of law and policy over more people than does the institution of marriage. The primary function of the family in the western tradition was that prescribed to it by religion; namely, the begetting of children and their rearing in a religious environment to ensure the continuance of a religious tradition. Non-heterosexual relationships did not signify legitimacy with respect to this function, owing to a strong religious sanction against them and against any sexually deviant practice. Even childless marriages were regarded as abnormal and deficient, given that they did not fulfill the family's function of producing offspring, future workers, soldiers, or citizens. The family has always been over-determined by religious ideology and relationships of social, political, and economic power. Rationales grounded in biological imperative have dovetailed with, but do not overlap, the predominant understanding and function of the family, and they have never provided the justification for any particular family form.

Tying both family and marriage to children would seem to suggest that before having a child, a married couple is not yet a family, and that after any and all children are grown and have left the household, they return to not being a family, or not quite a family. Yet, in all societies there have been children who have no parents for one reason or another, and who nonetheless need parenting. Opening up parenthood to non-biological children has greatly benefited the social welfare, though once this step away from the traditional functional family has been made—such as in the nineteenth-century when the family came to include adopted children—the next step to allowing single persons or same-sex couples to adopt children and so too to be considered families is made more possible. However, these latter moves, which are on the increase in American society today, have been met with swift and stern religious objection.

Initially, political activism stemmed from individuals working from within divergent groups such as the women's movement and the gay and lesbian movement, taking their cues from the Civil Rights movement of the 1960s. These activists argued for greater freedom and privacy rights for women in general and also for sexual minorities. For women, the freedom sought was based in equality and recognized the inequality confronting many women who chose not to lead their lives in the traditional family setting. For sexual minorities, the freedom sought was also based in equality but was overtly pitched as a sexual liberation from old norms regarding sexual activity and the family structure and so directly challenged traditional normative understandings. Thus there arose in the 1970s a powerful reaction grounded in religious fundamentalism that sought via political means to corral both the women's liberation and gay and lesbian liberation movements, reverse their gains, and return the United States to an earlier era of stable family life and conformity with traditional sexual mores.[7] The very nature and function of the family and the purpose of human sexual powers were being contested very publicly, and many religious believers were challenged to engage with each other and their traditions to come to an understanding of themselves and their apparent political opponents. While many denominations chose to remain true to their traditions, a few broke away from them and, after a process of internal debate, came to affirm alternative family forms and expressions of sexuality, recasting old issues such as sex outside of marriage and gay and lesbian families as opportunities to expand their religious horizons and embrace social change.[8]

On the one hand, single parenthood, especially if by choice, indicates heterosexual activity outside the parameters of marriage, while on the other hand, same-sex parenthood denotes impermissible sexual activity outside the parameters of marriage. New technology that has made it possible to have children without sexual activity challenges both marital and familial norms and has evoked in the minds of some religionists the specter of Frankenstein, of attempting godlike powers. Curiously, the trend of single and married individuals who have relied on technology in order to have children and so form a family has proven to be far less of a morals issue overall than has same-sex marriage or gay parenting. Restricting the analysis to the naturalness of the recourse to technology, however, would seem to warrant the condemnation of unnatural technological intervention no less than putatively unnatural sexual relations between two persons.

The reason for this distinction is because heterosexual couples who resort to technology are thought to do so because of an unfortunate physical failing on their part, not because of a failure to want to conform and meet the traditional expectations of forming a family, while single individuals, by themselves, do not raise the specter of homosexuality, though single motherhood challenges traditional gender roles.[9] Legal recognition of same-sex marriage and acceptance of gay parenting, by contrast, implies new forms of the family, new types of household, and seems to break the link between sexual activity and parenting, lineage, intergenerationality, and identifying the community as a continuing iteration of a cherished tradition, one that assertions of political power have always secured until individuals were freed from the bonds of tradition to form their own, by their own lights.[10] To allow—and not condemn—this radical experimentation is to threaten how "we" understand "our" values and purpose on this Earth and to displace "our" community as privileged judge of right and wrong, one guided by longstanding religious insights. The family today is a site of contestation, where religious conservative adherents of tradition and their followers confront younger religious believers and many others who would inaugurate new traditions or recall and emphasize different aspects of the old, both sides simultaneously exercising and negotiating their freedom very close to that most cherished place of all, home.

THE CONTEMPORARY FAMILY

The contemporary American family is less defined by religion than it once was, and people are less inclined to accept legal discrimination against alternative family structures than once they were. The factors that have lead to the decline of the traditional understandings of the family and its functions include different family formations involving both heterosexual and non-heterosexual individuals and couples. The notion that the traditional family headed by the father and husband must be maintained because only through the generation of children within this institution can we be assured that the male head of household is heterosexual (and so the privileged positions in the social and political hierarchy will be occupied only by heterosexual males, in keeping with traditional religious understandings) is no longer widely held, though belief in it remains strong. The structure of the family has become more a matter of choice, expressing the liberty of individuals, than a matter of conformity to tradition. This has made possible new performances of family life, some in keeping with tradition, some not. Importantly, the unitary vantage point from which any family is judged as morally worthy, a vantage point overly determined by religion, has lost its hegemony. For example, not allowing a gay person to exercise his or her right to marry the adult individual he or she chooses because of religious tradition is increasingly viewed as illegitimate on the part of the law and the wider community. Still, some statutes from an earlier era will continue to remain on the books until people get around to addressing them and taking action. Hence, though the pace of change has picked up, there is still a back-and-forth articulation of tradition and revision with respect to legal and cultural understandings of the family.

The Law, Religion, and the Family

In the United States the traditional patriarchal family, a unitary arrangement in the law, is no longer the legal norm, though American law has been slower to adapt to twenty-first century practice than has the law in most western European countries.[11] While for the Supreme Court marriage remains a fundamental human right, one originally grounded in a religious view of marriage that was explicitly referenced in its early marriage cases, today divorce, childbearing by single individuals, adoption by gay or lesbian persons, and legal provision for surrogate motherhood—among other contemporary practices—are provided for in the law and increasingly utilized by individuals who are increasingly wont to form and reform their families as per their individual wishes. And these innovations in practice and in the law are reflected at the international level in legal conventions among countries that provide for marriage across a variety of divides, international adoption, divorce, and enforcement of maintenance obligations such as spousal and child support.

Arrival at this contemporary state of affairs with respect to the nexus between religion and the family is built, however, upon a slow but steady diminution in the traditional patriarchal family as the regulative ideal for the law, and so too as its anchor in religion. Oddly enough, just as the patriarchal aspect of the family is receding, the cultural understanding of fathers as parents in their own right and the legal relationship between father and child is arising. This suggests that patriarchy was always less about the practice of fatherhood and more about power and control legitimated by religion. In practice, with respect to the politics of gay and lesbian rights, which tends to be considered a morality issue, a politician's religious affiliation has been found to be an important predictor of his or her vote on any legislation, a backhanded way in which religion has influenced the law, in turn restricting or expanding the public space for experimentation in family forms. Religion also certainly plays a powerful up-front role with respect to anti-gay lobbying, influencing legislators without regard to their own personal religious or secular views.

Religion in the United States historically has conditioned who may marry, whom one may marry, and who may adopt which children. Given that marriage, though a civil contract, requires solemnization, prior to the advent of justices of the peace this meant that to be legitimate a marriage had to occur in front of clergy. The law sanctioned, and religion solemnized, marriages between almost any two adults, no matter how foolish or ill-conceived the marriage. This limited legitimate marriages to the faithful, in the first instance, and then constrained marriages and family formation within one or a limited number of faith traditions. So too was once the case with adoption of children; adopters without any religious affiliation were seen as morally unfit, a lawful practice that may still remain more as a rule of thumb for some adoption agencies, and children needed to be placed with a family of the same religion. The religious question also came into play in deciding which parent should be awarded custody of a child in case of divorce. From the perspective of religious adherents, these differences may turn on whether religious identify is itself regarded as a choice or as an inheritance and to what extent each side of the question of identity formation regards the other as either tolerable or as a threat.

The law has already eliminated bastard status for non-marital children, which was once a measure of legitimacy and a powerful reminder of the religious wellspring of our understanding of family legitimacy. The church of yesteryear preferred the product of licit sexual activity in a bad marriage to illicit sexual activity, even if neither the sexual activity nor the child were desired by either party. Children born out of wedlock were socially stigmatized, and this was reflected in the law and in the inheritance rights it afforded.[12] The illicit sexual relations that illegitimate children represented were seen to loosen the social fabric, and they also brought stigma and legal consequences on their parents—especially if either were themselves married—by echoing biblical injunctions against fornication and adultery. The changing perception of these once socially deviant practices and the different way the law is treating them by not pursuing individuals and criminalizing such behavior or otherwise disadvantaging any offspring of an illegitimate pairing suggests that there has been a cultural shift in values, and the blame for this is often laid at the doorstep of the sexual liberation movement and the women's movement that achieved national prominence starting in the 1960s.[13]

This slow progression in public opinion and evolution in the law stimulated by the Civil Rights movement, coupled with the greater realm of freedom afforded individuals in their private lives, a domain the law has increasingly protected, may have reached its zenith around the turn of the last century. For example, the Federal Defense of Marriage Act (passed in 1996) and the many subsequent related acts at the state level have sent a clear signal to nontraditional couples and families that they may not be respected in the law or that they will be treated differently or as less than ideal, at a minimum. Responses to such actions that reassert traditional religious understandings in the garb of secular purpose have included affirmations in the law of non-traditional families, especially of same-sex couples, through devices such as civil unions and domestic partnership registries, as well as provisions for the adoption or custody of children by gay men and lesbians. Most European countries have moved in a different direction at the level of national and European Union policy, with several allowing same-sex marriage, legally sanctioning alternative family forms, and accommodating the growing interests of transgendered people.

Cultural Understandings of the Family

Implicit in the changing legal understanding of the family and the diminution of religious influence over it is the emerging challenge to the law's privileging of married over single individuals, a distinction not found in the U.S. Constitution, though one hitherto palpable throughout American society and law. In the older, traditional understanding of the family, the marital union is more or less a vessel for intergenerational transmission of values—of society's hegemonic norms—rather than a vehicle for the secure reproduction of the species. In discussions of the family and the sexual relations implicit in it, the term *natural* is rarely used as a natural scientist would use it; rather, it is deployed within a cultural framework in which signification and meaning are ascribed to biological or physiological processes. The slippage between "cultural" and "natural" occurs when what is in fact cultural or understood in such valences is attributed to "nature," as if the morally-charged signifiers at issue were as accessible and obvious as the scientist's understanding of human reproduction. Instead, society today understands that no religious or ideological concept of the family is neutral or even suitably neutral by itself to ground the law and be the basis for discrimination in the distribution of political or economic privileges.

Because of the different functions of the family in contemporary lived practice and the diverse cultural understandings of it, many of which are quite free of religious determination, American law is starting to lag behind society in providing distinctions in the law that serve the people in their different relationships that the culture signifies as family. Now, society is challenged with crafting new laws to match the evolving nature of the family and the individuals who are asserting their political rights and civil liberties on the one hand, and, on the other hand, balancing all that against the social role the traditional family has played, a dominating role that continues in some American subcultures such as evangelical Christianity. As has always been the case, society needs to ensure that somehow a steady hand is rearing the future generation and that persons are able to have an intimate life and experience human companionship—historically universal needs whatever the cultural understandings or legal regime.

There is a dance, then, between individual aspirations and the social context within which they find fulfillment, though religious belief is not carrying the tune or determining the permissibility of this or that form of family. This gradually opening space has made possible greater diversity within traditional family forms, even as it more obviously creates room for diversity in the family form itself. Religions too are struggling with questions of the family, with some becoming more liberal in the process, others staying the same, and still others entrenching their orthodox beliefs and practices. Regardless of the debate among religious adherents, the older privileging of one gender over another and restrictions based on sexual orientation that once characterized social acceptability have been superseded widely enough so as to prevent any reversal in this trajectory, though this does not speak to the near-term outcome of this evolution or to the success of any new family form.

Addressing the new gender and sexual orientation aspects of family has become unavoidable in any case, regardless of whether religious ideology keeps pace, because technology exists to make it possible for practically anyone to form a family with almost anyone else and to extend the family into the wider community, much as it once was. Arguably, technology is having a greater impact on women's ability to form families of choice. Today a child can have several mommies or daddies and can have been both adopted and also the offspring of an original sperm donation carried by a surrogate mother, for example, vastly complicating legal accommodations and religious understandings (even when all the parties involved are heterosexual), thereby providing multiple opportunities for the family to become a new site of freedom. And this freedom is twofold, disentangling "family" from whether anyone has contributed genetic material to it and detaching its members from any socially hegemonic understanding of who is permitted to comprise it.

CONCLUDING OBSERVATIONS

The family and religion have been intertwined throughout recorded human history, making a general theory specific to this relationship difficult. From the Nietzschean perspective, the family stands in the light of religion in much the same way any other social institution does; namely, religion serves to undergird the dominant view of the nuclear family by bestowing upon it the quality of being morally good, which permits rightful enforcement of the reigning ideology upon individual people, once accomplished through assertions of ecclesiastical power and later through state power. Liberalism points in the direction of family being a matter of choice or of accepting a family that is simply the result of choice, provided there is the commitment one expects family members to have to one another, even if this commitment is not based in religion, which is perhaps the iconic form of commitment in the West.

To the extent, then, that there is occurring a revaluation of family values in the United States today, broadly speaking (and with differences in degree in practice and its reflection in law and policy), the family and religion nexus of yesteryear is definitely fading. And, due to the civil liberties afforded to individuals in western societies and the guiding ideals of equality and liberty, this transformation of the relationship between the family and religion might signal the further privatization of religious belief and the further secularization of society with respect to the reach of political power in support of any religious perspective, or even in favor of a general religious understanding over a non-religious perspective.

NOTES

1. The practice of polygamy was reintroduced by the Mormon Church, prompting a confrontation with the U.S. government that resulted in the Church being escheated of its property and polygamy being outlawed, the latter in the case of *Reynolds v. United States* (98 U.S. 145 [1878]), the first Supreme Court case directly relating to family formation, here intertwined with the beliefs of a new religious minority. Polygamy remains illegal in the United States.

2. Of course, many arguments *against* slavery and the later regime of Jim Crow discrimination against African-Americans during the Civil Rights movement were also couched in biblical language.

3. The chapters in Part One of Kieran Scott and Michael Warren, eds., *Perspectives on Marriage. A Reader, Second Edition* (New York: Oxford University Press, 2001) provide a good entry into early Christian views on marriage and the family.

4. Carole Pateman's *The Sexual Contract* (Stanford: Stanford University Press, 1988) is a political theorist's searching analysis of the patriarchal underpinnings of the social contract tradition and the lesser degree of freedom the classical social contract thinkers accorded to women.

5. Part II, "The Beginnings of a Gay and Lesbian Movement," in *We Are Everywhere: A Historical Sourcebook of Gay and Lesbian Politics*, ed. Mark Blasius and Shane Phelan (New York: Routledge, 1997), provides many of the original voices in this late-nineteenth and early-twentieth century discussion.

6. Indeed, it was not until the 1967 case of *Loving v. Virginia* (388 U.S. 1 [1967]) that the remaining anti-miscegenation laws prohibiting interracial marriage in six southern states were struck down by the Supreme Court.

7. Progress that favors gay or lesbian family formation tends to be less secure than other gains in the law. For example, even once same-sex couples are granted benefits by a state, this may be subject to later popular referendum or opponents' legal strategy, as happened recently in Michigan, where a state court repealed an earlier decision that allowed universities and government agencies to provide do-

mestic partner benefits, as reported by David Eggert, "Michigan Court Rules Gay Partners Can't Get Benefits," *The Orange County Register*, February 3, 2007.

8. Several denominations even recognize same-sex marriages, though one in particular—the American Episcopalian Church—is under siege by its worldwide fellow Episcopalian churches for the stances it has taken on this issue, which its new female prelate has championed.

9. For the first time in the history of the United States, single women, including unmarried, widowed and divorced women, outnumber married women, and comprise 51 percent of the adult female population, a demographic that has social, economic, and political consequences. Helen Fisher argues that this trend represents a return to the state of affairs before the institution of marriage in her op-ed essay "History Loves an Unmarried Woman," *Los Angeles Times*, January 21, 2007.

10. The essays in Part IV, "Family," in *Sex, Preference, and Family: Essays on Law and Nature*, eds. David M. Estlund and Martha C. Nussbaum (New York: Oxford University Press, 1997), address issues such as these.

11. For example, the State of North Dakota only very recently rescinded its law that criminalized unmarried cohabitation, a law that dates to its statehood in 1889 and is similar to those which remain on the books in seven other states. See "Living Together Is No Longer Criminal in North Dakota," *The Orange County Register*, March 2, 2007.

12. The Uniform Parentage Act, amended in 2002, extended the parent and child relationship equally to each child and each parent, regardless of marital status, and the Uniform Probate Code has replaced "bastard" with "non-marital children." See Walter Wadlington and Raymond O'Brien, eds., *Family Law in Perspective* (New York: Foundation Press, 2007), 105–106.

13. Not surprisingly, same-sex parents and adoptive parents have to negotiate the same class, health, education, and other issues that face any family, though often without the support of their religious leaders or their community. See the chapters in Part 2, "Parenthood," in *Queer Families, Queer Politics: Challenging Culture and the State*, ed. Mary Bernstein and Renate Reimann (New York: Columbia University Press, 2001), for illustrations and analyses of these tribulations.

FURTHER READING

These works were consulted in the preparation of this chapter and will be particularly helpful for further study of the issues related to the family and religion. Readers who want more in-depth treatments of the family and religion in historical context and with a focus on the United States will profit from consulting the edited works by Sands, *God Forbid: Religion & Sex in American Public Life,* and by Scott and Warren, *Perspectives on Marriage. A Reader*. The Estlund and Nussbaum edited volume, *Sex, Preference, and Family: Essays on Law and Nature*, and Winfield's *The Just Family* provide philosophical treatments of the family with an emphasis on ethical argument, while Pateman's *The Sexual Contract* remains the classic reference for the lack of inclusion of women and the family into modern liberalism. Blasius and Phelan's edited volume, *We Are Everywhere: A Historical Sourcebook of Gay and Lesbian Politics*, is invaluable because of the wide variety of sources it contains, all in their original voices, and Bernstein and Reimann's *Queer Families, Queer Politics: Challenging Culture and the State*, and Mason, Skolnick, and Sugarman's *All Our Families: New Policies for a New Century, Second Edition*, will be of interest specifically for their treatments of sexual diversity issues and the family, while Say and Kowaleski's edited work, *Gays, Lesbians & Family Values*, focuses attention specifically on the religious issues and arguments surrounding contemporary non-traditional families. For a discussion of family law, see Krause and Meyer's *Family Law in a Nutshell, Fourth Edition*, and Wadlington and O'Brien's *Family Law in Perspective, Second Edition* and *Family Law Statutes, International Conventions and Uniform Laws*.

The Creation-Evolution Debate in the American Public School Classroom[1]

Jason R. Edwards

Amid a chaotic courtroom and after an embarrassing display of ignorance on the witness stand, the now despondent and desperate Fredric March collapses to his death on the courthouse floor while the rushing crowd of moderns barely notices his passing. Thus marks the tragic climax of *Inherit the Wind*.[2] Sadly, it also all too often marks the public's common understanding of the Scopes "Monkey Trial" and even the larger debate over the teaching of origins in the American public school classroom. Far too often, historians, teachers, and lay people alike present the battle over origins in American public schools as a simple contest between benighted bumpkins clinging to fanciful mythology versus progressive, enlightened moderns senselessly having to defend scientific facts. Though simplistic renderings of the passing of ages from superstition to enlightenment serve ideally the purposes of one side, perhaps no debate encapsulates more fundamental issues regarding freedom, religion, government, morality, democracy, America, and human dignity than does the debate over the teaching of origins in America's public schools. Consequently, American citizens deserve and should demand a more nuanced understanding than those typically offered through the popular media and textbook publishers. Black-and-white filming was particularly appropriate for a preachy movie script, but a careful examination of the historical debate and wrangling over origins teaching provides a vibrant and colorful mosaic infinitely more interesting and valuable. In fact, while the debate continues to be couched in terms of "fundamentalism" opposing "freedom," when one fairly examines the evidence it becomes difficult to identify exactly which side deserves which label.

Sacco and Vanzetti, Leopold and Loeb, Hauptmann, and O.J. all have claims on the title, but the true "trial of the century" was ironically not, like these others, over a felony but a misdemeanor; its ramifications, however, were anything but minor. *Tennessee v. John Scopes*—"The Monkey Trial"—took place over merely ten days in the summer of 1925, but its impact continues to reverberate into the twenty-first century. The case remains significant today because it remains the focal point for the teaching of origins in American public schools. In turn, that debate will forever be crucial because it speaks to a variety of momentous moral and Constitutional issues such as parental rights, local authority, and freedom of religion. It is not atypical to find laments that the "evolution debate" continues into the twenty-first century over eighty years after *Scopes*, but the reality is that this debate actually has a far longer history, one that spans thousands of years. By examining fairly and anew the full history of the origins debate, one discovers that regardless of one's beliefs concerning the earth's origin, the use of the government to enforce any belief systems through the school—the true definition of "Progressivism" in the United States—rightly looms ominous to all lovers of liberty.

THE HISTORICAL AND PHILOSOPHICAL DEBATES

It is hard to escape the ancient Greeks in any great philosophical argument, and this debate proves no exception. Fifth- and fourth-century Athens found Plato and Aristotle defending the divine origins of man against the materialist claims of Democritus and Heraclitus. As the ancients knew and moderns should appreciate, the answers to questions over man's origins carry ramifications and determinations regarding all of life's metaphysical, epistemological, and axiological questions.

Though enormous in consequence, the significance of origins is rather straightforward. If one believes that God created mankind (particularly if He did so in His image), man has purpose and meaning. In addition, man could only truly understand himself through grasping and accepting his relation to his Creator. Likewise, man would be beholden to God's laws and commands, which thereby provide a moral universe of consequence for man's existence, decisions, and actions. On the other hand, if man is a result of a great cosmic accident, a higher purpose and meaning beyond survival becomes elusive. Likewise, if man is rendered a beast, truly justifying any moral system beyond survival of the fittest becomes nigh impossible. Finally, if man is ultimately a result of the playing out of accidental and arbitrary physical laws and chemical processes, not only does the universe cease to be a moral stage, but each man's actions become best understood not as the result of freedom and choice but material determinism. A world bereft of true freedom and moral consequence, one devoid of objective beauty and morality, a world unknowable but through easily tricked senses, is the one that spiritual leaders from Plato to William Jennings Bryan have resisted accepting.

Besides the broad philosophical ramifications, the argument over origins also has more specific, but no less significant, constitutional implications for the United States. In a nation that embraces "freedom," the proper place for authority is always contested. In this instance, the right of parents to rear their children in the way that they see fit has come into conflict with the right of teachers to instruct these same children according to their conscience and expertise. Intellectual and academic freedom has historically been celebrated and protected in the United States; however, so has the right of citizens to pass laws that reflect their beliefs and values. When teachers are hired by parent-citizens and paid through the tax dollars of those same parent-citizens, the expectation has always been that the school and its employees are answerable to the society they serve. While freedom of speech extends to instructors in their private lives, few would argue that this freedom would remain as robust within schoolhouse walls. In fact, the very reason teachers cannot proselytize their religions in the classroom is the same reason it can reasonably be questioned whether only one explanation for man's origins can lawfully be instated. Indeed, as was noted above, the answer to origins determines one's metaphysics, epistemology, and axiology; in other words, it establishes one's religion and thereby appears outside the Constitutional purview of the state. Finally, in the midst of this clash of parental, state, and academic freedoms stands the individual student who also arguably has the right to a sound education, albeit one that liberates rather than indoctrinates. Which education best captures that heralded goal, however, remains highly contested.

The common hurdle to understanding the origins debate philosophically and particularly constitutionally is to get bogged down in whether one personally believes in macroevolution.[3] While the truth of Darwin's claims is no doubt of utmost importance, it can distract from an understanding of the full legal debate and a healthy respect for the opposing side. Certainly there exists a *prima facie* assumption that the "truth" should be taught in American schools; however, the reality is that all sides are equally convinced they are the sole possessors of the truth, and so neither will ever back down. To avoid this significant hurdle, one should put aside personal allegiances and fairly examine the history of this debate. Through focusing on the political and educational history of the conflict rather than the epistemological merits of Darwinists and their opponents, one can better understand the constitutional particulars in this specific interaction between the church and the state as well as perhaps understand the difficulty of church-state relationships generally. Ultimately, one discovers that freedom is fundamental to Americans but terribly difficult to create *ex nihilo*, and its maintenance is thwarted as freedom's definition constantly evolves.

THE AMERICAN SCHOOLING DEBATES

To examine the American origins debate one must start, of course, at the beginning—the founding of American public schools. To understand that event one should first consider that "progressives," of whatever beliefs or era, historically look to schools to create the idealized societies they envision. The United States provides an ideal example of this generalized rule. Religious progressives desiring to create a "shining city on a hill" began arriving on northern American shores in 1620 and quickly established both elementary and higher educational institutions.[4] In the early-nineteenth century, progressives in Massachusetts specifically and New England generally continued efforts to mold the future by developing the "common school."[5] Significant to the history of church-state relations, it should be noted that these institutions so vehemently endorsed Protestant beliefs that Catholic citizens revolted from the system and established their own parochial school system that thrives into the twenty-first century.

As the nineteenth century progressed and the North subdued the South in the Civil War, progressives imposed their Northern model of common schooling on their conquered neighbors. Then, heading into the twentieth century and the official "Progressive Era," forced government schooling expanded from the elementary years to the teen years in the form of newly founded high schools throughout the United States.[6] However, when this pattern of governmental intrusion into the lives of its citizens combined with a scientific theory that threatened the deepest religious beliefs of a citizenry, a showdown was inevitable.

The offending theory actually arrived in Western consciousness in 1859 when Charles Darwin published *On the Origin of Species by Means of Natural Selection, or the Preservation of Favoured Races in the Struggle for Life* and quite simply started a revolution.[7] It is difficult to overstate Darwin's impact in the field of science, but as has been alluded to earlier, his revolution spread throughout essentially all fields of human thought. Though the concept of evolution was not original to Darwin and his specific arguments have been modified throughout the years, Darwin's thesis that the variety of life was a result of blind natural selection rather than divine design ushered in a new era. As Darwin promoter Michael Shermer states:

We live in the age of Darwin [emphasis Shermer's]. Arguably the most culturally jarring theory in history, the theory of natural selection gave rise to the Darwinian revolution that changed both science and culture in ways immeasurable. On the scientific level, the static creationist model of species as fixed types was replaced with a fluid evolutionary model of species as ever-changing entities. The repercussions of this finding were, and are, astounding. The theory of top-down intelligent design of all life by or through a supernatural power was replaced with the theory of bottom-up natural design through natural forces. The anthropocentric view of humans as special creations placed by a divine hand above all others was replaced with the view of humans as just another animal species. The view of life and the cosmos as having a direction and purpose from above was replaced with the view of the world as the product of the necessitating laws of nature and the contingent events of history. The view that human nature is infinitely malleable and primarily good was replaced with a view of human nature in which we are finitely restricted by our genes and are both good and evil.[8]

In other words, Darwinism is a complete philosophical and societal revolution; it is an idea that wages total war against others and allows for no quarter or compromise.

When faced with unconditional surrender demands, any army or faith will do three things: attempt to take the high ground, bring up the artillery, and fight to the last man. Both sides in the origins debate have done just that in America. Both claim to be defending truth, justice, and the American way; both seek the help of the government because the government controls the big guns; and each continues to fight through victory and defeat decade after decade.

Though widely accepted in scientific circles today, Darwin was not embraced by all scientists in his own time. Sir John Herschel famously described Darwinism as "the law of higgledy-piggledy" and Darwin's former geology professor at Cambridge told Darwin that when he read *Origins* he "laughed till his sides ached."[9] In the United States, Darwin's most notable opponent was none other than Harvard's world-renowned zoologist and geologist, Louis Agassiz. Nevertheless Darwin, who was personally not inclined to public debate, had no shortage of vocal supporters. "Darwin's Bulldog," Thomas Huxley, vehemently defended Darwin in England and helped spread his word throughout Europe, while in America the United

States' greatest botanist, Harvard's Asa Gray, ably supported Darwin's theories. As the nineteenth century succumbed to the twentieth, Darwin's ideas gained increasing cachet, but had these arguments remained behind the ivy-covered walls of academia, it is unlikely that any great court trials would have resulted. However, what is believed and then taught in higher education classrooms inevitably trickles down into the secondary and elementary ones.[10] And when those elementary and secondary classrooms are filled through governmental fiat and paid for by tax dollars, an explosive legal battle becomes inevitable.

By 1920, the combustible combination of a revolutionary meta-narrative and government-enforced schooling provoked a citizen uprising. Though often misunderstood as solely a Southern movement, the effort to ban the teaching of Darwinism in American public school classrooms enjoyed broad support. In fact, legislation opposing the teaching of evolution was proposed in New York, Kentucky, and Minnesota before the first anti-evolution legislation was passed in Oklahoma.[11] Ultimately, forty-five bills in over twenty states were voted on throughout the 1920s, but the Oklahoma state legislature in 1923 established the first anti-evolution law by prohibiting state distribution of textbooks that included Darwinian teachings.[12]

While states debated the governing of their schools, the most widely adopted textbook (in the very recently formed field of biology[13]) in schools across the country was George W. Hunter's *A Civic Biology*.[14] In it, Hunter endorsed Darwinism, and so in 1925, when a twenty-four-year-old general science teacher and part-time football coach in Dayton, Tennessee, agreed to claim he had taught evolution by using Hunter's textbook for a test review while substituting for a colleague, the trial of the twentieth century was nigh.

FUNDAMENTAL PROGRESSIVISM

Due to common misperceptions, it is important to revisit the history of progressivism in the United States before discussing the specifics of the trial. All too often, the 1920s are understood as a battleground between progressive modern forces taking on traditional fundamentalists who bitterly fought a rear-guard action against enlightenment and perhaps time itself. This common perception is simply wrong. Anti-evolution laws, just like the misunderstood Prohibition Amendment before it, fit perfectly within the penumbra of typical progressive politics. Progressives (both generally and specifically tied to the American Progressive Era) seek to create an ideal society through governmental fiat and action. So, at the beginning of the twentieth century, the thinking followed that if men are falling into vice at the saloon and workers are inefficient because they are hung-over, the state should use its power to ban alcohol.[15] If the distribution of wealth grows offensive to sensibilities, use the power of the government to cap the income of the wealthy through taxation.[16] If the ruling elite, traditional deference, and political machines thwart democratic ideals, use the power of the government to provide for the direct election of Senators and award the franchise to women.[17]

Time and again, the first decades of the twentieth century witnessed attempts by progressives to determine the future through the retooling and extension of government authority. No less than four amendments to the Constitution were passed in this short timeframe and progressives backed each one. In fact, arguably the greatest individual champion for each of these amendments was none other than the Great Commoner himself, the three-time Democratic presidential candidate and President Wilson's Secretary of State, William Jennings Bryan. And Bryan was now ready to bring progressivism to the American classroom.

"Fundamentalism" had arisen in the first decades of the twentieth century and Bryan had become one of its brightest lights. Bryan was arguably the most important leader of both Fundamentalism and Progressivism and hardly thought of the two as contradictory. The Fundamentalists acquired their name through the publication of a series of pamphlets published from 1905 to 1915 which outlined "fundamental" tenets of the Christian faith in order to fend off the rise of German modernist and social gospel theologies (or heresies as the Fundamentalists considered them). Interestingly though, even some of these first pamphlets accepted the possibility of a theistic evolution and Bryan himself was not a literal six day creationist (which would actually cause him great problems on the witness stand). In fact, Bryan connected his historic progressive fights against the "malefactors of great wealth" to his opposition to Darwinism as he witnessed capitalists time and again justify their economic success and behavior as merely a result of "survival of the fittest."

It is also commonly assumed that Bryan advocated the teaching of the Genesis account in public schools; on the contrary, his acceptance that the doctrine of a separation of church and state prohibited the teaching of a particular religious tradition in the public school led to his new crusade. To Bryan, while the Bible could not be officially endorsed in public schools, it should also not be attacked. Likewise, the government could not establish another religion by teaching evolution. Bryan sought freedom and fairness by removing the contentious origins debate from public school classrooms altogether. Barring that, he felt freedom and fairness demanded both sides be taught. As he had done for all his decades before, Bryan lent his considerable popularity and sonorous voice to the progressive ideal of constructing an ideal democracy where the common people would rule through the creation of appropriate laws guaranteeing protection by and from the government. Anti-evolution laws were simply the next battle in his life-long progressive crusade.

Though Bryan had sounded the clarion call for anti-evolution legislation, he was not even aware of the Oklahoma statute when it first passed. Tennessee, on the other hand, had sought both Bryan's help and advice with their legislation. Bryan always advocated leaving origins studies out of the schoolroom in order to protect the rights of the people, and he never advocated making teachers who taught evolution criminals. The Tennessee legislature was more aggressive than Bryan, though, and in 1925 passed the Butler Act, which banned the teaching of evolution in Tennessee schoolrooms and made violation of the act a misdemeanor punishable by a $100–$500 fine. When Tennessee Governor Austin Peay signed the bill into law, he likely thought the law would serve as an advisory but would not be strictly enforced.[18] Governor Peay focused too much on the actual debate and consequently underestimated both a recently established New York organization seeking any opportunity to "progress to a new social order" and the entrepreneurial spirit of Dayton, Tennessee, town leaders, who upon finding an advertisement in the *Chattanooga Daily Times* by the American Civil Liberties Union (ACLU) saw an opportunity to put Dayton, Tennessee, "on the map."

The ACLU's fame (or infamy, depending upon one's perspective) had skyrocketed by 1925. Formed as the Civil Liberties Bureau during the First World War to defend the rights of Americans opposed to the war, the ACLU subsequently had expanded its focus to defending civil rights generally, but particularly in the realm of free speech. Comprised primarily of Eastern social activists and liberal lawyers, the ACLU's membership had generally supported Bryan's progressive crusading in the past but departed from Bryan's current understanding of freedom and progressivism in the origins debate.

Concerning the specifics of origins teachings, the first position statement by the ACLU ironically delineated that the "attempts to maintain a uniform orthodox opinion among teachers should be opposed" and that the "attempts of education authorities to inject into public schools and colleges instruction propaganda in the interest of any particular theory of society to the exclusion of others should be opposed."[19] Twenty-first century advocates of Intelligent Design of course embrace these statements by the ACLU, but in its historical context the ACLU meant to protect the free speech of evolutionists.

The ACLU considered the banning of evolutionary theory in school an ignorant act that smacked of an intrusion of fundamentalist religious belief and consequently a violation of the First Amendment's Establishment Clause. Therefore, the ACLU actively sought a case that would allow it to challenge not just the Tennessee law, but through appeals, the constitutionality of all anti-evolution laws in the United States. The ACLU understood early on that by using the judicial system and the growing power of the Supreme Court, it could eliminate the ability of legislatures across the country to legislate the wishes of the unwashed masses. When at the behest of Dayton town leaders John T. Scopes called, the ACLU seemingly had found its case.

By July 1925, the stage was set. Dayton's fathers would have their publicity stunt as Scopes obediently confessed to teaching evolution and the legal system charged and tried him.[20] The ACLU would have its test case and was eager to strike a blow for modern science and academic freedom. The Fundamentalists would also have their opportunity to publicize and gather further support for their effort to protect the rights of citizens and defend their faith. The press, too, now not limited to print but armed with the wireless radio and even newsreel, would have its true "trial of the century" to draw the nation's eyes to its daily wares. And so with the parties gathered all around, two giants strode onto this cacophonous media stage to duel. On the one side, none other than "the attorney for the damned"[21] Clarence Darrow strode out, eager to strike a blow for individual liberty and to topple "the idol of all Morondom."[22] Across the aisle, William Jennings Bryan, the man most responsible for both the legislative and religious revolutions of the three decades prior to then, prepared to strike another blow for "the faith of our fathers" and majority rule. With so much at stake and the anticipation so high, perhaps all parties were destined to be disappointed.

THE TRIAL OF THE CENTURY

The specific unfolding details of the trial are worth knowing, and fortunately the definitive account of the trial has been recorded. In 1997 Edward J. Larson published *Summer for the Gods: The Scopes Trial and America's Continuing Debate over Science and Religion* and promptly won the Pulitzer Prize for History.[23] This essay relies on Larson's retelling but need not reproduce it in detail. For the purpose of examining the interaction between church and state, it is sufficient to note that the prosecution in the Scopes trial had an "open and shut" case. The elected legislature of Tennessee had passed a statute prohibiting the teaching of evolution in the public school classroom, and John T. Scopes had confessed to breaking this law. As long as the trial stuck to these plain facts, they really could not lose. Wisely, the prosecution team recognized this situation and so planned and agreed that this straightforward explication of the basic facts would be their approach; they stuck to this plan except for one fatal (and famous) exception. Though Darrow and his defensive team were in Dayton officially to defend Scopes, their true mission was to put the anti-evolution Butler Act on trial. To do this, Darrow sought to parade before the jury a series of expert witnesses that would testify both to the truth of evolution and, contrary to his own beliefs, evolution's compatibility with the Scriptures. The prosecution objected to these witnesses on the sound legal ground that they could not speak to the facts of the case (whether or not the law had been broken) and the judge agreed. So, though Darrow fumed at the exclusion, his witnesses were barred from the court.

Before the defense rested, Darrow made a surprising move, calling William Jennings Bryan to the stand as an expert on the Bible. The prosecution team encouraged Bryan to refuse and the judge told Bryan he would support the refusal, but Bryan was eager for a showdown. Though this decision to take the stand by Bryan is considered a momentous blunder, he knew he was largely already trapped. Though well aware that Darrow would try to embarrass him on the witness stand, Bryan also knew that if he refused the challenge, H.L. Mencken and the rest of the hostile press would have a field day labeling him a coward embarrassed by his own fundamentalist beliefs. So he agreed to take the stand only after securing the right to then question Darrow and his ACLU team as well. Bryan felt this to be a valuable trade-off because if Darrow and the ACLU took the stand, he could expose their hostility to Christianity and consequently undermine their credibility. Though agreed to and promised, Bryan would never get his chance.

Though one of the most gifted orators in American history and trained as a lawyer, William Jennings Bryan simply proved to be overmatched by Darrow's trial courtroom acumen. Darrow pounded Bryan with questions regarding miraculous events recorded in the Bible, and though the prosecution offered up multiple objections, Bryan always responded that if "Darrow wants to attack the Bible . . . I will answer." Consequently, the judge allowed the blistering interrogation to continue. While Bryan initially scored some witty verbal retorts to Darrow's pointed questioning, his eventual admission that portions of the Bible where rhetorical and called for interpretation and that even the word "day" in Genesis might stand for an "age" meant Darrow had Bryan just where he wanted him. By the end, the "expert" on the Bible appeared confused about its teachings and offered an interpretation of the book that complied neither with strict literal interpretations nor with modernist theology. Even more damaging, Bryan had appeared to embrace an anti-intellectual approach to theology that has haunted Fundamentalism specifically and perhaps Christianity and religion generally ever since. He certainly provided grist for Mencken and others hostile to religion in the public square to mill.

Though Darrow's questioning of Bryan remains key to this historic event as the element most celebrated in the press of that day and the textbooks and movies of today, it actually had no role in the outcome of the trial. The judge had allowed the questioning to take place due to Bryan's agreement, but he had not let the jury be present for it because, like the expert testimony on evolution, the information to be gleaned from an "expert" testimonial on the Bible was not germane to the case. As such, the jury never heard or witnessed the famous exchange.

Apparently weary of sidebar theatrics, the judge reneged on Bryan's promised interrogation of Darrow. Disappointments continued to pile up for Bryan, for when the time came for closing arguments, Darrow directed the jury to declare Scopes guilty and thereby denied Bryan the opportunity to deliver his long prepared pro-Christian and anti-evolution oration. Consequently, after meeting for just seconds in the hallway, the jury returned from "deliberation" to pronounce Scopes guilty and the judge assessed a $100 fine—a fine Bryan had already offered to pay. And so the trial of the century was officially over, ending not with a bang, but with a whimper.

Despite its anticlimactic end, the reverberations of the trial have long continued. Though often portrayed in historic accounts as despondent and heart-broken, biographers have countered that if so, Bryan showed no signs of it.[24] He immediately traveled to Chattanooga and Winchester, Tennessee, to continue the anti-evolution crusade and returned to Dayton five days after the trial's end to give a speech but died in his sleep. The defense team immediately prepared for an appeal to the Tennessee Supreme Court which was heard in January of 1927. Again, the ACLU's ultimate goal was to have the conviction upheld so that it could then appeal the decision and challenge the constitutionality of the law in the U.S. Supreme Court. Its plans were thwarted though when the Tennessee High Court overturned the decision on a technicality (the judge, rather than the jury, had determined the fine) and then directed the Attorney General not to prosecute any more Butler Act cases. As such, clear victory could not be declared by either side. The Butler Act, as well as several other state statutes prohibiting the teaching of evolution, remained on the books for decades, but the negative media attention that engulfed Tennessee as a result of the trial guaranteed that the broadly supported Fundamentalist effort to outlaw evolution in schools essentially ended.

Death would not take Darrow until 1938, but G.K. Chesterton would best him in a public debate over religion and evolution at New York City's Mecca Temple in 1931.[25] Thankfully for Darrow, no transcript of that equally lopsided debate exists, nor were any dramatizations created.[26] Finally, John T. Scopes, the person who the trial was officially about but who seemingly could not have played a less important role, returned to teaching and lived out his life in general obscurity, unable or unwilling to capitalize on his fame due to his lack of knowledge regarding evolution and his admittance after the trial that he never really had broken the law. Used by outsiders, however willingly for their own gain and not his, Scopes, until his death in 1970, seemingly became the stereotypical man without a country, for he was a traitor to his own people and a largely discarded tool by his "defenders."

Before completely abandoning the Scopes Trial, it is worth exploring perhaps the most significant church-state legal issue raised by the Butler Act and the subsequent fight over teaching evolution in schools. Bryan was aware of this issue but never effectively raised it, and Darrow assumedly wanted to avoid it, for it demonstrated a hypocritical element to his stance. One year before the Scopes Trial, Darrow defended the infamous murderers Nathan Leopold and Richard Loeb. In an attempt to avoid the death penalty for the killers, the material determinist Darrow had argued that the blame for the murder of the fourteen-year-old Bobby Franks lay not with his killers Leopold and Loeb but on a society that had provided Leopold and Loeb access to the teachings of Friedrich Nietzsche. According to Darrow's mostly successful argument, society had to take into account the likely results (rather than just the truth or falsehood) of teachings it allowed in schools and even libraries. Contrastingly, one year later, in the Scopes Trial, Darrow argued that intellectual freedom for teachers must be protected and that if something was most likely true it should not be banned from public school instruction, even to young children, regardless of its consequences.[27] Bryan, as well as state legislatures that considered banning the teaching of evolution, had indeed focused attention on the logical consequences of teaching evolution to the young as the primary reason why it could and should be banned from the public school classroom. However, arguments over "truth"—not "consequences"—dominated the proceedings.

Knowing that schools create society makes a simplified understanding of the Scopes Trial, or a taking up of sides in evolution debates solely on one's position regarding the truth of macroevolution, inappropriate. Public school instruction is not simply about teaching the "truth," if for no other reason than all truth cannot be covered, so selection is inherently part of the process. Furthermore, public schools create a "public" by what is selected to teach. Therefore, the Constitution guarantees that all citizens—religious and secular—have a right to participate in determining what kind of society they wish to build and protect.

Progressives of both the religious and secular orders are always on the forefront of trying to determine educational content, because they are the most focused on the formation of their ideal society. Consequently, progressives often attempt to exclude others from the decision-making process by declaring opponents' views illegal. In the first quarter of the twentieth century, religious progressives known as Fundamentalists attempted to use legislatures to legislate their beliefs at the expense of others and enjoyed limited success. In the second half of the twentieth century, secular progressives, typically known as secular-humanists (who also had written out their fundamentals in manifestos), attempted to legislate their beliefs through the American court system; unlike their earlier religious cousins, they won an almost complete victory.[28]

THE ESTABLISHMENT OF SECULAR PROGRESSIVISM

After the 1920s, the country seemingly embraced what historian Edward Larsen described as a "thirty-year truce" in the war over origins teachings.[29] After the Scopes Trial, a wide variety of states had anti-evolution legislation introduced, but only two southern states, Mississippi and Arkansas, actually passed statutes. However, though evolutionists faced little legislative opposition, textbook publishers had no desire to lose sales due to publishing unpopular scientific theories, so they generally avoided putting evolution into their works.[30] As such, religious progressives won a *de facto* victory but not a *de jure* one. Secular progressives had made strides *de jure* but not *de facto*. In effect, political power returned to the people where local school boards could make their own decisions regarding what would be taught in their schools. This very American-styled democratic peace was shattered ironically by the nation that Fundamentalists considered the champion of atheistic secular humanism—the Soviet Union.

In 1957, the Soviet Union launched Sputnik and officially surpassed the United States technologically. In the brief span of twelve years, the United States had gone from the only true technological superpower to a seemingly distant second. As in all times of American crisis, the federal government once again took on broad power to stem the national emergency. So, like Lincoln in the Civil War or Franklin Roosevelt facing the Great Depression and a worldwide Fascist threat, President Eisenhower joined hands with Congress to fight the Cold War, and American schools would be considered the first line of defense. In 1958, the National Defense Education Act was passed, forever altering science education in the United States. Though the focus of the bill was flooding graduate study and universities with research funds for applied science, the ramifications trickled down quickly to secondary schools as well. Local opinions, interests, and rule seemed *passé* in a national emergency, and so the nation embraced scientific authority, which embraced evolution. A vast reworking of teaching was being dictated to the nation:

These reforms included the biological sciences, especially after the National Science Foundation began funding the Biological Science Curriculum Study (BSCS) in 1959. Like its counterpart for physics, the BSCS set about rewriting high-school textbooks, and the leading biologists serving on the Study (which included Hermann Muller) boldly embraced evolution. The appearance of the BSCS texts in the early sixties shattered the thirty-year truce in legal activities enveloping the anti-evolution issue.[31]

With this tide rising, the secular progressives were determined to take it at the flood. Fear had provided them with their chance to use the power of the national government to rework American education, the nation's long-standing church-state relations, and consequently the nation itself.

Though easily forgotten in the twenty-first century, to understand the revolution that occurred in the 1960s in church-state relations it must be remembered that the Supreme Court's interpretation of the Establishment Clause was quite literally turned on its head in the second half of the twentieth century. No court in the 1920s would have seriously considered the notion that an anti-evolution law violated the Constitutional injunction against establishing religion. The clause's original intent was to prohibit an American state church as understood by the Founders through their experience with the Church of England. Indeed, states were not only free to but did establish official state churches supported by public tax dollars. Though that practice disappeared in the first half of the nineteenth century, the Supreme Court did not seriously alter its understanding of the Establishment Clause until the Northern states established through the power of the sword the indivisibility of the nation and the supremacy of the national government over the states. With the forced passage of the Fourteenth Amendment, the states were now limited by the Bill of Rights and could not deprive "any person of life, liberty, or property, without due process of law."[32] Even so, it was not until 1947 that the Supreme Court first considered using the Establishment Clause to restrict state authority even when the state was not trying to establish an official church. The court "incorporated" the First Amendment's Establishment Clause only by reinterpreting the clause to mean aiding religion generally rather than establishing a particular denomination.

In *Everson v. Board of Education of Ewing Township*, the Court considered whether a New Jersey law that reimbursed parents whose children attended parochial schools for the cost of bus transportation to and from school unconstitutionally established religion. Ultimately, the Court decided that this law was constitutional because the First Amendment requires the state to be neutral towards religion and not its adversary. The Court found (5–4) that this law did just that by providing assistance to parents to get their children, regardless of their religion, safely and expeditiously to and from accredited schools. Though technically a victory for the church, this decision nevertheless established a foundation for the removal of religion from the public square. Through his majority opinion, Justice Hugo Black set the precedent that the religion clauses of the First Amendment were now applicable to the states through the Fourteenth Amendment, and his conclusion that this particular law did not breach "a wall between church and state" established a new standard by which church-state relations would henceforth be judged.[33]

Using *Everson* as their legal foundation, a new generation of radical secular progressives rose up in the 1960s to remake American society through judicial fiat. Scoring a series of dramatic victories, these progressives used the Supreme Court to remove religion from the public square. Their targets typically centered on the American public school. In 1962, the *Engel v. Vitale* decision declared that prayer in the public school system, even if voluntary and non-denominational, was unconstitutional.[34] A year later the Court found in *School District of Abington Township, Pennsylvania v. Schempp*, that recitations of the Lord's Prayer or beginning a school day with a reading from the Bible was a breach in the separation of church and state and even potentially "psychologically harmful to the child."[35] The *Schempp* case established the even more religiously proscriptive position that "to withstand the strictures of the Establishment Clause there must be a secular legislative purpose and a primary effect that neither advances nor inhibits religion."[36]

With a new strict standard in place, the removal of religion from the classroom has continued unabated from the 1960s forward. Selecting just a few from many examples, in *Wallace v. Jaffree* (1985) the court struck down as a violation of the Establishment Clause an Alabama law that required a "moment of silence" at the beginning of each school day.[37] In *Lee v. Weisman* (1992) the court outlawed clergy-led prayer at public school graduation ceremonies,[38] and in 2000 the Court ruled that student-led, student-initiated prayer at football games violated the First and Fourteenth Amendments in *Santa Fe Independent School District v. Doe*.[39] Ironically, the crucial *Schempp* decision stated that "the State may not establish a 'religion of secularism'"—Bryan's exact position—but their decision seemed to do just that.[40]

In the second half of the twentieth century, few areas proved more fruitful to scientific fundamentalists than the long-standing origins debate. The legal trends of the day almost assured victory if the progressives challenged anti-evolution laws while the social tumult stemming from civil rights and war protests ushered in more and more political radicalism. Even "conservatives" had impetus to rework the teaching of science in American public schools due to the Cold War and the perceived need to "catch-up" with the Russians.

In 1968, the Supreme Court Chief Justice Earl Warren and his Court in a fascinating bit of historical irony would decide another momentous case tied to Little Rock Arkansas' Central High School.[41] In 1965, Susan Epperson, a first-year biology teacher at Central High, agreed to the Arkansas Education Association's request to stand as the plaintiff in a lawsuit against Arkansas' anti-evolution statute. The legal counsel for Epperson argued this was a simple case of First Amendment freedom; a science teacher had a right and duty to teach evolution since it was the dominant and most widely accepted scientific theory of origins. In contrast to the Scopes Trial, it was the state that wished to widen the parameters and parade a host of experts before the court to demonstrate the reasonableness of the statute by putting evolution on trial. However, as with the Scopes Trial, the judge essentially disallowed outside expert testimony in an effort to focus the case on the law itself and ruled that the law was unconstitutional.[42]

The Warren Court heard the case on appeal after the Arkansas Supreme Court reversed the initial *Epperson* ruling in 1967, declaring that the law was "a valid exercise of the state's power to specify the curriculum in its public schools."[43] The Warren Court certainly appeared predisposed to ruling on behalf of evolution, though finding Constitutional reasons for doing so was problematic. The justices almost all agreed the law must be unconstitutional but they really could not agree why.[44] Ultimately, the court declared the Arkansas statute in place since the 1920s banning the teaching of evolution in the public schools an unconstitutional violation of the Establishment Clause. With one stroke of the pen all remaining anti-evolution laws, including Tennessee's famous Butler Act, were apparently null and void. Scientific fundamentalism, at least in the crucial field of origins, had seemingly been established by the state.

Though the heady days of banning evolution had passed for the creationists, one avenue seemingly remained open. The *Epperson* decision endorsed neutrality, not hostility, to religion, and so demanding equal time for conflicting views on origins in the classroom appeared to be a constitutionally legitimate option. Indeed, Bryan's endorsement of banning evolution had been motivated by equal treatment (both Genesis and Darwinism would be banned) not exclusivity. With the Court's ruling that states could not bar Darwin from passing beneath the schoolhouse door, seemingly the author of Genesis would be equally welcome. Reality proved otherwise.

Creationists faced daunting opposition from the courts that early on simply refused to hear their cases that had accused the state of establishing secularism in public schools. In 1971, the Supreme Court continued to build the wall between church and state ever higher by setting up a three-pronged test for Establishment Clause cases. In Chief Justice Warren Burger's majority opinion in *Lemon v. Kurtzman*, the "Lemon Test" was born. Under the *Lemon* Test, to not violate the Establishment Clause a law had to: (1) have a secular legislative purpose, (2) have its primary effect be one that neither advances or inhibits religion, and (3) not foster an excessive entanglement with religion.[45] The first requirement dated to 1963's *Abington v. Schempp* while the second was established in 1968's *Board of Education v. Allen*.[46] The third element was new and added a particularly difficult hurdle for creationists. Though the Lemon Test remains in the twenty-first century a crucial element to Establishment Clause cases, it has been criticized by both the political Left and Right as unworkably vague and unfailingly capricious in application. Nevertheless, it both exemplified and served as a significant barrier for creation science, much less religious epistemology, in the American public school classroom.

SCIENTIFIC FUNDAMENTALISM SECURES POWER

Especially when considering the legal history of the Establishment Clause in the later twentieth century and before one becomes too embroiled in it or easily passes over the names of court cases, it is important to carefully note the beliefs of the general populace and the ruling elite as well the constant sparring over control of language. The common mistake made when examining Supreme Court cases is to simply equate "creationism" with religion and "evolution" with science. While obviously these terms do have undeniable correlation, treating them as synonyms can irreparably cloud the important church-state issues at stake. Though it has already been established that one's beliefs regarding origins will undoubtedly affect, if not determine, one's worldview, philosophy, and religion, it is reasonable to question whether the Establishment Clause should be considered in a state or school's decision regarding what to teach in science class. It is only by the assumption that belief in creationism can stem solely from an *a priori* allegiance to a religious text that courts would argue teaching it in a public school equated with establishing a religion. By the end of the twentieth century, creationists would insist that concluding that the world was designed, not only can be but is a conclusion derived purely through the scientific method. If this argument is generally acknowledged, the banning of any origins theories other than the materialistic one fundamental to secular-humanism would seemingly violate the neutrality required by the U.S. Constitution.

Quickly reviewing the twentieth-century history of the origins conflict in regards to language should make clear how an arguably inappropriate equation of creationism and religion was established. At the beginning of the twentieth century, the general populace did not widely accept the theory of evolution and reasonably assumed its adoption would cause a civic decline. Having been embraced in higher academia for the better part of a century, by the last few decades of the twentieth century evolution had broadly filtered down into the general public and no longer seemed such a dire threat to essential moral and civic virtues. Since the anti-evolution efforts had been spearheaded by the religious progressives known as Fundamentalists who proudly defined all of their philosophy as stemming from divine revelation in the Holy Scriptures, it became easy for the courts and public to equate belief in creation with a literal interpretation and faith in the book of Genesis. Consequently, when "creationism" is used by adherents and foes alike as simply another word for Fundamentalist Christianity, there is little doubt that the modern era's court system would ban it from schools as a violation of the Establishment Clause. The history of the 1970s and forward then becomes one where creationists must demonstrate the legitimacy of concluding that the world was created by relying on the scientific method, while secular progressives have striven to prove that the identification, recognition, and conclusion of design not only falls outside the purview of science but stems solely from religion.

Creationists honed their scientific arguments during the 1970s and refined their legal approach to focus on America's natural inclination for "equal time." Though no major victories were won in the court system, limited victories had been won in state legislatures such as California, Kentucky, Texas, Indiana, and Tennessee, where either creationism was increasingly recognized as science or, more commonly, legislatures dictated that evolution had to be taught as a theory and not as a fact. In addition, the publicity generated by these state actions likely encouraged many school districts nationwide to adopt their own particular policies for providing an even-handed and citizenry-sensitive approach to origins teaching.

With the election of Ronald Reagan in 1980, creationists had reason to hope for even more. The fortieth president was elected on a platform that in regards to education called for the elimination of the newly created Department of Education as a Cabinet-level post, the support of tax credits for tuition paid to private schools, as well as a return of prayer to the public school classroom. All three of these elements likely encouraged creation scientists. Returning educational authority from the federal government back to local officials would bode well since "equal time" enjoyed widespread public support. Tax credits would indicate that the extremely high wall of separation exemplified by the *Lemon* Test's "entanglement" verbiage might not remain. And, of course, the removal of prayer, which like rulings regarding origins teaching had been easy for the Supreme Court to declare but much harder to enforce, if removed, would lend credence to the idea that the government did not need to root out any vestige of religion from the public school.

In the area of education, Reagan promised much more than he could deliver. Likewise, a decade that began with such promise ended in utter defeat for creationists. Before the defeat, though, came victory. In 1981, Arkansas easily passed a law that required schools that taught evolution to also teach creationism. If origins were to be taught at all, both theories were to be treated as theories, with the best evidence of each side presented. Louisiana passed similar legislation that same year, which was particularly significant because even though Louisiana was also southern and so at first glance fell into regional stereotypes, it more importantly was urban. Much more than regional, the origins debate has tended to divide along rural and urban lines, but in Louisiana urban and rural parishes joined hands in approving "equal time" legislation.

The ACLU wasted little time in challenging creationism's latest legislative victories. The Reverend Bill McLean was the lead plaintiff in the grievance filed against the Arkansas law in Little Rock's federal district court. Judge William R. Overton presided over the case but seemed predisposed to strike the law, and the professionalized "small-print" lawyer-style that had emerged over the course of the twentieth century caused what the media tried to dub "Scopes II" to be a "box-office" failure. After two weeks of argument, Judge Overton ruled on January 5, 1982, against the Arkansas statute. Judge Overton equated creation science with religion rather than science and so considered its appearance in public school a violation of the Establishment Clause.

Louisiana's equal-time law was more skillfully and neutrally constructed than Arkansas' law, and so the ACLU knew that a victorious challenge of this law might lead to final victory and the complete banishment of creation science and religious epistemology from the public school science classroom, regardless of popular sentiment. It took literally years of legal wrangling (mostly victories for opponents of the "equal time" law), but the law's legitimacy would eventually be determined by the U.S. Supreme Court when the Court heard the case in December of 1987.

Before the Court, the state argued that lower courts had inappropriately and arbitrarily defined creation science as religious belief rather than actual science.[47] The state had compiled reams of evidence to prove that creation science was indeed science and therefore deserved a hearing in the public classroom to serve the secular purpose of academic freedom and fairness. The opposition presented the court with a multitude of statements primarily culled from scientific organizations that stated creation science was not science and that creationism had no place in the public school classroom. The court rendered its decision six months later in four different written opinions reflecting very different interpretations of creation science. In any event, the majority decision in *Edwards v. Aguillard* struck down the law as an unconstitutional violation of the Establishment Clause by tying creation science to Fundamentalism and ergo an establishment of religion.[48] The decade that had begun so promisingly for the creationists ended in nearly complete defeat.

The key element to understanding the origins debate in the 1990s lies once again in an understanding of progressive politics. Progressives of whatever political or religious stripe always attempt to impose their beliefs through the power of the government. Typically such efforts have two main prongs of attack: (1) mandate the teaching of one's beliefs; and (2) outlaw the teaching of all competing beliefs. As has just been seen, by the end of the 1980s, the Supreme Court effectively outlawed creation science from the public school classroom, thereby achieving one-half of any progressive's dream. The 1990s would largely witness the completion of the first goal: the instilling of one's beliefs through legal fiat.

In 1988, the Republican progressive George Bush ran for president in a campaign that declared he would be the "education president." His initiative was *America 2000*, a standards-based federal education plan designed for adoption throughout the United States. This plan was renamed *Goals 2000* when Democratic progressive Bill Clinton became president in 1992. Capitalizing on the nation's remaining concern over its failing educational system as documented in the famous 1983 Congressional report, *A Nation at Risk,* both progressive Republicans and Democrats looked to the government to remake American schools in their officially prescribed image.[49]

Such a governmental effort made the evolutionists' dream of once and for all establishing evolution in American public schools an imminent possibility as the government looked to the vehemently evolutionist National Academy of Science to recommend the standards for science.

The evolutionists' opportunity was almost lost when the entire *Goals 2000* project was nearly aborted after the history standards were released in 1994 and caused a political firestorm over the controversial inclusions and exclusions on the list. In fact, opposition to *Goals 2000* helped sweep the Republican Party into control of both the House and Senate—something that had not happened since the midterm elections of 1952. As a result, the teeth of *Goals 2000* were largely removed as states would be given the right to establish their own specific standards using federal government ones as a guideline rather than a mandate with funding tied to compliance. With their autonomy largely maintained, the states set out to devise their own standards. By 2000 every state but Iowa had science teaching standards in place and these standards would frequently be enforced through accountability testing. While not a federal mandate, this standardization process, as such processes essentially always do, proved a victory for the progressives—in this case evolutionary ones, as the vast majority of standards endorsed evolution. With the dawn of 2000, the evolutionary progressives' victory was essentially complete: their beliefs were required and tested throughout the United States while their opponents' ideas had been outlawed.

THE INTELLIGENT DESIGN REVOLT

Representing either survival of the fittest or the power of myth, in the twenty-first century the anti-evolution phoenix arose yet again from the ashes of defeat. From the publication in 1978 of "Freedom of Religion and Science Instruction in Public Schools" in the *Yale Law Journal* to his closing arguments in the 1987 *Edwards v. Aguillard* Supreme Court case, Wendell Bird had led the anti-evolution fight in the United States.[50] However, with the publication of *Darwin on Trial* in 1991 by University of California Law Professor Phillip E. Johnson, the anti-evolution torch passed to a new group, and the strategies used to oppose evolution changed rather radically.[51]

Creationism's association with Fundamentalism had ultimately doomed it and Henry Bird to defeat due to the Court's modern Establishment Clause stance. In fact, Phillip Johnson lamented that in both the public's and the government's eyes the debate had come to be defined as an either-or choice between faith and science. To Johnson, the problem was science's strict adherence to the philosophy of materialism, which disallowed supernatural scientific explanations by linguistic fiat.

To Johnson it was regrettable that previous opponents of naturalism had too often tied the broad idea of creationism to specific Genesis accounts such as the six-day creation and the flood. Johnson argued, in contrast, that a more accurate understanding of creationism generally would more effectively counter materialism. Johnson's efforts did not revolve around establishing a particular faith, but uniting people of faith and non-faith who recognized that materialist assumptions and explanations did not always adequately explicate natural phenomena.[52]

Johnson's far broader understanding of origins held much less chance of being accused of establishing a religion because a wide variety of religions and non-religions fell under this general distrust of pure naturalism. Likewise, the scientific appeal was far greater because it was not motivated *a priori* to the defense of particular religious beliefs; in fact, the position rested on scientific observation and evidence, as well as a healthy amount of mathematical and probability theory, to induce that the world had to be designed. Simply understood, scientists—not theologians—argued that random chance cannot account for the "irreducible complexity" found in things as immense as the universe itself to things as small as microscopic bacterial flagellum. Johnson's call for an inclusive and scientifically based opposition to evolutionary theory became known as "Intelligent Design," and it has continued the debate against evolution from the 1990s into the twentieth century.

Johnson has been joined by a substantial number of scientists and mathematicians, the leading lights being Michael Behe and William Dembski.[53] As scientists, these Intelligent Design advocates maintain that science itself is best served when all evidence is evaluated and theories remain open to questioning, particularly when new evidence is discovered. The position maintained by the Intelligent Design movement—and it is an attractive position for many Americans—is to "teach the controversy." In other words, Intelligent Designers maintain that evolution does have a rightful place in the curriculum, but as a scientific theory rather than a fact. Evolution continues to have many "holes" in its account that scientists cannot explain and assertions that scientists cannot prove. Consequently, it makes sense—particularly in a science class—to examine all the evidence and let students draw their own conclusions. In fact, the Intelligent Designers argue that their scientific discoveries should lead to nothing less than a revolution in science, for they will change how science is pursued by opening up the door once again to supernatural explanations of events when the material evidence suggests that a supernatural conclusion makes the most scientific sense.

The basic tenets of the Intelligent Design movement enjoy wide public support, as Americans overwhelming reject the tenets of materialist evolutionists, but after finally establishing full control over the American public school classroom, the evolutionists obviously have no plans to willingly relinquish their power or make room for others.[54] The fight rages on to determine if they will have to. Thus far, results have been mixed at best for the Intelligent Designers. A major victory was achieved in 2005, when the Kansas Board of Education voted to allow local school boards to include criticisms of Darwinian theories if they so choose and adopted science standards that allowed for supernatural explanations.[55] However, in 2006, Cobb County, Georgia, backed down from its decision to require the placing of stickers on biology textbooks that reminded students that macroevolution was an unproven theory.[56] And, in 2005, Intelligent Design suffered a stinging defeat due to creation scientists borrowing the "intelligent design" moniker for their *Of Pandas and People* textbook. In *Kitzmiller et al. v. Dover Area School District*, U.S. District Court Judge John E. Jones III ruled that the school board of Dover, Pennsylvania's decision to have ninth-grade biology teachers note that Darwinism is a theory and to make books that document problems in evolutionary theory available to students who had an interest in the subject was a violation of the Constitution's Establishment Clause.[57] The Dover School Board's use of the creationist *Of Pandas and People* textbook, whose authors had simply gone through and replaced the word "creation" with "intelligent design," led the judge to equate Intelligent Design with creation science, thereby making the Establishment Clause decision predictable.

FINDING ABSOLUTES IN AN ENDLESSLY EVOLVING DEBATE

Going forward, the debate shows no real sign of disappearing. On the one hand, evolution advocates have an almost unassailable position as a result of three key pillars of strength. The scientific community's allegiance to Darwinism and materialism remains almost airtight despite Intelligent Design advocates' efforts to obtain a place at the table. The ACLU and a host of other civic and legal organizations jealously guard America's school house doors, ever vigilant to keep out those who would question evolutionary dogma. And, from the very beginning, the evolutionists have enjoyed the powerful support of the media. Though perhaps primarily attracted to conflict and controversy, and while at times irritating to evolutionists who do not want their opponents granted any legitimacy through airtime, the media has been an invaluable ally in the evolutionists' efforts to gain control of the schools and mark creationism beyond the intellectual pale. One only has to consider the likelihood of a postmodern-day Mencken rising up to make a mockery of evolutionists or the media creating a show trial on behalf of creationists to recognize the crucial role the media plays in establishing evolutionism.

Despite nearly a century of legal defeats, opponents of evolution nevertheless remain strong enough to fight for the foreseeable future. In fact, though facing formidable odds, there remain a variety of reasons why opponents of materialistic evolution have reason to hope. Though evolution has been taught in American schools now for decades, the vast majority of Americans still rejects its primary tenets and continues to believe in some form of creationism. This both attests to the effectiveness of churches and independent educational organizations in propagating their ideas and gives hope for legal change because in a democracy, the laws tend to eventually represent majority opinion. Interestingly, though evolutionists have historically tried to label adherence to creationism as merely an American (or even a sectional) oddity, the "shrinking" world should allow a "broad-tent" Intelligent Design approach to flourish as Islam, Judaism, and many Eastern faiths also reject evolutionary materialism.

Within the American legal system, evolution currently controls the high ground, but new appointments to the Supreme Court make new interpretations of law a continual threat. Furthermore, the more often evolutionary champions such as Richard Dawkins, Daniel Dennett, and others announce that evolutionary theory necessarily leads to atheism, the more likely it becomes that the Supreme Court will rule the teaching of evolution a violation of the Establishment Clause, as it did creationism.[58]

Finally, though facing an uphill battle within the scientific community, the research being done by the Intelligent Designers demands attention and has garnered a great deal of it from the popular press; and, since it is still in its relative infancy, if Intelligent Design can successfully build on its research it could conceivably become a force with which to be reckoned within the scientific community. Even failing that, though, Intelligent Design's endorsement of "teaching the controversy" will almost assuredly resonate with the American populace because it embraces fair play, respects citizens' beliefs, and avoids the natural rankling that occurs whenever beliefs are dictated to Americans.

Since 1620, religious progressives have attempted to use American schools to establish their beliefs in the succeeding generations. These religious progressives have had different beliefs and have gone by a myriad of names including Puritan, Unitarian, Progressive, Fundamentalist, and Secular-Humanist, but their goals are always the same: use the power of the government to establish their beliefs, their faith, their "shining city on a hill." To progressives of all stripes, separation of church and state tends to mean that their beliefs are true and therefore rightly established by the government while all contrasting beliefs result from a false religion and are therefore banned from the public square by Constitutional decree.

The debate over origins is perhaps best understood as one of the most important battlegrounds in the far broader war for true liberty. Unless one rejects logic altogether, the answers one gives to origins questions will determine one's answers to essentially every other metaphysical, epistemological, and axiological question. Consequently, to suggest that teaching answers regarding origins is not establishing a religion is disingenuous at best. As G.K. Chesterton wrote, "anybody who really understands that question will know that it always has been and always will be a religious question . . . "[59]

Recognizing the true nature of the origins debate in American public schools leads to one final conclusion, and it is the essential debate in church-state relations. However, this answer is not determined but is a difficult choice of personal application. Does one embrace religious progressivism and fight for the establishment of one's faith, or does one defend religious freedom by keeping church and state separate by allowing others the freedom to think and believe as they choose, shining city be damned? The authors of *Inherit the Wind* recognized the value of the Scopes Trial in serving as a metaphor for an abusive use of government power and actually wrote the play to criticize not Fundamentalism but the McCarthy hearings;[60] the Scopes Trial and the debate over origins teachings can remain a potent tool for understanding freedom, but only if one demands the story be seen in Technicolor, not black-and-white.

NOTES

1. I would like to thank Grove City College's The Center for Vision and Values for their support of this project. Without their generous assistance, this research and project could not have been undertaken.

2. *Inherit the Wind*, VHS, dir. Stanley Kramer (1960; Santa Monica, CA: MGM/UA Home Video, 1996).

3. It is appropriate to keep in mind that no debate exists over the existence of "microevolution"—the process within which species adjust to their environment. The debates always revolve around "macroevolution," which argues that all of life has a common ancestor (species can evolve into other species) and there is a material/natural explanation for the initial creation of matter and the world.

4. The first college formed in the colonies was Harvard in 1636. The first compulsory school law in the colonies was passed in Massachusetts in 1642 and the famous "Old Deluder Satan Act" was passed in Massachusetts in 1647.

5. Horace Mann, the "father of the common school," began his twelve year run as Secretary of the Massachusetts School Board in 1837.

6. The Federal Commission of Education did not record national high school enrollment figures in 1880. In 1890, 202,963 pupils, representing 3.8 percent of the 14–17 age group were enrolled. This statistic doubled every decade during the rest of the Progressive period, jumping to 519,251 pupils in 1900, to 915,085 pupils in 1910, and to 1,851,968 pupils in 1920. The number of public high schools also increased dramatically, rising from 2,526 schools in 1890, to 6,005 schools in 1900, to 10,213 schools in 1910, and to 14,326 schools in 1920. This information was collected and presented by Edward J. Larson, but he notes that the rise in high school attendance cannot be attributed to compulsory attendance laws because these were not effectively enforced until 1920. See *Trial and Error* (New York: Oxford University Press, 2003), 26, 220.

7. Charles Darwin, *On the Origin of Species by Means of Natural Selection, or the Preservation of Favoured Races in the Struggle for Life* (Birmingham, AL: Gryphon Editions, 1987).

8. Michael Shermer, *Why Darwin Matters* (New York: Henry Holt and Company, 2006), xxii.

9. Robert B. Downs, *Books that Changed the World*, rev. ed. (New York: Signet Classics, 2004), 284.

10. This "trickle-down" effect is almost always first seen in textbooks that are commonly written by college professors. This first wave is followed closely by new generations of teachers educated at the university. The history of Darwinism's spread is no exception. Edward Larson writes that by "the turn of the century, evolution had clearly supplanted creationism in high-school textbooks... To the extent that textual content was an indication of teaching, public high schools were teaching evolution decades before the anti-evolution crusade, with the presentation seeming to grow more dogmatically Darwinian over time. A review of teaching journals, policies, and manuals reinforces this conclusion." *Trial and Error*, 22, 23.

11. Larson, *Trial and Error*, 48.

12. Ibid., 7.

13. It was only around the turn of the century that high school botany, zoology, and historical zoology began to be combined into the single course of biology. The first high school biology textbook appeared in 1907. Larson, *Trial and Error*, 21.

14. Ibid.

15. The Eighteenth Amendment to the Constitution banning the production and sale of alcoholic beverages was ratified in 1919.

16. The Sixteenth Amendment to the Constitution making income tax legal was ratified in 1913. It originally was only applied to the top one percent of income earners in the nation.

17. The Seventeenth Amendment to the Constitution was ratified in 1913 and

provided for the direct election of Senators. The Nineteenth Amendment to the Constitution was ratified in 1920 and guaranteed women's right to vote.

18. Larson, *Trial and Error*, 57.

19. Ibid., 59.

20. It is probably worth noting to counter popular mythology that John T. Scopes was never jailed and never faced jail time. Everything was arranged in the summer through friendly handshakes at a local soda fountain.

21. Clarence S. Darrow, *Attorney for the Damned*, ed. Arthur Weinberg (New York: Simon and Schuster, 1957).

22. Clarence S. Darrow, *The Story of My Life* (New York: C. Scribner's Sons, 1932), 249.

23. Edward J. Larson, *Summer for the Gods: The Scopes Trial and America's Continuing Debate over Science and Religion* (Cambridge, MA: Harvard University Press, 1997).

24. Ibid., 197.

25. William K. Kilpatrick, "The Wild Man: Why Gorillas Don't Build Libraries But Men Do," *Touchstone* (September 2006), 21–23.

26. A poll was taken of the audience which numbered well over 3,000 after the debate regarding who "won," with Chesterton garnering votes at over a two-to-one clip. American Chesterton Society, "Chesterton Quotemeister," http://www.chesterton.org/qmeister2/darrowdebate.htm (accessed February 9, 2007).

27. For a brilliant and more detailed analysis of this flip-flop in Darrow's rhetorical argument, see Richard Weaver's *The Ethics of Rhetoric* (Davis, CA: Hermagoras Press, 1985), 27–54.

28. American Humanist Association, "Humanist Manifesto I," http://www.americanhumanist.org/about/manifesto1.html (accessed February 9, 2007); American Humanist Association, "Humanist Manifesto II," http://www.americanhumanist.org/about/manifesto2.html (accessed February 9, 2007); American Humanist Association, "Humanist Manifesto III," http://www.americanhumanist.org/3/HumandItsAspirations.htm (accessed February 9, 2007).

29. Larson, *Trial and Error*, 81.

30. Edward Larson cites evidence compiled among others by Maynard Shipley in 1930 that found "70 percent of public high schools omitted teaching evolution" due to its omission in textbooks. Likewise, Larson cites Gerad Skoog's quantitative analysis of texts published between 1930 and 1959, which "found only about 3 percent of the words in texts . . . dealt with evolutionary topics, compared with over 8 percent in texts published during the sixties after evolution generally returned to the classroom." *Trial and Error*, 85–87.

31. Ibid., 91.

32. The Constitution of the United States, Amendment 14, Section 1.

33. Hugo Black famously borrowed the "wall" language from a letter Thomas Jefferson wrote while he was president to the Danbury Baptists assuring them that their religious freedom would be protected.

34. *Engel v. Vitale*, 370 U.S. 421 (1962).

35. *School District of Abington Township, Pennsylvania v. Schempp*, 374 U.S. 203, 209 (1963).

36. Ibid., 222.

37. *Wallace v. Jaffree*, 472 U.S. 38 (1985).

38. *Lee v. Weisman*, 505 U.S. 577 (1992).

39. *Santa Fe Independent School District v. Doe*, 530 U.S. 290 (2000).

40. *School District of Abington Township, Pennsylvania v. Schempp*, 225.

41. Little Rock Arkansas' Central High was of course the location for the famous federal-state showdown stemming from the Warren Court's momentous *Brown v. Board of Education of Topeka, Kansas* decision in 1954. When the Governor and citizens of Arkansas resisted the integration of the "Little Rock Nine" in 1957, President Dwight Eisenhower sent in the 101st Airborne to occupy the school and enforce the federal court's ruling.

42. For an outstanding and detailed recording and analysis of the entire *Epperson* case history, including a rather disturbing account of the disingenuous writing of the Court's opinion by Justice Abe Fortas, see Chapter Four of Edward Larson's *Trial and Error*, 93–124.

43. Larson, *Trial and Error*, 107.

44. Ibid., 113.

45. *Lemon v. Kurtzman* declared unconstitutional both a Rhode Island law and a Pennsylvania law that allowed the state to support salaries of teachers of secular subjects in parochial and private schools.

46. *School District of Abington Township, Pennsylvania v. Schempp*; *Board of Education v. Allen*, 392 U.S. 236 (1968).

47. The state was trying to have the Supreme Court order a lower federal court to have a full hearing on the case that they previously had refused to do, striking down the law without trial.

48. *Edwards v. Aguillard*, 482 U.S. 578 (1987).

49. National Commission on Excellence in Education, *A Nation at Risk: The Imperative for Educational Reform* (Washington, D.C.: U.S. Government Printing Office, 1983).

50. Wendell Bird, "Freedom of Religion and Science Instruction in Public Schools," *The Yale Law Journal* 87, no. 3 (January 1978): 515–570.

51. Phillip Johnson, *Darwin on Trial* (Downers Grove: InterVarsity Press, 1993).

52. Ibid.

53. Michael J. Behe, *Darwin's Black Box: The Biochemical Challenge to Evolution* (New York: Free Press, 1996).; William A. Dembski, *The Design Inference: Eliminating Chance through Small Probabilities (Cambridge Studies in Probability, Induction and Decision Theory)* (Cambridge: Cambridge University Press, 2006).

54. 2006 Gallup polls for instance suggest that 13 percent of the American public believes in pure materialistic evolution while 82 percent believe man was created by God. Gallup Organization, "Evolution, Creationism, Intelligent Design," http://www.galluppoll.com/content/?ci=21814&pg=1 (accessed February 9, 2007).

55. Jodi Wilgoren, "Kansas Board Approves Challenges to Evolution," *New York Times*, November 9, 2005, National Edition.

56. American Civil Liberties Union, "Georgia School Board Drops Defense of Anti-Evolution Stickers," http://www.aclu.org/religion/intelligentdesign/27745prs 20061219.html (accessed February 9, 2007).

57. *Kitzmiller et al. v. Dover Area School District*, 400 F.Supp.2d 707 (M.D. Pa. 2005).

58. Richard Dawkins, *The Blind Watchmaker: Why the Evidence of Evolution Reveals a Universe Without Design* (New York: Norton, 1996); Daniel C. Dennett, *Darwin's Dangerous Idea: Evolution and the Meanings of Life* (New York: Simon & Schuster, 1995).

59. G. K. Chesterton, *The Everlasting Man* (San Francisco: Ignatius Press, 1993), 25.

60. *Inherit the Wind* was written by Jerome Lawrence and Robert Edwin Lee and first opened on Broadway in 1955.

FURTHER READING

When trying to understand any issue, one should begin with an historical exploration of the topic. The debate on origins is no different and thankfully contains Pulitzer Prize-winning work. Edward J. Larson has established himself as the foremost historian on the debate and his works can be enjoyed both for the quality of the research and for the quality of the literary presentation. His *Summer for the Gods: The Scopes Trial and America's Continuing Debate over Science and Religion* is the essential book on the Scopes Trial specifically and his *Trial and Error: The American Controversy over Creation and Evolution* is an invaluable retelling of the origins debate generally. Excellent biographies are also available for many key players in the debates, including a recent important biography, *A Godly Hero: The Life of William Jennings Bryan* by Michael Kazin. However, one may prefer to let historical figures speak for themselves, and it is easy to do in this case as Bryan, Scopes, Darrow, and Chesterton all published autobiographies that record their thoughts and feelings regarding the origins debate and their role in it: William Jennings Bryan and Mary Baird Bryan's *The Memoirs of William Jennings Bryan*, John T. Scopes and James Presley's *Center of the Storm: Memoirs of John T. Scopes*, Clarence S. Darrow's *The Story of My Life* and G.K. Chesterton's *The Autobiography of G.K. Chesterton*.

For those seeking to explore more specific arguments from the various sides, an endless parade of sources awaits. Essentially the first chapter of any science textbook will lay out the basic tenets of evolutionism in a dry textbook style, although one not inclined to indicate any debate exists regarding the material. The works of Richard Dawkins, such as *The Blind Watchmaker: Why the Evidence of Evolution Reveals a World Without Design*, provide a combative advocacy of evolution that will include explanations as to why all evolutionists must be atheists. Agreeing with Dawkins' conclusions about evolution and atheism but not the validity of evolution, Ken Ham is arguably the key spokesman for creation science, producing works such as *The Lie: Evolution*. The book that launched the Intelligent Design movement was Phillip Johnson's *Darwin on Trial*, while Michael Behe's *Darwin's Black Box: The Biochemical Challenge to Evolution* is the most significant scientific work in the Intelligent Design field.

3

Freedom, Commitment, and the Challenges of Pledging of Allegiance in America's Public Schools[1]

Lee Canipe

It is, perhaps, one of the great historical ironies of American culture that the Pledge of Allegiance has become an ongoing source of public controversy. Intended as a patriotic statement of unity and devotion, the pledge—almost from the moment of its composition at the end of the nineteenth century—has instead provided a symbolic battleground for American ideals that are often at odds with one another. The problem with the Pledge of Allegiance, it seems, lies not so much in its *content* (although after 1954, this, too, became problematic) as in how (and where) it has been used. Most states now require their public schools to include the Pledge of Allegiance as part of their daily classroom exercises. Even though the laws in almost all of these states (Delaware is the exception) make explicit provisions for students to opt out of the ritual, the fact that their participation is assumed—if not *expected*—strikes some Americans as implicitly coercive. In a nation which places a high premium on individual freedom, even the *perception* of state-endorsed coercion can be problematic when the freedom in question is the first one mentioned specifically in the Bill of Rights: "Congress shall make no law respecting an establishment of religion or prohibiting the free exercise thereof."

At the same time, however, Americans have long recognized the precarious nature of their collective identity in a country where citizenship is based not on a shared ethnicity, religion, or even, in some cases, history. Instead, the United States is a nation founded, in Thomas Jefferson's words, on the self-evident truths "that all men are created equal" and are "endowed by their Creator with certain unalienable rights." These truths *may* be self-evident, but they are not necessarily self-perpetuating. They must be constantly taught and re-taught as new generations of Americans are born (or naturalized). It was in this context—the need to communicate and conserve a collective sense of American identity—that the Pledge of Allegiance was written. Indeed, when Americans pledge their allegiance to the flag and to the republic for which it stands, they are, by definition, binding themselves to support the essential American ideals of liberty and justice for all. In a nation founded on something as abstract as self-evident truth, regular recitation of the pledge trains Americans to think of themselves as citizens united by a shared love of country.

America's public schools have traditionally been the place where this citizenship training begins in earnest. Practically speaking, the public education system provides the state with direct access to the vast majority of its youngest citizens (the exceptions, of course, being those children educated either at home or at private academies) who are required by law to attend school during their most formative years. Early in the twentieth century, John Dewey recognized this vital role that free public education plays in transmitting democratic values from one generation to the next. Education, he believed, was a deliberate process that prepared children to function appropriately in society, with one of its primary aims being the cultivation of what he called "civic efficiency, or good citizenship."[2]

Not surprisingly, then, daily classroom exercises—saluting the American flag, reciting the Pledge of Allegiance, even, in some schools, singing patriotic songs—have for years been used to teach young Americans the virtues of patriotism and love of country. These exercises, however, can also be a source of anxiety for those citizens whose religious beliefs—or lack thereof—turn an oath like the Pledge of Allegiance into a crisis of conscience. At what point does the state's need to reinforce a collective identity trump an individual's freedom of conscience? When the pledge's specifically religious dimension—that is, the phrase "under God"—is factored into the equation, determining the proper boundaries between rights and responsibilities becomes even more problematic.

Written as a patriotic oath intended both to teach and encourage love of country, the Pledge of Allegiance has become a cultural battleground upon which contrasting views of freedom and commitment—not to mention church and state—have clashed repeatedly over the last several decades, with each side claiming that its perspective best reflects the most essential of American ideals. In this instance, at least, both sides *may* be right.

THE PLEDGE IN HISTORICAL CONTEXT

The Pledge of Allegiance was born in 1892 when Francis Bellamy, a Baptist minister from Little Falls, New York, composed a short patriotic oath in honor of the 400th anniversary of Christopher Columbus's arrival in the New World. Bellamy's "oath of allegiance" first appeared in the September 8, 1892, issue of the popular magazine *Youth's Companion*: "I pledge allegiance to my Flag and to the Republic for which it stands; one nation indivisible, with liberty and justice for all."[3] Later that fall—and at Bellamy's request—President Benjamin Harrison publicly declared his support for the new pledge and proclaimed that the flag should "float over every school house in the country, and the exercises be such as shall impress upon our youth the patriotic duties of American citizenship."[4]

Harrison's endorsement of the pledge as a means of both teaching and reinforcing the responsibilities of citizenship reflected the widely held view at the time that the United States' ever-expanding immigrant population posed a threat to the nation's cultural unity. Among the more vocal adherents of this viewpoint was Josiah Strong, a Congregationalist minister whose popular book, *Our Country* (1885), boldly proclaimed the superiority of the Anglo-Saxon race and culture and the urgent need for Protestant missionaries to counterbalance the dangerous, anti-democratic influence of Roman Catholicism around the world. The continuous influx of foreigners into the United States, however, began to cast some uncomfortable doubt into the minds of "native" Americans as to how long the country would remain "theirs."

Indeed, throughout the latter half of the nineteenth century, millions of immigrants, primarily from Central and Eastern Europe, poured into the United States. The trend continued into the early 1900s. In fact, census figures from the first three decades of the twentieth century show that over 18.5 million people left their homelands to begin new lives in America during those years, more than the total for the previous eighty years combined.[5] The sheer, unprecedented number of immigrants—coupled with their wide diversity of national loyalties, languages, cultures, and religious practices—raised fears that the nation's ability to assimilate new arrivals could very easily be overwhelmed. By the end of the nineteenth century, writes cultural historian Merle Curti, alarmed officials at all levels of government had already begun to recognize "the need for a wholesale and thoroughgoing effort to Americanize the immigrant"—an effort that would focus, primarily, upon the public schools.[6]

In keeping with Harrison's proclamation in support of the pledge, then, thousands of schoolchildren recited Bellamy's oath during Columbus Day flag ceremonies on October 12, 1892. It did not take long for public schools across the nation to make saluting the flag and pledging allegiance part of their regular daily classroom practices. By 1918, a majority of states had passed laws requiring such ceremonies in their schools for the stated purpose of fostering patriotic devotion in the hearts of the nation's youngest—and, in some cases, newest—citizens.[7]

During the 1920s, two revisions to the pledge sought to clarify potential ambiguities in Bellamy's original text. Both were uncontroversial. The first change, made in 1923, replaced the phrase "my Flag" with "the flag of the United States" in order to prevent any lingering confusion in the minds of immigrant children concerning the proper object of their loyalty. Since they were now *Americans*, they would pledge allegiance to the *American* flag—not the flag of their ancestral homes. The second change, made a year later, added the qualifier "of America" to the description of the flag. Both revisions were intended to increase the pledge's effectiveness as an expression of a specifically American communal identity. In June 1942, an act of Congress made Bellamy's composition the "official" pledge of allegiance to the nation's flag.[8]

BECOMING "ONE NATION, UNDER GOD"

The pledge remained unchanged for the next twelve years. During that period, however, international politics and the United States' position in the world changed dramatically, creating new reasons for anxiety in American culture. Though victorious in the effort to defeat fascism—and, significantly, the only industrial power spared the devastation of World War II—the United States soon found itself staring across an ideological divide at the newly resurgent Soviet Union and the specter of "international communism." Soviet dictator Josef Stalin "no longer talked about allied unity," writes historian Ronald Oakley, "but instead warned of the inevitable battle between communism and capitalism."[9] In August 1949, the Russians successfully tested an atomic bomb, breaking the United States' monopoly on the weapon and shattering the American sense of security that came with it. By the end of the year, China had fallen to Mao Zedong and his Communist insurgents, advancing the "Red threat" one step closer to world domination. Sensational revelations about spies in the inner circles of American diplomacy and atomic research only heightened popular fears that

Communists were both attacking the United States from without and subverting it from within.[10] Just as anxiety over the culturally disruptive effects of immigration during the 1890s had prompted public school officials to incorporate flag salutes and the pledge of allegiance into their daily classroom routines, this widespread anxiety over the perceived communist threat led to the insertion of the phrase "under God" into the pledge in 1954.

According to Luke Hart, Supreme Knight of the Knights of Columbus, the idea to include the phrase in the pledge "originated at the Knights of Columbus meetings of Fourth Degree Assemblies in April 1951."[11] Adding "under God" to the pledge, the Catholic fraternal group believed, would acknowledge "the dependence of our Nation and its people upon the Creator of the Universe.[12] The Knights forwarded the resolution to Edmund Radwan, a Republican congressman from upstate New York, who entered it into the *Congressional Record* on March 25, 1953, without comment.

On April 21, 1953—and apparently without knowledge of the New York resolution—Michigan congressman Louis Rabault introduced House Joint Resolution (H. J. Res) 243 proposing that "under God" be added to the Pledge of Allegiance.

"It is my hope," Rabault explained, "that the recitation of the pledge, with this addition, 'under God,' by our schoolchildren will bring to them a deeper understanding of the real meaning of patriotism." Including God in the nation's pledge would send a clear message to the world that unlike communist regimes that denied God's existence, the United States recognized a Supreme Being. Official acknowledgement of God would further distinguish freedom-loving Americans from their atheist adversaries.[13]

Although public support for the change seemed strong in the wake of Rabault's proposal—according to one poll from May 1953, nearly seventy percent of all Americans favored the revision—the "under God" amendment lay dormant in Congress for almost a year.[14] In February 1954, however, the idea of adding God to the pledge gained new momentum. On February 7, George M. Docherty, pastor of the New York Avenue Presbyterian Church in Washington, D.C., lent his vocal support to the "under God" amendment. In a stirring "Lincoln Day" sermon, the pastor called for immediate revision of the pledge. Without "under God," Docherty noted, the Pledge of Allegiance could legitimately be the pledge of any republic, even that of the Soviet Union. God, he believed, is the difference between America and Russia and the Pledge of Allegiance should reflect that. Pointing out that Abraham Lincoln had used "under God" in the Gettysburg Address, the preacher concluded by urging Congress and President Eisenhower, seated with his wife in "Lincoln's Pew," to include the phrase in the pledge.[15]

On February 10, 1954, the "under God" proposal officially resurfaced on Capitol Hill, this time in the Senate, when Homer Ferguson, a Republican from Wisconsin, introduced his own joint resolution to revise the pledge. Again, the inclusion of God was not intended to serve any specific religious purpose. It was, instead, seen as a direct rebuttal of communist ideology and an essential contribution to the national defensive arsenal. "America must be defended by the spiritual values which exist in the hearts of and souls of the American people," said Ferguson. "Our country cannot be defended by ships, planes, and guns alone," he maintained, and the proposed modification of the pledge reflected this reality.[16] That same week, Rabault made his first comments on the pledge issue since the previous April. It is, he told the House of Representatives, "most proper that in our salute to the flag, the patriotic standard around which we rally as Americans, we state the real meaning of that flag. From their earliest childhood our children must know the real meaning of America. Children and Americans of all ages must know that this is one Nation in which 'under God' means 'liberty and justice for all.'"[17]

Over the next several months, other members of the House lent their public support to the effort to amend the pledge. Anticipating possible arguments against the revision, one congressman offered a pre-emptive rebuttal to the claim that invoking God in the pledge undermined the separation of church and state. "The phrase 'under God,'" declared Charles Oakman, a Republican from Michigan, "is inclusive for all religions and has no reference whatever to the establishment of a state church." He also dismissed the argument that the addition of God to the pledge violated freedom of religion. "The right to disbelieve in God is fundamental of a free democracy," he said. "However, there is a vast difference in making a positive affirmation on the existence of God in whom one does not believe, and on the other hand making a pledge of allegiance and loyalty to the flag of a country which in its underlying philosophy recognizes the existence of God."[18]

The potential presence of God in the pledge, then, did not carry any particular religious meaning at all for Oakman. One could believe in God, not believe in God, believe different things about God—it did not matter, for in the end, the pledge was not really about God at all. The pledge, ultimately, was about the flag of the United States of America and the democratic values it symbolized. For all the talk about "godless" communism, Oakman implied that a patriotic atheist could in good conscience pledge allegiance to the flag using the words "under God" because "God" here did not refer to a Supreme Being in the theological sense. "God," instead, represented an icon of democracy that lent transcendent significance to the American system of government. Christians, Jews, atheists, and agnostics alike could *all* say "under God" as long as they believed in America. In none of the conversations about the proposed revision did any member of Congress voice reservations—conscientious, theological, or otherwise—about including God in the pledge.

In May 1954, the judiciary committees of both the House and the Senate voted to recommend that their respective chambers approve the insertion of "under God" into the pledge, and in early June, both houses overwhelmingly passed a joint resolution to insert "under God" into the pledge.[19] As expected, President Eisenhower signed the resolution into law at a White House ceremony on Flag Day, June 14, 1954. "From this day forward, the millions of our schoolchildren will daily proclaim . . . the dedication of our nation and our people to the Almighty," Eisenhower said. "To anyone who truly loves America, nothing could be more inspiring than to contemplate this re-dedication of our youth, in each school morning, to our country's true meaning."[20] The pledge has remained unchanged since 1954.

CONSCIENTIOUS OBJECTIONS AND THE JUDICIAL SHIFT FROM *GOBITIS* TO *BARNETTE*

Despite its intended purpose as an instrument of national unity, the Pledge of Allegiance has nevertheless generated a good deal of controversy since its inception in 1892. The earliest reported opposition to the pledge arose in 1918 when the state of Ohio prosecuted a Mennonite because his daughter refused to recite the oath at school.[21] As John Concannon has noted, however, these early clashes "rarely led to direct court tests because most of these religious groups [e.g., the Mennonites, the Jehovah's Witnesses, the Elijah Voice Society, and the Church of God] refused to resort to the court to defend their children from school expulsion."[22] It was not until the late 1930s that public school policies requiring students to recite the pledge came under significant legal scrutiny. On five separate occasions between 1937 and 1939, the Supreme Court refused to hear cases dealing with the pledge and the public schools.[23] Although the particular personalities and circumstances varied from case to case, all ultimately addressed the same fundamental challenge: finding a balance between protecting the integrity of the individual conscience on the one hand and promoting a shared identity for the community on the other. By refusing to act on these cases, the Supreme Court in each instance effectively gave priority to the interests of the community—specifically, the need to educate children in the virtues of good citizenship and patriotism. In dismissing the case of *Leoles v. Landers* (1937), for example, the Court tacitly affirmed that "school officials acted lawfully in expelling students who refused to salute the flag incident to their duty to instruct children in the study of and devotion to American institutions and ideals."[24]

The Supreme Court's implicit endorsement of communitarian interests at the expense of individual rights became explicit in the spring of 1940 when the justices agreed to hear *Minersville (Penn.) School District v. Gobitis*.[25] The circumstances surrounding the case resembled those of the earlier pledge-related disputes. Twelve-year-old Lillian Gobitis and her ten-year-old brother, William, had been expelled from the Minersville public schools for refusing to salute the American flag and recite the Pledge of Allegiance during their school's daily patriotic ceremony.[26] Raised by parents who were Jehovah's Witnesses, the Gobitis children had been taught to obey the Ten Commandments as found in the Bible, particularly the first—"Thou shalt have no other gods before me" (Exodus 20:3)—and second—"Thou shalt not make unto thee any graven image" (Exodus 20:4). Pledging allegiance to anything or anyone except God and saluting the flag violated both of these commandments and were therefore forbidden by God. Unwilling to disobey God and shirk their religious obligations, the Gobitis children declined to participate in the required school ceremony as a matter of individual conscience. Their parents sued the school district and eventually the case arrived at the Supreme Court.

While recognizing that individual expressions of belief (or disbelief) were protected from interference by the government, the Supreme Court nevertheless decisively upheld the Minersville public school district's policy of expulsion for students who refuse to participate in mandatory patriotic exercises. The rights of an individual's conscience, it seemed, did have limits. Indeed, writing for the majority in the 8–1 decision, Justice Felix Frankfurter framed the issue as a matter of communitarian interest. "When does the constitutional guarantee [of freedom of conscience]," he wrote, "compel exemption from doing what society thinks is necessary for the promotion of some great common end, or from a penalty for conduct which appears dangerous to the general good?"[27]

Operating under the assumption that "national unity is the basis for national security," Frankfurter argued that the need to encourage patriotic loyalty in the hearts of its citizens provided the government with a compelling reason for limiting liberty of conscience.[28] "The ultimate foundation of a free society is the binding tie of cohesive sentiment," he continued, and in the United States, the national flag symbolized that sense of unity. So, could local authorities take appropriate measures such as requiring school children to salute the flag and recite the Pledge of Allegiance in order "to evoke that unifying sentiment without which there can ultimately be no liberties, civil or religious?"[29] Frankfurter answered his own rhetorical question affirmatively. Some methods of evoking patriotic sentiment, he admitted, "may seem harsh and others no doubt foolish. Surely, however, the end is legitimate."[30] Moreover, he concluded, making individual exceptions to communal civic exercises for reasons of conscience "might introduce elements of difficulty into the school discipline, [and] might cast doubts in the minds of other children which would themselves weaken the effect of the exercise."[31] In other words, when national security depended upon national unity, one bad apple might spoil the whole barrel.

As the lone dissenting vote in the decision, however, Justice Harlan Stone issued a scathing opinion in which he dismissed Frankfurter's equation of national security with national unity. Certainly the Constitution's guarantees of personal liberty are not absolute, he wrote. The selective service system, for example, compels individuals to enter the military whether they want to or not. The compelling interest of national security, Stone observed, justifies such compulsion. "But it is a long step," he continued, "and one which I am unable to take, to the position that government may, as a supposed educational measure and as a means of disciplining the young, compel public affirmations which violate their religious conscience."[32] The state may indeed be convinced that forcing young schoolchildren to recite a pledge of allegiance "will contribute to national unity," Stone conceded, but "there are other ways to teach loyalty and patriotism which are the sources of national unity, than by compelling the pupil to affirm that which he does not believe."[33] The Gobitis children's refusal to say the pledge hardly represented a grave threat to national unity (or national security, for that matter), Stone argued. Even if it did, though, the state's action was problematic:

The Constitution may well elicit expressions of loyalty to it and to the government which it created, but it does not command such expressions or otherwise give any indication that compulsory expressions of loyalty play any such part in our scheme of government so as to override the constitutional protection of freedom of speech and religion. And while such expressions of loyalty, when voluntarily given, may promote national unity, it is quite another matter to say that their compulsory expression by children in violation of their own and their parents' religious convictions can be regarded as playing so important a part in our national unity as to leave school boards free to exact it despite the constitutional guarantee of freedom of religion.[34]

The *Gobitis* decision struck many Americans as heavy-handed and immediately came under heavy criticism. The editors of over 170 newspapers, for example, sided with Stone in opposing the ruling. "We think the decision is a violation of American principle," opined the *St. Louis Dispatch*. "If patriotism depends upon such things as this—upon violation of a fundamental right of religious freedom—then it becomes not a noble emotion of love for country, but something to be rammed down our throats by the law."[35] At the same time, Jehovah's Witnesses across the country paid a stiff price for their convictions. Within two weeks of the *Gobitis* decision, the Justice Department had received hundreds of reports describing angry attacks by Americans incensed by the Witnesses' perceived lack of patriotism and apparent disloyalty.[36]

Three years later, the Supreme Court revisited the issue in *West Virginia State Board of Education v. Barnette*. By this time, however, the United States had been plunged into the Second World War and the shadows of fascism—particularly the spectacular Nazi propaganda program in Germany with its mass rallies, swastika flags, and straight-armed salutes to Hitler—cast the arguments over coerced expressions of patriotic devotion in a decidedly different light. Once more, the Jehovah's Witnesses were at the center of controversy over public school policies regarding the flag and the pledge.

Encouraged by the outcome of the *Gobitis* decision, the West Virginia State Board of Education had adopted a policy that added a flag salute and pledge to the daily public school program. Students who refused to participate would be considered insubordinate and subject to appropriate disciplinary measures. A group of Jehovah's Witnesses, again citing scrupulous obedience to the Ten Commandments as a religious obligation, petitioned the federal district court in West Virginia for an injunction to stop enforcement of the law. Several conscientiously objecting students had already been expelled from school—with some even threatened with reform school for juvenile delinquents—and their parents now faced criminal prosecution for encouraging the delinquency of minors.

In an abrupt reversal of both its decision in *Gobitis* and its implicit endorsement of community authority during the late 1930s, a divided Supreme Court ruled 6–3 in favor of the Jehovah's Witnesses claim that mandatory participation in flag ceremonies infringed upon individual rights of conscience. Writing for the majority, Justice Robert H. Jackson argued that, insofar as a compulsory flag salute and pledge required "an affirmation of a belief and an attitude of mind,"[37] the central question raised by the case was whether or not the government had the power "to force an American citizen publicly to profess any statement of belief or to engage in any ceremony of assent."[38] Echoing Stone's *Gobitis* dissent, Jackson firmly concluded that it did not.

With the example of Nazi Germany as a backdrop, Jackson observed that "those who begin coercive elimination of dissent soon find themselves exterminating dissenters. Compulsory unification of opinion achieves only the unanimity of the graveyard."[39] Against Frankfurter's assertion that voluntary participation in public school flag ceremonies would weaken the overall effectiveness of such exercises if some children opted out, Jackson noted that believing "patriotism will not flourish if patriotic ceremonies are voluntary and spontaneous instead of a compulsory routine is to make an unflattering estimate of the appeal of our institutions to free minds."[40] He then moved to address the central constitutional issue at stake in the case, which, for Jackson, was a matter of individual freedom of thought:

If there is any fixed star in our constitutional constellation, it is that no official, high or petty, can prescribe what shall be orthodox in politics, nationalism, religion, or other matters of opinion or force citizens to confess by word or act their faith therein . . . We think the action of the local authorities [in West Virginia] in compelling the flag salute and pledge transcends constitutional limitation on their power and invades the sphere of intellect and spirit which it is the principle of the First Amendment to our Constitution to reserve from all official control.[41]

The *Barnette* opinion, then, marked the tipping point with regard to the Pledge of Allegiance in the Supreme Court's attempt to negotiate a proper balance between the government's power to shape the collective loyalty of its citizens and the rights of each citizen to believe and behave in keeping with the mandates of individual conscience. Following *Barnette*, the burden of proof would be on the government to demonstrate a compelling interest for requiring citizens to make public oaths or affirmations of belief. Conscience had trumped community, at least at the level of constitutional jurisprudence. Even after *Barnette*, however, the spirit of *Gobitis*—that is, the belief that America's strength lies in its unanimity of will, even if that unanimity must, at times, be coerced—continued (and continues) to shape not only public school policies regarding the Pledge of Allegiance, but political conversations regarding the definition of patriotism as well. Indeed, the fact that as of June 2006 all but seven of the states in the union had laws either requiring or encouraging pledge ceremonies in the public schools certainly reflects this persistent American desire for a cohesive national community, even at the expense of individual liberty.

PLEDGE OR PRAYER?

The 1954 revision of the pledge added a new, quasi-theological dimension to the ongoing conversation about the Pledge of Allegiance's place in the public schools. At first, the invocation of God in the pledge caused hardly a ripple in the mainstream consciousness. In the relatively homogenous culture that sociologist Will Herberg famously described in 1955 as "Protestant-Catholic-Jew," most Americans at the time simply assumed that their fellow citizens shared a belief in God.[42] The specific content of that belief, however, was less important than the act of believing itself. "Our government makes no sense unless it is founded on a deeply felt religious faith," Eisenhower proclaimed in 1952, "and I don't care what it is."[43] This seemingly benign spiritual ambiguity, observed Herberg, could have negative, unintended consequences. "So thoroughly secularist has American religion become," he wrote, "that the familiar distinction between religion and secularism appears to be losing much of its meaning under present-day conditions" as both sides of the divide share the same basic "values and assumptions defined by the American Way of Life."[44] As long as the cultural lines between religion and secularism remained fuzzy, such vague invocations of God as found in the revised Pledge of Allegiance seemed harmless enough.[45]

All that changed, however, in June 1962, when the Supreme Court declared the practice of government-sponsored prayer in New York's public schools to be an unconstitutional establishment of religion. "It is neither sacrilegious or [sic] antireligious," wrote Justice Hugo Black for the majority in *Engel v. Vitale*, "to say that each separate government in this country should stay out of the business of writing or sanctioning official prayers and leave that purely religious function to the people themselves and to those the people choose to look to for religious guidance."[46] Although Black's opinion made clear that the constitutional problem lay not in the practice of prayer itself but, rather, in the fact that the New York State Board of Regents had written the prayer, the Court's ruling effectively signaled the end of officially-recognized prayer in the public schools.[47]

A year later, the Supreme Court struck down a Pennsylvania state law requiring that ten verses from the Bible be read without comment at the beginning of every public school day. The prescribed ceremony also included the Lord's Prayer, the Pledge of Allegiance, and any relevant announcements. Even though the law allowed students to be excused from participating for reasons of conscience, the Court nevertheless considered the practice to be an establishment of religion. By an 8–1 majority, the justices ruled in *Abington (Penn.) School District v. Schempp* (1963) that no state legislature or local school board could require that Bible readings or the Lord's Prayer be a mandatory part of the daily public school program.[48]

In the aftermath of *Engel* and *Abington*, the 1954 addition of "under God" to the pledge suddenly assumed a significance far beyond what Rabault, Ferguson, and the other sponsors of the revision originally envisioned. Indeed, as historian Garry Wills has observed, the combined effect of these two decisions meant that by the early 1960s, the Pledge of Allegiance had become the only place "in almost every school's daily regimen where God [could] still be mentioned."[49] The pledge had, in the minds of some Americans, become a kind of prayer: what had begun as an uncontroversial ideological device now loomed as a potentially divisive point of contention in a culture where the once-blurry distinctions between religion and secularism were slowly growing sharper.

In the nearly forty years following *Engel* and *Abington*, several complaints involving the Pledge of Allegiance made their way into the lower courts. In almost all of them, religion—specifically, the mention of God in the oath—played a central role. Old assumptions that all Americans could in good conscience affirm a belief in a widely shared, elastic concept of God no longer held true. In 1966, the New Jersey Supreme Court heard arguments on behalf of Black Muslim students who refused to participate in the pledge ceremony on the basis of their religious beliefs.[50] During the early 1970s, federal courts in Florida, Maryland, and New York struck down laws requiring all students to stand during the pledge, regardless of their willingness to participate in reciting the oath.[51] The courts' rulings were consistent: as long as non-participating students remained quiet and respectful during the pledge, they could remain seated without penalty by school officials.

Several teachers—again, for reasons of religious conscience—also objected to state laws that required them to *lead* their students in the pledge. In *Russo v. Central School District No. 1* (1972, 1973), a federal appeals court ruled that a teacher who remained silent while her students recited the pledge could neither be forced to join the ceremony nor disciplined by school officials for her refusal.[52] Seven years later, though, the Seventh Circuit Court of Appeals arrived at a different verdict in the case of an Illinois teacher who claimed that her religious beliefs prevented her from participating in the Pledge of Allegiance and other elements in her public school's daily patriotic ceremony. The court concluded that despite her religious scruples, the teacher did not have the freedom to disregard (as she had done) the entire prescribed curriculum for encouraging civic responsibility and national loyalty—a program that included not only the pledge, but patriotic songs and the observance of national holidays as well.[53] In so ruling, the appeals court effectively implied that the Pledge of Allegiance should properly be understood as a statement of patriotic—not religious—conviction. As Wills noted, though, not all Americans shared this assumption.

Among the notable judicial opinions concerning the pledge that emerged in the 1970s was a nonbinding advisory ruling issued by the Supreme Judicial Court of Massachusetts. The state legislature had passed a bill that would require public school teachers to lead their classes in reciting the Pledge of Allegiance at the beginning of each school day. In considering whether or not to sign the bill into law, Massachusetts governor Michael Dukakis asked the court to offer its opinion on the constitutionality of the measure—to state, in other words, how they *would* rule if a case ever arose involving the statute in question. Citing *Barnette* as a precedent, the court advised that such a law would likely be found unconstitutional as a violation of the First Amendment.[54] With the court's advice in mind, Dukakis vetoed the legislation in 1977.

This veto might have faded into obscurity had Dukakis not run for president in 1988. As the Democratic nominee, however, Dukakis quickly discovered the unfortunate political consequences of even *appearing* to oppose the Pledge of Allegiance. Vice President George H. W. Bush, the Republican candidate, used the 1977 veto to portray Dukakis as a dangerous liberal full of contempt for American patriotic values. "Should public school teachers be required to lead our children in the Pledge of Allegiance?" Bush asked rhetorically at the GOP convention. "My opponent says no—but I say yes."[55] Dukakis' meekly indignant response—"I can't imagine a President of the United States who knows a bill is unconstitutional and proceeds to sign it anyway"—failed to deflect the political impact of the charge.[56]

"It's very hard for me to imagine that the Founding Fathers—Samuel Adams, John Adams, John Hancock—would have objected to teachers leading students in the Pledge of Allegiance to the flag of the United States," the vice president told one audience while speaking from a platform adorned with dozens of large American flags.[57] Despite repeated efforts to explain his veto of the Massachusetts pledge bill, Dukakis' nuanced arguments about freedom of conscience and Supreme Court precedents came across as legal hair-splitting compared to Bush's blunt, emotional appeal. "Of course the pledge is taken all the time in Massachusetts," an exasperated Dukakis said. "We take it in ceremonies and everything else. I encourage schoolchildren to say the Pledge of Allegiance."[58] Dukakis' plaintive attempts to justify his veto decision, however, largely failed to sway those voters who feared that his stated concern for civil liberties masked a deeper, more serious threat.

This fear was especially prevalent among conservative, evangelical Christians whose influence in Republican politics had, by 1988, become impossible to ignore. In the years since *Engel* and *Abington*, the pace of secularization in America seemed to have accelerated at a dizzying rate, with public expressions of religious sentiment coming under attack in the name of civil liberty.[59] For these conservative Christians "who are dismayed when Christmas symbols are removed from public places, who fear ever for the mention of God on coins and public buildings," the historian Wills wrote in 1990, "the words in the pledge are a bastion they must rally to defend. Prayer may be forbidden, but one act of homage is still allowed."[60]

Robert Dornan, a Republican congressman from California, effectively reduced the issue to a concise sound bite during a debate in the House of Representatives on the merits of the pledge. The problem, he said, "is there are some people in this country who resent that pledge . . . [because] they resent the word that we see over your head, Mr. Speaker: God."[61] While Democrats accused Dornan, Bush, and other Republicans of creating a false controversy for purely political purposes, their arguments nevertheless struck a responsive popular chord. In the minds of many Americans, then, preventing students from reciting of the Pledge of Allegiance seemed tantamount to excluding God from the public schools once and for all.

THE *NEWDOW* CHALLENGE

Around the same time that the Pledge of Allegiance briefly took center stage in a presidential campaign, a specific legal challenge to the phrase "under God" emerged in Illinois when atheist Rob Sherman filed suit on behalf of his son, a student in the local public schools. The invocation of God, Sherman claimed, represented a form of religious establishment and thus constituted a violation of the First Amendment. His argument, however, failed to persuade the courts. Upholding the district court ruling against Sherman, the Seventh Circuit appeals court observed that like the phrase "In God We Trust," the pledge's invocation of God carried no real religious significance. Rather, the judges asserted, it was simply a ceremonial expression used to convey a sense of ritual solemnity.[62] The theological vacuity of "under God," in other words, enabled it to pass constitutional muster.

The *Sherman* verdict—or, rather, the assumptions behind it—went to the heart of the matter surrounding the Pledge of Allegiance as a quasi-religious statement of belief. How did the invocation of God in the pledge function? As a theological affirmation of faith or a patriotic declaration of American ideals? The original intent behind the 1954 revision, of course, suggested the latter. Free, democratic Americans believed in God; atheistic communists did not. Under what God, though, did the United States exist? The God who Christians believed was revealed in Jesus Christ? The God who established a covenant relationship with the people of Israel? The "Nature's God" to whom Thomas Jefferson referred in the Declaration of Independence? Something else entirely? The precise *theological* nature of the

God invoked in the pledge certainly did not concern the congressmen and senators who proposed and endorsed the change.

In keeping with this ambiguous definition of God, the *Sherman* ruling left it up to individual Americans to supply their own theological interpretations of this "ceremonial expression." Still, for most people, the name of God is not an empty vessel that, depending upon the circumstances, may or may not carry any significance. Certainly this is true for individuals with strong religious convictions. It is also true, however, for individuals of no religious convictions beyond the belief that God does not exist. For atheists like Sherman, the mere invocation of God—with its implication that God, however God might be defined, exists—represented a distinct statement of religious belief, regardless of its alleged neutrality.

On these grounds, Michael Newdow, an atheist in California, mounted the most successful (to date) legal offensive against the practice of having public school students recite the Pledge of Allegiance in its revised form.[63] The phrase "under God," he argued, violated the First Amendment's prohibition against the establishment of religion by giving the government's implicit endorsement to the belief that God exists. In 1998, a judge dismissed Newdow's first attempt to put the pledge on trial—Newdow's daughter, on whose behalf he was acting, was too young for public school and, hence, too young to participate in public school patriotic ceremonies. His appeal two years later was also dismissed. In 2002, however, he won a surprising victory when Judge Alfred T. Goodwin and the Ninth Circuit Court of Appeals ruled that, in light of previous Supreme Court decisions, the phrase "under God" in the pledge did indeed represent an unconstitutional establishment of religion.[64] A revised opinion, issued soon after the original, focused specifically on the precedent set by *Lee v. Weisman* (1992), in which the Supreme Court declared unconstitutional the practice of nonsectarian prayer at public school graduation.

In his majority opinion on *Lee* a decade earlier, Justice Anthony Kennedy had observed that, although attendance at graduation exercises was voluntary, the practice raised serious "concerns with protecting freedom of conscience from subtle coercive pressure in the elementary and secondary public schools."[65] In other words, leaving young students who objected to public prayer with only two options—violate their beliefs or protest the ceremony—placed them in an emotionally and psychologically vulnerable position that was essentially equivalent to the kind of official coercion prohibited by the Establishment Clause. A slim majority (5–4) of the Court agreed with him. Guided primarily by the *Lee* precedent, then, Goodwin reasoned that if a nonsectarian prayer offered *once* at a *voluntary* school event could not pass constitutional muster, then a nonsectarian invocation of God recited *daily* in classrooms where attendance was *mandatory* could hardly withstand the same scrutiny.

Reaction to the Ninth Circuit's decision was swift and severe. President George W. Bush called it "ridiculous."[66] Televangelist Pat Robertson condemned the ruling as "a senseless act of judicial tyranny."[67] James Dobson, founder of the influential conservative Christian organization Focus on the Family, declared it a "cockamamie edict" and the latest example of "the liberal judiciary running amok in our land." Clearly, he wrote, "these liberal judges must have believed that, in view of all the other successful assaults on religious faith taking place in recent days, it was time to go for broke."[68]

Not all Americans objected to the decision. The northern California chapter of the American Civil Liberties Union (ACLU), for example, hailed the Ninth Circuit Court for "breath[ing] life into the Pledge's stirring ideal of a country 'with liberty and justice for all.' The decision secured liberty for children of minority faiths who have quietly been denied religious freedom for nearly fifty years, when pressured at public school to pledge allegiance to a God they do not worship."[69] Supporters of the ruling, however, formed a distinct minority. A poll taken by *Newsweek* on June 30, 2002, showed that almost ninety percent of the country believed that "under God" should remain in the pledge.[70]

The Elk Grove Unified School District, where Newdow's daughter then attended public school, petitioned the Supreme Court to review the Ninth Circuit's decision. When the justices agreed to hear the case—a milestone in and of itself, marking the first time a legal challenge to "under God" had reached the high court—activists on both sides hoped for an emphatic ruling to settle the question once and for all. Instead, the Court's anticlimactic decision in June of 2004 sidestepped issues of church and state almost entirely. The justices *did* reverse the Ninth Circuit ruling, but they did so on the purely technical ground that Newdow lacked the legal standing to bring a lawsuit on behalf of his daughter.[71] Justice John Paul Stevens wrote the majority opinion, which focused almost exclusively on matters of family law and the definition of standing.

In a concurring opinion, however, Chief Justice William Rehnquist directly addressed the First Amendment questions that Newdow's case had raised. The phrase "under God," he argued, does not automatically convert recitation of the Pledge of Allegiance from a patriotic exercise into a religious one. Instead, he continued, when taking the pledge, "participants promise fidelity to one flag and one nation, not to any particular God, faith, or church."[72] The burden on Newdow, the chief justice wrote, was to demonstrate that the pledge's reference to God "tend[ed] to the establishment of a *religion* in violation of the First Amendment."[73] Insofar as the

Pledge of Allegiance was a *patriotic*—instead of a religious—exercise, Rehnquist doubted that such a successful demonstration was possible.[74]

With the Supreme Court's reversal of the *Newdow* verdict, "under God" survived its most serious challenge yet—but only by a technical knockout. The Court's unwillingness to offer a conclusive ruling (Rehnquist's concurrence—along with those of O'Connor and Thomas— notwithstanding) on the case satisfied few observers on either side of the issue and almost certainly ensured that legal wrangling over God's place in the Pledge of Allegiance would continue into the future.

CONCLUSION

As of June 2006, 43 of the 50 states in the union had statutes either requiring or strongly encouraging public school students to recite the Pledge of Allegiance daily.[75] Wisconsin's law made the pledge mandatory in private schools as well. In the wake of the *Newdow* challenges, several of these state laws have faced legal opposition. Some of these efforts have succeeded. In 2004, for example, the U.S. Third Circuit Court of Appeals struck down Pennsylvania's pledge law as unconstitutional because it required school officials to notify the parents of children who chose not to take the oath. Interestingly, the court ruled that the notification requirement violated the students' right to free *speech*—not their *religious* freedom.[76]

The Pennsylvania decision, however, represents a rare exception to the general trend upholding these laws on the grounds that the pledge should be properly understood as a patriotic ceremony. Echoing Rehnquist, Judge Karen J. Williams of the Fourth Circuit Court of Appeals took this approach in her 2005 opinion in support of Virginia's pledge law. Unlike prayer, she wrote, the Pledge of Allegiance "is not a religious exercise or activity, but a patriotic one." As such, its use in the public schools "does not amount to an establishment of religion."[77] Still, in an increasingly multicultural and multireligious society, the pledge's invocation of God remains problematic—even for jurists who generally support its use in the public schools. While joining Williams in upholding the Virginia law, for example, Judge Diana Gribbon Motz acknowledged that for atheists or for those citizens from a polytheistic religious traditions, "requiring recitation of the Pledge, with its invocation of a monotheistic God, might well be seen as both favoring religion over nonreligion and 'preferring' one religious tradition over another."[78]

Motz's concerns reflect the reality of an American culture that is significantly more diverse today than it was in 1954 when Congress added "under

God" to the Pledge of Allegiance. In those days, sociologist Will Herberg could describe almost the entire American religious spectrum in shorthand: Protestant-Catholic-Jew. Not so in a twenty-first century where new religious movements continue to mushroom across the nation's spiritual landscape. A survey conducted by the City University of New York in 2001, for example, revealed that the fastest growing religion in the United States between 1990 and 2001 was the neo-pagan practice of Wicca, or witchcraft.[79] While the number of self-described witches in America represents but a tiny sliver of the overall population, the spectacular growth of the Wiccan movement (from 8,000 to 134,000 in eleven years) is indicative of a trend toward greater religious diversity that shows no signs of slowing down. In such an environment, public invocations of God in *any* context will likely provoke increasingly more opposition from those Americans who fall outside the traditional boundaries of "Protestant-Catholic-Jew." When the specific context is a public school patriotic exercise, though, the potential for future legal conflict will remain high as long as the Supreme Court declines to rule decisively on the First Amendment status of God in the pledge.

That the Pledge of Allegiance should be a continuing source of public controversy is indeed ironic, given its originally intended purpose as a statement of American unity. Given the famously dichotomous character of what Alexis de Tocqueville described as "Anglo-American civilization," however, perhaps this ongoing tension should not be surprising. The American character, wrote Tocqueville in *Democracy in America*, "is the result (and this should be constantly present to the mind) of two distinct elements, which in other places have been in frequent hostility, but which in America have been admirably incorporated and combined with one another. I allude to the spirit of Religion and the spirit of Liberty."[80]

During the first 62 years of its existence, the Pledge of Allegiance served as a frequent battleground for two understandings of American liberty: an individual citizen's freedom to follow the dictates of conscience and a democratic community's freedom to define itself and its values. Since 1954—and, especially, since the early 1960s—it has also become a bone of contention in the ongoing American struggle between freedom *for* religion and freedom *from* religion. As such, then, it *could* be that the pledge (and the attendant controversy surrounding it) performs a most valuable—if sometimes conflicted—service to the nation's democracy, forcing citizens of different ideological and theological persuasions to discuss once again not only what it means to be an American, but also how best to define an allegiance that is worth pledging.

NOTES

1. Many thanks to Emilee Simmons of the Baptist Joint Committee on Public Affairs for her assistance in providing valuable research materials for this essay.

2. John Dewey, *Democracy and Education: An Introduction to the Philosophy of Education* (New York: Macmillan, 1916; rpr. 1924), 3–4, 140ff.

3. "Under God," *Time*, May 17, 1954, 101. Bellamy's pledge replaced an earlier, decidedly less poetic—but infinitely more exclamatory—ode to the flag written by Col. George T. Balch: "We give our Heads!—and our Hearts!—to God! and our Country! One Country! One Language! One Flag!" See Balch, *A Patriotic Primer for Little Citizens* (Indianapolis: William B. Burford, 1895), 16.

4. *The Youth's Companion* 65 (1892): 457.

5. Sydney Ahlstrom, *A Religious History of the American People* (New Haven, CT: Yale University Press, 1972), 749–750.

6. Merle Curti, *The Roots of American Loyalty* (New York: Columbia University Press, 1946), 185. For an excellent account of how the flag ritual developed in American public schools, see Scot M. Guenter, *The American Flag, 1777–1924: Cultural Shifts from Creation to Codification* (Rutherford, NJ: Fairleigh Dickinson University Press, 1990), 114ff.

7. See Guenter, 132. See also, David Manwaring, *Render Unto Caesar: The Flag-Salute Controversy* (Chicago: University of Chicago Press, 1962), 1–16.

8. *New York Times*, April 22, 1953.

9. Ronald Oakley, *God's Country: America in the Fifties* (New York: Dembner Books, 1986), 5.

10. The most notorious of these revelations dealt with scientists Julius and Ethel Rosenberg, who were executed in 1953 for selling atomic secrets to the Soviets, and the high-profile congressional investigation that led to the conviction on perjury charges of former State Department attaché (and alleged spy) Alger Hiss in 1950. For a good account of how the "Red Scare" manifested itself in American culture, see Richard Fried, *The Russians are Coming! The Russians are Coming! Pageantry and Patriotism in Cold War America* (New York: Oxford University Press, 1998).

11. "Letters," *Newsweek*, June 21, 1954, 2, 6. See also Christopher Kauffman, *Faith and Fraternalism: The History of the Knights of Columbus, 1882–1982* (New York: Harper and Row, 1982), 385.

12. Congress, House, Resolution of the New York Fraternal Congress, entered into the record by Congressman Radwan of New York, 83rd Cong., 1st sess., *Congressional Record* 99, pt. 10 (March 25, 1953): A1494.

13. Congress, House, Congressman Rabault of Michigan introducing H.J. Res. 243 to amend the Pledge of Allegiance, 83rd Cong., 1st sess., *Congressional Record* 99, pt.10 (April 21, 1953): A2063. In February of 1953, FBI director J. Edgar Hoover offered a word of advice to the nation's parents that accurately captured the spirit of the argument: "Since Communists are anti-God, encourage your children to go to church." See William Lee Miller, "Piety Along the Potomac," *Reporter*, August 17, 1954, 28.

14. A Gallup poll released on May 9, 1953, indicated that 69 percent of the American public favored the idea of adding "under God" to the pledge, 21 percent opposed it, and 10 percent had no opinion. See *The Gallup Poll: Public Opinion, 1935–1971, Vol. 2,* 1140.

15. George M. Docherty, "Under God," sermon preached at the New York Avenue Presbyterian Church, Washington, D.C., February 7, 1954. The full text of the sermon can be found on the New York Avenue Presbyterian Church's website at http://www.nyapc.org/congregation/Sermon_Archives/?month=1954-02. Excerpts of Docherty's sermon were entered into the official record of Congress by Rep. Rabault. See Congress, House, Congressman Rabault of Michigan speaking for the Joint Resolution on the Pledge of Allegiance, H.J. Res. 243, 83rd Cong., 2nd sess. *Congressional Record* 100, pt. 2 (February 12, 1954): 1700.

16. Congress, Senate, Senator Ferguson of Wisconsin introducing the Joint Resolution on the Pledge of Allegiance, S.J. Res. 126, 83rd Cong., 2nd sess. *Congressional Record* 100, pt. 2 (February 10, 1954): 1600–01.

17. Congress, House, Congressman Rabault of Michigan speaking for the Joint Resolution on the Pledge of Allegiance, H.J. Res. 243, 83rd Cong., 2nd sess. *Congressional Record* 100, pt. 2 (February 12, 1954): 1700.

18. Congress, House, Congressman Oakman of Michigan speaking for the Joint Resolution on the Pledge of Allegiance, H.J. Res. 371, 83rd Cong., 2nd sess. *Congressional Record* 100, pt. 2 (February 12, 1954): 1697–98.

19. It is interesting to note that the only significant debate about the revision that did occur in Congress revolved around the question of who would get official credit for it. Understandably, both the Republican Ferguson and the Democrat Rabault (and their respective parties) wanted to claim responsibility for the change, and their bickering on the question threatened to undo the bipartisan goodwill that the pledge amendment had generated. In an unusually gracious political move, Ferguson finally endorsed Rabault's bill as the "official" proposal to revise the pledge. For a more detailed account of this episode, see Gerard Kaye and Ferenc Szasz, "Adding 'Under God' to the Pledge of Allegiance," *Encounter* 34 (1973): 52–56.

20. U.S. President, *Public Papers of the Presidents of the United States* (Washington, D.C.: Office of the *Federal Register*, National Archives and Records Service, 1960), Dwight D. Eisenhower, 1954, 141.

21. See *Troyer v. State* 21 Ohio N.P. (n.s.) 121, 124 (1918).

22. John J. Concannon, III, "The Pledge of Allegiance and the First Amendment," *Suffolk University Law Review* 23 (1989): 1022.

23. The cases were *Nicholls v. Mayor of Lynn, Mass.* (1937), *Leoles v. Landers* (1937), *Hering v. New Jersey State Board of Education* (1938), *Johnson v. Town of Deerfield, Mass.* (1939), *Gabrielli v. Knickerbocker* (1939). For a good, concise summary of these cases, see Charles J. Russo, "The Pledge of Allegiance: Patriotic Duty or Unconstitutional Establishment of Religion?," *School Business Affairs* (July/August 2003): 23.

24. Ibid., 23.

25. For an extensive account of this case, see Peter Irons, *The Courage of Their Convictions: Sixteen Americans Who Fought Their Way to the Supreme Court* (New York: Penguin Books, 1990), 15–24.

26. Lillian Gobitis Klose recalls her experience at the center of the flag salute controversy in Irons, 25–35.

27. *Minersville (Penn.) School District v. Gobitis* 310 U.S. 586 (1940), at 593.

28. Ibid. at 595.

29. Ibid. at 597.

30. Ibid. at 598.

31. Ibid. at 600.

32. Ibid. at 603, J. Stone dissenting.

33. Ibid.

34. Ibid. at 605.

35. As cited in Francis Heller, "A Turning Point For Religious Liberty," *Virginia Law Review* 29 (January 1943): 452–453. Not only does Heller list all the major newspapers that raised editorial objections to the *Gobitis* decision, but his article is also a helpful, contemporary look at the Jehovah's Witnesses' legal agitation for religious liberty.

36. Irons, 23. The violence was not entirely vigilante. In some instances, local law enforcement officials participated in the humiliating, disruptive, and sometimes even abusive, harassment of Jehovah's Witnesses.

37. *West Virginia State Board of Education v. Barnette* 319 U.S. 624 (1943), at 633.

38. Ibid. at 634.

39. Ibid. at 641.

40. Ibid. In their concurring opinion, Justices Hugo Black and William O. Douglas flatly dismissed the national security argument that Frankfurter had advanced in *Gobitis*. "Neither our domestic tranquility in peace nor our martial effort in war," they wrote, "depend on compelling little children to participate in a ceremony which ends in nothing for them but a fear of spiritual condemnation." See id. at 644.

41. Ibid. at 642.

42. Herberg's argument that "Protestant," "Catholic," and "Jew" represented three equally valid subheadings under the broad category of "American" certainly reflected the religious homogeneity of the day. While the specific content of the three faiths differed, all affirmed a belief in (more or less) the same God and all served to support the essential democratic assumptions of American culture. See Will Herberg, *Protestant-Catholic-Jew: An Essay in American Religious Sociology* (Chicago: University of Chicago Press, 1955).

43. *New York Times*, December 23, 1952, 16.

44. Herberg, 270–271.

45. Opposition to the invocation of God in the pledge *did* exist in the years following the revision, though on a very small scale. The Freethinkers of America, an atheist organization, petitioned the New York State Commissioner of Education

to drop "under God" from the pledge as recited in New York's public schools. It was, they claimed, a violation of the First Amendment's guarantee of religious freedom. When the case went to trial in 1957, the Freethinkers' request was rejected by the state supreme court. See *Lewis v. Allen* 159 N.Y.S. 2d 807 (1957). The U.S. Supreme Court refused to hear an appeal.

46. *Engel v. Vitale* 370 U.S. 421 (1962), at 435.

47. The prayer composed by New York's State Board of Regents, in the spirit of Eisenhower's comment (above), was deliberately vague and inclusive: "Almighty God, we acknowledge our dependence upon Thee, and we beg Thy blessings upon us, our parents, our teachers, and our Country."

48. See *Abington (Penn.) School District v. Schempp* 374 U.S. 203 (1963). For a good, concise summary of the Supreme Court's post-1947 interpretation of the Establishment Clause as it relates to the public education, see John Witte, Jr., *Religion and the American Constitutional Experiment: Essential Rights and Liberties* (Boulder, CO: Westview Press, 2000), 165ff.

49. Garry Wills, *Under God: Religion and American Politics* (New York: Simon and Schuster, 1990), 81.

50. *Holden v. Board of Education, Elizabeth*, 216 A.2d 387 (N.J. 1966).

51. The Florida case was *Banks v. Board of Public Instruction of Dade County*, 314 F. Supp. 285 (S.D. Fla. 1970), *aff'd*, 450 F.2d 1103 (5th Cir. 1971); in Maryland, *State v. Lundquist*, 262 Md. 534, 278 A.2d 263 (1971); and in New York, *Goetz v. Ansell*, 477 F.2d 636 (2nd Cir. 1973).

52. *Russo v. Central School District No. 1*, 469 F.2d 623 (2nd Cir. 1972), *cert. denied*, 411 U.S. 932 (1973).

53. *Palmer v. Board of Education*, 603 F.2d 1271 (7th Cir. 1979), *cert. denied*, 444 U.S. 1026 (1980).

54. *Opinion of the Justices*, 363 N.E.2d 251 (Mass. 1977).

55. "Taking the Pledge," *Time* (September 5, 1988): 14.

56. Ibid. Time and again, Dukakis' measured, "technocratic" responses to emotional campaign issues frustrated his managers and hampered his ability to connect with voters on a personal level. See Jack W. Germond and Jules Witcover, *Whose Broad Stripes and Bright Stars? The Trivial Pursuit of the Presidency 1988* (New York: Warner, 1989), 3ff.

57. Ibid., 15.

58. Ibid.

59. See, for example, *Lynch v. Donnelly* 465 U.S. 668 (1984). In this 5–4 decision, the Supreme Court narrowly upheld a local municipality's practice of placing a nativity scene in a public park during the Christmas season. For many Christians, the very fact that such a seemingly innocuous display of religious devotion—a display that would have caused hardly a ripple of dissent forty years earlier—could end up on trial in the Supreme Court (and survive by such a razor-thin majority) highlighted the seriousness of the apparent threat to traditional values posed by the American Civil Liberties Union (ACLU) and other like-minded organizations.

60. Wills, 81.

61. Congress, House, Congressman Dornan of Michigan, 100th Cong., 2nd sess. *Congressional Record* 134, pt. 2 (September 14, 1988): H7608.

62. *Sherman v. Community Consolidated School District 21 of Wheeling Township*, 980 F.2d 437 (7th Cir.1992), *cert. denied*, 508 U.S. 950 (1993). Cf. Justice Brennan's assertion in 1984 that the reference to God in the pledge could "best be understood . . . as a form of ceremonial deism, protected from Establishment Clause scrutiny chiefly because [it has] lost through rote repetition any significant content." See *Lynch v. Donnelly* 465 U.S. 668 (1984), at 716.

63. For an excellent summary of Newdow's legal challenges, see Richard J. Ellis, *To The Flag: The Unlikely History of the Pledge of Allegiance* (Lawrence, KS: University Press of Kansas, 2005), 142ff.

64. *Newdow v. U.S. Congress* 292 F.3d. 597 (2002).

65. See *Lee v. Weisman* 505 U.S. 577 (1992), at 592. In his original opinion, Goodwin cited three "tests" that had been used by the Supreme Court in previous cases: the three-pronged "Lemon Test" first outlined in *Lemon v. Kurtzman* (1971), the "endorsement" test formulated by Justice Sandra Day O'Connor in *Lynch v. Donnelly* (1984), and the "coercion" test articulated in *Lee v. Weisman* (1992).

66. George W. Bush, quoted by David Kravets, "Federal Appeals Court Rules Pledge of Allegiance Unconstitutional Because of Words 'Under God,'" *Associated Press*, June 26, 2002.

67. Pat Robertson, "Pat Robertson Lambasts Court Ban on Pledge," June 26, 2002, http://www.patrobertson.com/ PressReleases/PledgeOfAllegiance.asp.

68. James Dobson, "One Nation Under —?," August 2002, http://www.focusonthefamily.com/docstudy/newsletters/000000364.cfm.

69. Margaret Crosby, "The Values of the Pledge of Allegiance," *ACLU News* (November/December 2002), http://www.aclunc.org/aclunews/news021126/pledge.html.

70. See "Vast majority in U.S. support 'under God,'" http://archives.cnn.com/2002/US/06/29/poll.pledge/.

71. *Elk Grove Unified School District v. Michael A. Newdow* 542 U.S. 1 (2004).

72. Ibid.

73. Ibid., emphasis added.

74. Two other justices wrote concurring opinions. O'Connor, applying her endorsement test from *Lynch v. Donnelly*, concluded that "under God" represented a form of ceremonial deism (cf. *Sherman*) that did not favor any one specific religion. Thomas, while agreeing with the decision, suggested that the more fundamental problem lay not with the Ninth Circuit's reasoning but rather with the precedent set by *Lee v. Weisman*. The Ninth Circuit, in other words, had correctly applied a flawed legal argument (that is, Kennedy's coercion test).

75. The exceptions were Hawaii, Iowa, Maine, Nebraska, Oregon, Vermont, and Wyoming. For a summary of all 43 state laws and references, see Peyton Cooke's report for the First Amendment Center at http://www.firstamendmentcenter.org/analysis.aspx?id=17035.

76. See *Circle Schools v. Pappert* 381 F.3d 172 (3d. 2004). More and more in

American jurisprudence, First Amendment disputes that once might have been considered under the religious freedom clauses are now treated as free speech cases. See, for example, *Westside Board of Education v. Mergens* 496 U.S. 226 (1990), *Rosenberger v. University of Virginia* 000 U.S. U10270 (1995), and *Capitol Square Review and Advisory Board v. Pinette* 000 U.S. U10267 (1995).

77. See *Myers v. Loudoun County Public Schools* No. 03–1364 (4th Cir. 2005) at 19, 21.

78. Ibid. at 25. In deference to Supreme Court precedent, however, Motz declined to oppose the Virginia law.

79. Barry Kosmin, Egon Mayer, Ariela Keysar, *American Religious Identification Survey 2001* (The Graduate Center of the City University of New York, 2001), 12–13, http://www.gc.cuny.edu/faculty/research_studies/aris.pdf.

80. Alexis de Tocqueville, *Democracy in America*, ed. Richard D. Heffner (New York: Mentor, 1956), 47.

FURTHER READING

On the history of the Pledge of Allegiance, the best place to start is Richard J. Ellis, *To The Flag: The Unlikely History of the Pledge of Allegiance* (Lawrence, KS: University Press of Kansas, 2005). Ellis' book has the advantage of including the *Newdow* cases in its discussion of the pledge. Scot M. Guenter places the pledge in the context of the various flag rituals that have developed in the United States in *The American Flag, 1777–1924: Cultural Shifts from Creation to Codification* (Rutherford, NJ: Farleigh Dickinson University Press, 1990). For a good examination of the pre-"under God" controversies involving the Pledge of Allegiance, see David Manwaring, *Render Unto Caesar: The Flag-Salute Controversy* (Chicago: University of Chicago Press, 1962). Finally, John J. Concannon, III, provides a thorough overview of the various legal challenges to the pledge in his article, "The Pledge of Allegiance and the First Amendment," *Suffolk University Law Review* 23 (1989): 1019–1047.

4

Student Religious Expression within Public Schools

William Lester

The American public school is a quintessentially American experience. Even with the ever larger numbers of students and their parents choosing private schools or home schooling, the vast majority of America's children will attend a public school. This makes the public school a unique place in a community. It is one of the few places where broad cross sections of Americans meet on a regular basis. Thus, public schools provide the focal point for much of a community's interaction. Since children are required by law to receive schooling, this means that America's free public schools will draw virtually all of society's groups into its environs. Practically every group in America has an interest through their children and grandchildren in what goes on in the public school. Further, each one of these groups brings their own norms and values into the schoolhouse. To be sure, the interaction of diverse groups has many advantages for society, but this interaction can also cause tension when diverse values come into conflict.

Few topics elicit a response from people that is more visceral than their children's care and direction in life. When society's groups meet at the public schoolhouse and the debate centers on religious values, it can be quite contentious. In this contentious environment, how can we maintain and nurture respect for diverse religious or nonreligious values? How do we insure that minority viewpoints are not discriminated against in the public school setting? These questions and more become particularly important in the shared societal space of the public school. Indeed, it is in the public school where many of our children will learn important lessons about how to interact with others and will carry these lessons into adulthood.

SEPARATION OF CHURCH AND STATE: VARYING VIEWPOINTS

The major competing viewpoints regarding issues of church and state are the separationist approach, the perspective of neutrality, and the accomodationist perspective, with each providing an important framework for understanding the debate surrounding student religious expression in public schools.

Those supporting strict church-state separation are often called "separationists" and believe that for religious freedom to be protected, religion must be truly separate from government with no government interaction with religion.[1] Separationists believe that government must not become entangled in religious issues or questions because to do so would tend to prejudice the government toward one group over another with this interaction becoming destructive to both entities. Religion should avoid entanglement with the government in order to keep it from becoming subservient to government interests while the government should avoid entanglement so as not to become captured by any particular religious viewpoint. Separationists would argue that any other position puts both religion and government in jeopardy. They believe that the Free Exercise Clause and the Establishment Clause of the First Amendment were put into place to bar government from favoring religion over non-religion and to bar support or promotion by government of religious beliefs and practices, even if that promotion is religiously generic and supports no specific sectarian group.[2] Particularly troubling to separationists is the perceived vulnerability of America's schoolchildren to government-supported religious messages in the public school system, since the school population is a largely captive audience composed of young impressionable minds.

Yet separationists would agree that America's history is filled with examples of government connection to religion and that these connections continue today. Examples would include but are not limited to government-sponsored chaplains in the military; aid to religious hospitals, religious social service agencies, and religious colleges; references to God on currency and in the Pledge of Allegiance; and the invoking of God's name by government officials during holidays and in public speeches. This places America's history and often current practices squarely in conflict with separationist thought. The practical result is that the debate about what constitutes acceptable practice can often end up in the courts.[3]

Nonetheless, the American public is generally supportive of the ideal of separation of church and state espoused by separationists but fall off markedly in their support when specific religious practices like school prayer are mentioned.[4] This reveals a level of confusion among the American people regarding issues of government and religion that can often be found in the debates around student religious expression. On the one hand, the American public seemingly supports separation of church and state, but on the other hand, they support various religious practices that involve the state.

Neutrality is another opinion regarding church and state issues that has been espoused over the years and has found some resonance with the Supreme Court. Basically, the neutrality position tries to avoid religion, particularly in court decisions. The goal is neither to promote nor impede religion. However, this does not mean that religion and government cannot have contact as separationists might prefer. Instead, the contact must be incidental to the government's fulfillment of a secular purpose. This contact can be both to the advantage and disadvantage of religion. Basically, the effects on religion are ignored in the equation.[5] The legal foundation for neutrality lies in the Supreme Court's decision in *Lemon v. Kurtzman* (1971), where the Court held that a law does not constitute excessive government entanglement with religion as long as the law's purpose and effect are secular. For example, under the doctrine of neutrality, it is acceptable for government to provide bus service to religious school students for their attendance at their religious school since getting students to their school safely and their basic education serves a secular purpose. Separationists would see this as unconstitutionally aiding religion with state funds. Separationists depart from neutrality by believing that religion should receive no benefit from government even if the benefit is only ancillary to the government's purpose.[6]

The "accomodationists" viewpoint holds that government should be allowed under the First Amendment to have substantial leeway in supporting or promoting religion. They see nothing wrong with the government sponsoring organized prayer, displays of religious symbols on government property, or supporting religious observances for the general public. Government as an instrument of the people, according to accomodationists, should allow the people to express themselves through their governing bodies and in the use of public facilities even if this expression favors one religious group over another religious group.[7] For instance, a government-sponsored crèche would be appropriate even if it excluded other religions from the display. Accomodationists would have no difficulty with this arrangement.

An important subset of the accomodationist viewpoint is the "non-preferentialist" view. Non-preferentialists believe that the government can support or encourage religious beliefs and practices only if that encouragement does not specifically favor one religious group over another. For example, while non-preferentialists would not want sectarian prayers in a public forum, they could be supportive of non-sectarian prayer. Basically, accomodationists from both groups believe that public expression of religious values is interwoven into the history of America and that government has and should continue to recognize the importance of religion in American society by its actions.[8] To them, government silence on religion is sending a message to America's public schoolchildren that the proper place for religion is in one's private life and not in the nation's public life. To accomodationists, this sends a deeper message that religion cannot legitimately enter public debate on issues before the government because religion is being confined purely to the private realm.[9]

Americans bring all of these diverse positions and more into the debate regarding what is the proper role of religion in America's public schools. Common ground on this issue is often hard to find. Yet, despite the often conflictual positions, we have come to some agreement that public school students do not lose their rights to freedom of religion, freedom of expression, and freedom of association just because they enter the public schoolhouse.[10]

The point of this discussion thus far has been to demonstrate just how rocky the path to compromise is when such divergent viewpoints are involved in fashioning public policy regarding the proper role of religion in public education. Nevertheless, we have been able to arrive at some positions regarding student religious expression, though the legal environment remains fluid. It should be noted that it is a "student's" religious expression that is protected. Government may not mandate religious practice or impose a religious teaching or viewpoint on a captive public school audience. We have largely settled this question. However, the individual student can bring their religious freedoms into the public schoolhouse. Just how far do these individual freedoms reach in the public school setting? Do these individual freedoms also extend to corporate religious activity? The remainder of this chapter will explore student rights to religious expression and the limits to these rights in the American public school.

RELIGIOUS EXPRESSION IN PUBLIC SCHOOLS

The First Amendment

The First Amendment to the U.S. Constitution reads, "Congress shall make no law respecting an establishment of religion, or prohibiting the free exercise thereof; or abridging the freedom of speech, or of the press; or the right of the people to peaceably assemble, and to petition the Government for a redress of grievances."[11] The First Amendment provides some definition of freedoms and the limits of religious expression in American society. When courts rule on issues regarding freedom of religious expression, they apply the First Amendment. In fact, it is not only the Establishment Clause and the Free Exercise Clause that impact student religious expression, but freedom of speech, freedom of the press, the right to peaceable assembly, and the right to petition government all have important impacts as well. Some cases that have religious issues are decided or have elements of their decisions decided outside of the Establishment Clause and the Free Exercise Clause. For instance, a case like *Lamb's Chapel v. Center Moriches Union Free School District* (1993) has free speech, freedom of association, and freedom to assembly implications that can be used alongside establishment and free exercise arguments. In *Lamb's Chapel*, all of these issues were present and argued in the case, which eventually affirmed in the right of Christian clubs to form at public schools on multiple first amendment grounds.[12]

Another example is provided in public schools when students assemble peaceably and associate with other students on campus for both religious reasons like "See You At The Pole" and for nonreligious gatherings and clubs that students propose and lead on campus. The First Amendment rights to speech, assembly, and association can be used by both religious and nonreligious students in whatever context they find themselves in within the public schools. Freedom of religion can often be defined as coextensive with freedom of speech, freedom of association, and freedom to peaceably assemble when these cases go forward through the court system.

Though the First Amendment provides the basis for how we decide between competing values in the public school setting, it is not an easy task to arrive at what the First Amendment means. All of the societal perspectives regarding church and state mentioned earlier can find aspects of the First Amendment that support their viewpoints and historical precedent that seemingly supports what they believe. With all of these divergent opinions emanating from the courts, scholars, and interest groups about the meaning and application of the First Amendment, it makes for a highly dynamic environment around the issue of student religious expression. Still, even in this dynamic and at times highly charged environment, the Supreme Court has provided some definition to the application of the First Amendment that can be used in discerning the boundaries.

Before turning explicitly to an examination of student religious expression in the public schools, it is beneficial to look at a brief legal history of public school and religion cases brought before the Supreme Court. Certainly, there were some cases involving religion in public schools like *West Virginia State Board Of Education v. Barnette* (1943), *McCollum v. Board of Education District 71* (1948), and *Tudor v. Board of Education of Rutherford* (1953) that predate *Engel v. Vitale* (1962). The *Barnette* case is discussed later in this chapter when the topic turns to optional attendance during classes where students and/or their parents find the subject matter to be religiously objectionable. However, in *McCollum* the Supreme Court struck down religious instruction in public schools, and in *Tudor* the Supreme Court let stand a lower court ruling against the distribution of Bibles by outside groups like the Gideons. Still, the *Engel* decision in 1962 marked the beginning of challenges to many longstanding religious practices in America's public schools and is often an accepted line of demarcation for cases that now come before the Supreme Court dealing with student religious expression, whereas the previous cases dealt with government-sponsored and compulsory religious activities.[13]

The issue of prayer introduced in *Engel* deals very forcefully with religious expression in the form of prayer. In a sense, *Engel* begins this genre of cases that delve into private and noncompulsory religious expression since prayer at the school in question was not compulsory as the previous cases had been. So, beginning with *Engel v. Vitale* (1962), which is a case in which the Board of Education of New Hyde Park, New York, had adopted a prayer written by the New York State Board of Regents, the U.S. Supreme Court began to examine these religious issues in public schools. The State Board was becoming increasingly concerned about the moral decline of schoolchildren and felt that a nonsectarian prayer would aid in the moral and spiritual training of the children. The New Hyde Park Board of Education required the recitation of the prayer at the beginning of each school day with a student allowed to "opt out" with written parental permission. Some of the district's parents filed suit on behalf of themselves and their children stating that this was clearly a breach of the Establishment Clause since the state wrote and mandated the prayer. Under their position, the fact that it was an attempt at being nonsectarian prayer was irrelevant. The Supreme Court agreed that the school board had violated the Establishment Clause by even engaging in the practice of writing the prayer.[14]

The very next year, the Supreme Court agreed to hear *Abington Township v. Schempp* (1963) with the Supreme Court combining two cases from Maryland and Pennsylvania. Basically, both states required reading from the Bible without commentary often followed by a recitation of the Lord's Prayer. As in *Engel,* students could be excused with parental permission. The Supreme Court ruled once more that this was a violation of the Establishment Clause since the reading and recitation was required by state law. The Court ruled that the violation occurred with the enactment of the legislation. Therefore, whether or not a student could voluntarily remove themselves from the exercise was moot since the legislation itself was unconstitutional.[15]

These two decisions have been upheld over the years and it now seems to be settled that government may not require religious observance even if a student can opt out of the requirement. Indeed, the legislation itself was considered a violation of the Establishment Clause. So the state or its representatives or employees may not use government to lead or to mandate religious activities.

These decisions along with others have led to confusion about what can and cannot be done vis-à-vis religion in the public schools. Some state officials and administrators have misread these opinions and others to mean that students and student groups cannot use their free exercise and free speech rights in the public school domain. This has led to cases where religious expression has been denied even when it is not emanating from the government, but rather from the individual. This has happened even though these decisions went to pains to state that individual students, teachers, and administrators still had these free exercise rights as individuals.[16] With the issue of overt government sponsorship largely settled, it now fell to the Supreme Court to decide what levels of free exercise rights can be afforded individuals and groups within the public school system. However, cases dealing with a student's First Amendment rights under the Free Speech Clause merit attention since these cases have an impact on student expression generally and hence on religious expression specifically.

Tinker v. Des Moines Independent Community School District (1969), though not overtly a case dealing with a student's right to religious expression, does deal generically with a student's right to expression in the public school environment. This obviously is important to any type of student speech, be it religious or not, under the First Amendment's Free Speech Clause. The case dealt with three students who decided to wear black armbands to their public school in protest of the Vietnam War. The school district suspended the students because they were in violation of a policy barring armbands that was passed by the board right before the students actually wore the armbands.[17]

The parents of the students filed suit in U.S. District Court claiming that this violated their children's free speech rights. The U.S. District Court ruled in favor of the school district. The U.S. Court of Appeals tied on the matter and the case was taken up by the U.S. Supreme Court. The Court ruled that the First Amendment applies to public schools. This was an important extension of the First Amendment to citizens that were not considered full adults. This raised the bar that school administrators must now meet in order to deny first amendment rights to public school students. Though the rights are not exactly the same for minors, the older students become, the more adult-like the rights conferred become. Therefore, administrators would have to demonstrate a constitutionally valid reason to abridge a student's right to free expression. Specifically, in this case, the wearing of the armbands did not cause disruption in the school's primary educational function and could actually be seen as furthering the basic function of teaching the students to be active and involved citizens.[18]

It should be noted that this decision did not endorse unbridled free speech in the public schools. Expression can be curtailed if it is disruptive to the primary purpose of the public school, which is to provide education in a safe and nondisruptive environment. Now, the question as to what constitutes "disruptive" behavior is open to wide interpretation. For instance, in Tinker, it was only three students who donned armbands in protest. What if it had been hundreds of students? Would that then constitute disruptive behavior? The justices seemed content to stay with the specifics of the case in *Tinker*. Indeed, it is this lack of definition that plagues this question of just what constitutes disruption.

Public school administrators have to make these decisions in a very fluid environment. The best one can do in this fluid environment is to understand that the threshold for disruption is higher among secondary students, and that it is important to examine Court decisions for clues about what constitutes a disruptive environment.[19] Certainly, a student's free expression rights, especially when combined with free exercise rights, presents administrators with a very high threshold for establishing whether or not a certain form of expression is disruptive.

An example of limits to free expression for public school students can be found in *Bethel School District v. Fraser* (1986), where a student was suspended from school and barred from speaking at his graduation ceremony due to a speech he had given nominating a classmate for Associated Student Body Vice President. His speech was filled with sexual innuendo and was deemed by the school to be a violation of the school's prohibition of obscene language. The Supreme Court ruled that the school's actions did not violate the First Amendment because the school has an obligation to insure a nondisruptive environment.[20] Another case dealing with limits to student expression, *Hazelwood v. Kuhlmeier* (1988) dealt with public school students and their rights to freedom of the press. In this case, the Supreme Court ruled that a student newspaper could be censored by administrators if it had not been established as forum for student opinion and if it was a school-sponsored newspaper. Still, the administrators do not have carte blanche to censor anything they like; they must demonstrate that censoring the newspaper serves a legitimate educational purpose.[21]

These three decisions, though not directly dealing with rights to student religious expression, provide another approach that can be used to argue for these rights: free speech rights under the First Amendment being extended to public school students. *Tinker* makes it apparent that public school students do not jettison their free speech rights at the schoolhouse door. Yet these free speech rights are certainly more limited than they would be if the student were an adult in the public square. The Supreme Court's limit is that the free expression must not be disruptive to the general purpose of the public school. This is seen in the limits put on *Tinker* by the *Bethel* and *Hazelwood* decisions. Still, the impact of *Tinker* is important to public school religious expression cases. The question now becomes whether or not the student's religious expression is disruptive to the school mission, which is fundamentally the education of all students in a disciplined and nondisruptive environment.

The Equal Access Act (1984)

In 1984, the "Equal Access Act" was passed by the U.S. Congress with overwhelming majorities in both chambers. The Act allows student-led non-curricular clubs to form on a secondary public school campus provided the school allows even one other student-led non-curricular club to form on campus. The Equal Access Act generally prohibits public schools from discriminating against any student group based on the religious, political, philosophical, or other content of their group's speech. The Act requires equal access and privileges for student groups if the school possesses three characteristics. First, the school must be a public secondary school. Second, the school has to be receiving federal funding. Third, the school must have a "limited open forum," meaning that it allows non-curricular student groups to meet on school property during non-instructional time or at a time set by school officials before or after classroom instructional time. For instance, a model-building club or a political club led by students, if allowed on campus, would mean that other student-led groups have the right to form. There could not be discrimination against one group as long as another is allowed to form and operate. Further, equal access to facilities must be provided. The only way that a public school can deny access to a student-led group is if it denies access to all non-curricular groups.[22]

The background to the development of the Equal Access Act is instructive. Various lower court decisions in the 1970s and 1980s had led some school district administrators to a strict interpretation of the Establishment Clause to such an effect that they denied students any organized religious activity on campus.[23] Some administrators even interpreted various court decisions to mean that no religious expression was allowed in a public school even if it was an individual's private expression. There are anecdotal accounts of students being denied their right to pray over their food at lunch or being told that they cannot even discuss religion or even mention the name of God while on public school property.[24] Even if these accounts show no systemic effort to deny religious rights to students, the perception among many in the early 1980s was that Christian activity was being singled out as constitutionally impermissible in the public square and particularly in public schools.

While not a public school case, *Widmar v. Vincent* (1981) provided a case at the college level where a Christian group was denied access to university facilities by the University of Missouri at Kansas City because the university felt to allow access would violate the Establishment Clause. Yet the university allowed a myriad of other groups to use the facilities. A student religious group brought suit against the university on the grounds that their First Amendment rights to free exercise of religion and free speech were being violated by the university. The Supreme Court ruled that the university had to allow access to the religious group on an equal footing with all other groups. This was not considered a violation of the Establishment Clause because providing a forum to all groups does not necessarily mean that the university endorses any particular group. The purpose of free expression serves an overall secular purpose and any benefit that a religious group attains from this policy is purely incidental since the policy is applied to all groups.[25]

The *Widmar* decision certainly encouraged those believing that public school students had been similarly discriminated against. Led by conservative Christian groups and others, pressure was put on the Congress to pass legislation supporting the rights of public school students to form groups on campus and for the schools not to discriminate against these groups vis-à-vis other groups in granting equal access to campus facilities. In 1984, as discussed earlier, the Congress responded to this pressure by passing the Equal Access Act, guaranteeing secondary public school students the right to form groups and to access public school facilities as long as the group was engaging in lawful behavior or not causing disruption of the school's primary function.

After the Equal Access Act was passed, there was a large increase in the number of Christian student-led organizations operating on public secondary school campuses. One source put the number of Christian clubs in operation on public school campuses at about 100 in 1980 and around 15,000 in 1995.[26] As the Equal Access Act went into effect, it was almost inevitable that there would be challenges in the courts given the different positions taken on the Establishment Clause and the Free Exercise Clause. The challenge to the Equal Access Act came in *Westside Community Schools v. Mergens* (1990). A public secondary school in Nebraska had not allowed students to form a Christian Club despite allowing other "limited open forums" to exist within the school. The school district disallowed the club by denying the club a school district staff member for club oversight, which was required under the Equal Access Act. The students countered that this was a violation of the Act by singling them out due to their religious foundations. The Supreme Court ruled in a solid 8–1 majority that the school district had violated the Equal Access Act and that the school district must provide access and a club sponsor.[27] Thus, the constitutionality of the Act had been firmly upheld.

Another case, which did not make it to the Supreme Court, further underscored how entrenched the Equal Access Act has become in public secondary schools. *Prince v. Jacoby* (2002) dealt with a two-tier system set up by the Bethel School District in Washington State. One class of organization received benefits like access to the public address system, purchase of supplies by the school district, use of school vehicles for field trips, and a free page in the school yearbook. The other class of organization, while allowed to organize, did not get access to these benefits. Religious organizations were placed into the disadvantaged class of organizations. A student seeking to start a Christian club called "World Changers" filed to become a recognized club in the school. The club was placed into the disadvantaged category. A suit was brought against the school district in federal district court, where the students lost. However, upon appeal to the U.S. Ninth Circuit Court of Appeals, the lower court ruling was overturned as a violation of the student's rights under the Equal Access Act and the First Amendment's Free Speech Clause. The Supreme Court subsequently refused to hear an appeal of the case, thus providing more support for the Equal Access Act.[28]

The First Amendment provides boundaries for the debate about what the proper limits of religious expression should be in the public school. The meaning of the First Amendment and the proper limits of the boundaries it sets are vociferously debated by a variety of societal groups interested in the public schools. Even with this ongoing debate, there has been some direction provided through decisions of the Supreme Court and legislation about what can and cannot be done in public schools. Agreement seems to have been reached that public elected officials, public employees, and outside groups may not use the public school as a forum for their own particular religious beliefs.

Conversely, neither is a public school to be a religion-free zone. Students do not check their religious rights and liberties at the schoolhouse door. The First Amendment provides secondary-level public school students with rights that cannot be abridged haphazardly by school administrators. Still, these public school students do not have the same level of constitutional rights that adults enjoy. These First Amendment rights can be limited if the exercising of these rights interferes with the school's primary function, which is the education of its students. However, educators must tread lightly, for how can educators teach a student about the importance of free expression and thought and then not afford the student at least a measure of freedom?

Going back to the *Tinker* decision, Justice Abraham Fortas wrote, "It can hardly be argued that either students or teachers shed their constitutional rights to freedom of speech or expression at the schoolhouse gate."[29] Further, Fortas states, "In our system state-operated schools may not be enclaves of totalitarianism. School officials do not possess absolute authority over their students."[30] Additionally, the decision states, "we do not confine the permissible exercise of First Amendment rights to a telephone booth or the four corners of a pamphlet, or to supervised and ordained discussion in a school classroom."[31] Basically, the question becomes, "How can we develop true citizens in a deliberative democratic republic if we do not allow students to engage in free debate and expression in the very public schools where these values are held up as important to democratic governance?"

The Court has come down firmly on the side of allowing a large measure of free expression to secondary public school students because such activity is important to developing active and engaged citizens. With this bent toward developing engaged citizens in place, we have ostensibly chosen to err on the side of student-led free expression in public schools. Legislation like the Equal Access Act was enacted to make sure that students and student-led groups are not discriminated against in the use of school facilities due to their activity being religious in nature. Religious expression is protected by the First Amendment and extends to public school students. Congress and the Supreme Court have come down on the side of free expression and free religious expression where possible. The bar for silencing expression generally and religious expression particularly has been set high. The next section deals with how a public school administrator can navigate the difficult terrain between allowing students to use their rights to religious expression and at the same time provide a welcoming and safe environment for all students.

U.S. DEPARTMENT OF EDUCATION GUIDELINES REGARDING PUBLIC SCHOOL PRAYER

As is often the case in public administration, departments and agencies must implement guidelines in order to communicate policy and procedure. The development and dissemination of guidelines are often needed to make operational sense of a confusing environment.[32] Hence, the U.S. Department of Education has released guidelines in order to help the public school administrator make sense of what can and cannot be permitted in the controversial area of school prayer and related types of religious expression. The issuance of these guidelines, it was hoped, would aid in sound decision making regarding the topic by providing administrators with the most accurate and up-to-date information. The introduction to the guidelines states,

Section 9524 of the Elementary and Secondary Education Act ("ESEA") of 1965, as amended by the No Child Left Behind Act of 2001, requires the Secretary to issue guidance on constitutionally protected prayer in public elementary and secondary schools. In addition, Section 9524 requires that, as a condition of receiving ESEA funds, a local educational agency ("LEA") must certify in writing to its State educational agency ("SEA") that it has no policy that prevents, or otherwise denies participation in, constitutionally protected prayer in public schools as set forth in this guidance.

The purpose of this guidance is to provide SEAs, LEAs, and the public with information on the current state of the law concerning constitutionally protected prayer in the public schools, and thus to clarify the extent to which prayer in public schools is legally protected. This guidance also sets forth the responsibilities of SEAs and LEAs with respect to Section 9524 of the ESEA. As required by the Act, this guidance has been jointly approved by the Office of the General Counsel in the Department of Education and the Office of Legal Counsel in the Department of Justice as reflecting the current state of the law. It will be made available on the Internet through the Department of Education's web site (www.ed.gov). The guidance will be updated on a biennial basis, beginning in September 2004, and provided to SEAs, LEAs, and the public.[33]

This introduction to the guidelines clearly states that funding from the federal government is at stake if constitutionally protected prayer is not guaranteed by a school district. Further, it states that the guidelines will be regularly updated in order to reflect current law. The guidelines communicate very forcefully that some prayer by students is protected and that the federal government will attempt to help school administrators navigate the law with the issuance of these guidelines.

The opening section of the guidelines deals with how a school district can certify that they are in compliance with the law regarding constitutionally acceptable prayer in public schools. The section entitled "Overview of Governing Constitutional Principles" is a brief lesson to administrators on pertinent Supreme Court decisions. The opening paragraph of this section states, "The relationship between religion and government in the United States is governed by the First Amendment to the Constitution, which both prevents the government from establishing religion and protects privately initiated religious expression and activities from government interference and discrimination."[34] This gives the administrator the initial understanding that establishment is forbidden, but also that individuals have religious rights that government must respect if privately initiated. Thus, in the guidelines, public school administrators are introduced to the very real tension between establishment and free exercise.

The guidelines then go on to explain several Supreme Court decisions and their impact on the school prayer issue. First is *Everson v. Board of Education* (1947), which states that government must be neutral in its treatment of religion without showing either favoritism or hostility toward religion. The guide goes on to explain that the First Amendment means that government may not sponsor religion or religious activities, but it must protect privately initiated religious activity since both the Free Exercise Clause and Free Speech Clause protect it. Administrators are told succinctly that "teachers and other public school officials may not lead their classes in prayer, devotional readings from the Bible or other religious activities. Nor may school officials attempt to compel students to participate in prayer or other religious activities."[35] Likewise, the guidelines go on to state that public school officials may not decide to interject prayer into a public school event. This would be considered a favoring of religious speech over secular speech as ruled in *Lee v. Weisman* (1992) and *Santa Fe Independent School District v. Doe* (2000). The guidelines then go on to state,

Although the Constitution forbids public school officials from directing or favoring prayer, students do not "shed their constitutional rights to freedom of speech or expression at the schoolhouse gate," and the Supreme Court has made clear that "private religious speech, far from being a First Amendment orphan, is as fully protected under the Free Speech Clause as secular private expression." Moreover, not all religious speech that takes place in the public schools or at school-sponsored events is governmental speech. For example, "nothing in the Constitution . . . prohibits any public school student from voluntarily praying at any time before, during, or after the school day," and students may pray with fellow students during the school day on the same terms and conditions that they may engage in other conversation or speech. Likewise, local school authorities possess substantial discretion to impose rules of order and pedagogical restrictions on student activities, but they may not structure or administer such rules to discriminate against student prayer or religious speech. For instance, where schools permit student expression on the basis of genuinely neutral criteria and students retain primary control over the content of their expression, the speech of students who choose to express themselves through religious means such as prayer is not attributable to the state and therefore may not be restricted because of its religious content. Student remarks are not attributable to the state simply because they are delivered in a public setting or to a public audience. As the Supreme Court has explained: "The proposition that schools do not endorse everything they fail to censor is not complicated," and the Constitution mandates neutrality rather than hostility toward privately initiated religious expression.[36]

This extensive passage from the guidelines demonstrates that the current judicial understanding as espoused by the Supreme Court is that students do possess rights to prayer within the public schoolhouse as long as the exercise of these rights is not demonstrably interfering with the school's primary purpose of providing an education to all students. A public school administrator receiving these guidelines would understand that there is a zone of religious expression that is protected by the U.S. Constitution as pronounced by the Supreme Court and delineated in the U.S. Department of Education guidelines.

Even though the guidelines have been very useful in aiding public school administrators through the constitutional jurisprudence around the issue of school prayer, the guidelines go even further by offering a section dealing with the different contexts in which school prayer may take place and what constitutes a proper action on the part of the public school officials. First, the topic of "Prayer During Noninstructional Time" is tackled. Basically, students have the right to pray, pray with other students and study religious materials collectively, read their Bibles or other scriptures, and say grace over meals. As long as the activity is taking place during noninstructional time and is not causing material disruption of educational activities, it is permitted. It goes on to state that while the school may curtail student activity generally to maintain order, it cannot single out religious activity for this kind of treatment.[37]

In the section "Organized Prayer Groups and Activities," it states that students maintain their right to association and may organize religious activities in the same fashion that other non-curricular groups are allowed to organize. Further, in keeping with the Equal Access Act, public schools may not deny access to school facilities or resources unless these facilities and resources are denied to all groups whether the groups are religious or not.[38] Events like "See You At The Pole," where millions of public school students gather around their school's flag pole before classes begin in order to pray,[39] serves as an example of a constitutionally protected practice. Since the event is student-led and organized, it is a case of students using their rights to free exercise, freedom of expression, and freedom of association under the Constitution.

The next section of the guide deals with teachers, administrators, and other school employees and what they may or may not do in the public school context. Basically, they may not act in their official capacity as a representative of the school in any matter that promotes or denigrates religion. However, teachers may participate in religious observances when the overall context makes it clear that they are not doing so as representatives of the school. Teachers may also engage in religious discussions, prayer, and Bible study or other religious studies in the same way that they would be allowed to if the activity were nonreligious. This applies if the activity takes place during their off times like lunch, before or after school, or in a break room. Also, baccalaureate services are specifically mentioned in the guidelines. Teachers may participate in them as private citizens.[40]

However, it should be reiterated that teachers, administrators, and other school officials may not participate with students in religious activities while on school grounds or at school activities as long as they are representing the school in any capacity, which usually means while on the job. However, this does not preclude school district personnel from participation in a private religious use of a school facility like a baccalaureate service as long as they are not there representing the public school district. School district personnel do possess private rights to religious expression.

Moments of silence are next mentioned in the guidelines. School officials may not encourage or discourage prayer during these times. They may enforce the time as being silent, but they may not suggest prayer as something that should or should not be engaged in by the students.[41] This is an example where the school is not mandating a specific activity to take place during this time, it is up to the individual student to use this time of silence as they see fit. If a student chooses to silently pray, that is their right under the Constitution.[42] Teachers during the moment of silence would be necessarily engaged in the enforcement of the policy, but nothing precludes a teacher from praying silently during this time while attending to his or her duties.

Accommodation of prayer during instructional time is the subject of the next section in the guidelines released by the U.S. Department of Education. Schools have discretion about whether or not to dismiss students for off-campus religious observances on the same level as dismissing students for off-campus secular purposes. The school, however, must not treat requests for absences for religious purposes any differently from requests for absences for nonreligious purposes. The request can neither be favored nor disfavored because it is religious in nature. For example, if a school allows absences for special trips with parents for nonreligious purposes, they must also accommodate religious requests for absences. The guidelines specifically mention the possible need for a Muslim student to leave during Ramadan. The school must provide equality in deciding whether or not to grant absences between religious and nonreligious purposes. On that basis, the request for a religiously based absence in order to pray, or for any other religious reason, cannot be denied on its face.[43]

There has been some confusion as to whether or not a public school student can bring religious discussion or religious themes into an assignment or classroom discussion. The guidelines from the Department of Education state that a student can do so if it is germane to the assignment.[44] The threshold for allowing this is quite low because many assignments could conceivably have a religious element. Still, a student cannot interject his or her view on creationism into a history assignment like the Battle of Stalingrad. A teacher could rule this use of free expression out-of-bounds and disruptive. However, a religious viewpoint pertaining to war could be relevant to such a discussion.

In oral assignments, paintings, and performances where the student is given discretion about what to present, religious viewpoints and information cannot be censored purely because of its religious content. However, this does not give a student the right to conduct a religious service as their presentation to a captive public school audience. Still, a public school student has the right to introduce a religious viewpoint into assignments and this cannot be discriminated against.[45]

At its "street-level" assessment, the classroom teacher is the arbiter of what constitutes acceptable religious discussion within the classroom and whether or not this discussion constitutes classroom disruption. A student would have to appeal a teacher's adverse decision regarding religious expression be it in a discussion or an assignment to an administrator. An adverse decision at the local administrative level can often be appealed to a state-level education administrator. Beyond these appeals, as can be seen in the various court cases, the American court system is available for a redress of grievances regarding a student's First Amendment rights.

Certainly, with the many thousands of classrooms and the many thousands of teachers, the standards can vary from classroom to classroom. When the various situations exist within their own unique circumstances, this makes variance even more likely. Hence, consistency can be a problem. The environment that public school teachers and administrators exist in is very fluid and requires close attention to legal advice and court decisions. The courts are at times the last place to go in a quest to achieve some form of consistency across local and state boundaries in issues of student religious expression.

An area that has been quite contentious is a student's right to religious expression as it pertains to student assemblies and extracurricular events. The guidelines given by the Department of Education provide the school administrator with some guidance in this area as well. First, student speakers may not be selected in a way that favors or disfavors religious speech. The process must be neutral. The student's right to free expression, whether religious or not, cannot be abridged by the school district if the student is given primary responsibility for the content of their speech. However, where the public school maintains substantial control over the content being delivered, prayer or other religious speech cannot be undertaken, or it would constitute government endorsement of the speech. A school can publicize disclaimers clarifying that the student's speech is her or his own and not the school's.[46]

Santa Fe Independent School District v. Doe (2000) involved all of the issues above. The Sante Fe Independent School District in Texas had been allowing student-initiated and student-led prayer before public high school football games for quite some time. An elected student chaplain was selected to give the prayer. However, a suit was brought in federal court on behalf of students who objected to the practice of praying at the football games. In response to the suit, and while the litigation was proceeding, the school district refined its procedures for allowing the prayer by holding two different student elections linked to the question of whether or not to pray at the high school football games.[47]

The first election allowed the students to decide whether or not to pray before the football games. When the outcome of this balloting showed that the majority of students wanted there to be prayer, a second election was held to choose a student representative to deliver the prayer. The school district felt that by allowing the students to decide, they were adequately removing themselves from the issue. The Supreme Court disagreed.[48]

Writing for the majority, Associate Justice John Paul Stevens said, "The delivery of such a message—over the school's public address system, by a speaker representing the student body, under the supervision of school faculty, and pursuant to a school policy that explicitly and implicitly encourages public prayer—is not properly characterized as 'private' speech."[49] The majority was not persuaded that the student expression was private in nature given the school district's control over the election process and content of the speech being given by the student. Therefore, it is apparent that the process for choosing a speaker must be completely neutral and that the context of the delivered speech matters greatly. If the neutrality of the process is established, religious expression is granted only when it is obviously the student's privately formulated speech.

A related issue handled by the guide is student prayer at graduation exercises. The rules regarding graduation prayer are quite similar to that governing student assemblies and extracurricular events. First, the school may not require or organize prayer at graduation ceremonies. Second, any student or invited speaker must be chosen using truly neutral and impartial criteria for speaker selection. It cannot be tilted toward favoring or disfavoring religious speech. Further, it must be apparent that the speaker is in control of their own remarks and that they cannot be attributed to the school. Like the student assembly and extracurricular section of the guide, schools may make a disclaimer in which they disavow sponsorship of the speaker's expression.[50] This basically creates a free expression zone around the speech being delivered. The expression can be religious, antireligious, and/or offensive to many. This issue, like the issue of student assemblies and extracurricular activities, is difficult to navigate. Still, the basic doctrine is one of school neutrality and even-handedness throughout the process of choosing a speaker and then allowing the speaker to have free expression rights without prior censorship.

Much of the confusion around this issue stems from *Lee v. Weisman* (1992) in which the Supreme Court determined whether or not an invited rabbi could offer a prayer at graduation. In a tight 5–4 decision, the Supreme Court ruled that a guest invited for the purpose of delivering a prayer is at its very core favoring religion over nonreligion. Therefore, the basic action of the school district violated the Establishment Clause.[51] Part of the confusion comes from the mistaken view that this means all graduation prayer is banned. While the issue can be difficult and a school administrator caught in the crossfire may want to outright ban the practice, prayer at graduation can be done legally. The *Lee* decision does not ban all prayer. What is being banned is prayer that is endorsed by the government in the public school ceremony. Free speech being exercised by a speaker chosen in a neutral process, whether the speaker is a student or outside invitee, cannot be abridged if the speaker is given primary control over their own expressive content. Thus, the speaker may pray or not. Conversely, the speaker may also criticize the school or make a political statement. The bottom-line is that the speech cannot be vetted by the school and the selection process must be neutral in regards to the choice of speaker. Religion cannot be a criterion for selection or exclusion. Certainly, this opens a Pandora's Box for a school administrator, but it is mistaken to state that graduation prayer is a banned practice.

The last area handled in the "U.S. Department of Education Guidelines Regarding Public School Prayer" addresses baccalaureate ceremonies. Very directly, it is stated, "School officials may not mandate or organize religious ceremonies."[52] Therefore, organization and execution of a baccalaureate service by a public school is constitutionally impermissible. However, if a school allows other outside community groups to use school facilities, it must also allow religious groups to use the facilities. A private community group requesting the use of school facilities for a baccalaureate service should receive the same consideration as all other community groups and cannot be favored or disfavored in the process. Hence, a private baccalaureate service can be held on school property and students may engage in religious speech while at the service.

These guidelines published by the U.S. Department of Education have provided public school administrators with a valuable resource for discerning what actions to take in permitting or not permitting student religious expression. While the guidelines are not exhaustive, they do provide public school administrators with a solid nucleus of information for navigating through these often difficult decisions while dealing with all of the different societal groups that have a stake or position in these issues. It should be noted that these are "guidelines" and that there is much controversy and litigation that continues to surround these issues. The guidelines are subject to change and/or reinterpretation. Still, these guidelines provide public school officials with an invaluable resource as they attempt to make decisions that respect all involved parties and that line up with current constitutional principles.

COMMON SOURCES OF CONFLICT AND CONFUSION

While the guidelines provided by the U.S. Department of Education give public school administrators guidance on issues surrounding prayer and religious expression, there are multiple areas of conflict that an administrator must recognize. Many of these are not covered in the guidelines. The issue of religious clothing or jewelry can be a subject of contention. This issue goes back to *Tinker v. Des Moines Independent School District* (1969), which was discussed earlier, where it was ruled that public school students have a right to free expression that is connected to peaceful and nondisruptive expression. In *Tinker*, the students were engaging in symbolic expression by the wearing of black armbands to protest the Vietnam War. *Tinker* also extends to symbolic religious expression. Therefore, as long as the article of clothing or jewelry does not cause a disturbance to the primary purpose of the public school, its wearing cannot be considered a violation of any school policy. Further, a school administrator cannot deny the right to wear such clothing just because it might make people uncomfortable or clash with others' viewpoints. As long as the message of the clothing is not deemed to be vulgar or causing disruption, it can be worn.[53] *Tinker* is the operative standard when it comes to student religious expression through clothing or jewelry.

This should not be taken to mean that a school cannot have a dress code. It simply means that there is a certain level of free expression rights accorded to public school students. Speech of a political or religious nature is a form of expression that—even when symbolic as in *Tinker*—is highly protected. However, this cannot be equated with a student having a right to wear sagging pants that expose underwear or to have a right to any bizarre or vulgar fashion that comes to the mind of the student. Numerous court cases have been able to parse between protected expression and unprotected expression and have given public schools some latitude in this regard. The National School Boards Association has published an article that helps public school administrators with this issue. They end the article with some guidelines for public school students' rights related to clothing and/or jewelry.

1. *Protect Students' Religious Expression.* Dress codes must accommodate students whose legitimate religious beliefs require or encourage certain types of dress or accessories.

2. *Protect Students' Rights of Expression.* Dress codes must not interfere with students' rights to make political or philosophical statements about the world, as long as that expression does not cause a substantial disruption of or a material interference with school activities, or interfere with the school district's educational mission.

3. *React to Actual, Not Perceived Threats.* Before banning specific items of apparel because of gang activity or other violence, the school district must have evidence to support such a ban.

4. *Consistent and Reasonable Application Is the Key.* The school district must be sure that there is reasonableness and consistency in the application of a student dress code. A student dress code that is applied in a manner that holds different groups of students to different standards will not be upheld by the courts.[54]

So, public school officials must be very circumspect when it comes to the issue of public school students' rights to free expression in their clothing and jewelry. Also, it should be noted that religious expression is a particularly important and highly protected form of this expression.

OPTING OUT OF ASSIGNMENTS AND ACTIVITIES

Another area rife with conflict and confusion in the debate surrounding religious rights of public school students is the question about whether or not a student can "opt out" when certain subjects are brought up in the school's curriculum. Basically, the right to "opt out" would allow students to avoid participation when certain controversial subjects come up. The right to "opt out" on religious grounds would be based upon the student's and the parent's religious conviction. This is an area that is at best confusing with many different voices contributing to the debate. First, unless the student is an eighteen-year-old or older high school student, the right to "opt out" does not rest with the student. It is the student's parents or official guardians that possess this right. Even with some level of confusion surrounding this issue, there are some things that are known about the right to "opt out." According to the "Protection of Pupil Rights Amendment" (PPRA) passed in 1998, parents have the right to inspect materials that will be used in any U.S. Department of Education-funded survey of their children and to subsequently exempt their children from participation in the survey. There is also a requirement that parents be notified and that written permission be obtained before a student participates in any survey, analysis, or evaluation.[55]

In 2002, the PPRA was amended (Tiahrt Amendment) as part of the "No Child Left Behind Act" to include parental rights to inspection of survey, analysis, and evaluation instruments that are not U.S. Department of Education funded and to make decision about their student's participation or nonparticipation based upon their findings. Further, the Tiahrt Amendment allows the parents of students to access any curriculum that their children may encounter while in a public school.[56] Based upon the parent's findings after examining the curriculum, they may choose to opt their children out of the activity or lesson by communicating their desire to the school administrators. While the law covers more than religious reasons for opting out, it certainly allows for religious objections in making this determination.

In fact, there existed and still exists a right independent of PPRA for parents to opt their children out of school activities on religious grounds. For instance, *West Virginia State Board of Education v. Barnette* (1943) found that an ordinance requiring the salute of the American flag by the children of Jehovah's Witnesses was an unconstitutional restraint due to the Free

Exercise Clause. On religious grounds, these children were allowed to "opt out" of this activity because it clashed with their religious practices as Jehovah's Witnesses. As it relates to the Amish community in *Wisconsin v. Yoder* (1972), it was found that the state's desire to educate children could not override the Amish community's deeply held religious belief that education should not go past the eighth grade. This allowed the Amish to "opt out" of the compulsory attendance laws.[57] Parents have had a right to challenge the public schools on religious grounds in the education of their children for many years.

Yet, while the PPRA as amended provides parents with a right to inspection and to opt their children out of numerous public school functions, services, and curricular activities, it does have its limits. This is where the confusion lies. For instance, it is not a violation under PPRA or under any past court decision for a student merely to be exposed to what some would consider to be offensive ideas, as was found in *Mozert v. Hawkins City Board of Education* (1987) U.S. Court of Appeals, Sixth Circuit. In *Mozert*, students were required to read from a series of readers that many parents in the school district objected to on religious grounds. The parents involved in the suit stated that much of the required reading violated their own religious values.[58]

Originally, the school district provided a way for the children to "opt out" of the assignment and receive an alternative assignment. However, this option was withdrawn and the children were then required to read the material. The parents then filed suit in federal court claiming that their free exercise rights were being violated.[59]

Ultimately, the U.S. Court of Appeals, Sixth Circuit found that the student's mere exposure to material is not grounds for establishing a violation of free exercise rights. Fundamentally, the public school is not liable for a violation of the free exercise clause because part of the task of a school is to provide exposure to different sets of ideas and experiences. Hence, the public school was merely performing its duty by requiring a certain level of exposure. Merely requiring interaction with a variety of viewpoints and experiences was found not to be the same as endorsement of the viewpoints and experiences.[60] For example, this line of reasoning from *Mozert* could be used to allow public schools to expose students to literature from different religions and political viewpoints during their public education years without having to provide a cafeteria approach to assignments that allow students and their parents to "opt out" at every objection. However, it is obvious under PPRA that parents have the right to examine material used within the public school. Should they find something objectionable, they may request that their child be opted out of the lesson or other activity.

Does this mean that the public school administrator must grant the request? This is where there seems to be conflict between PPRA and *Mozert*. PPRA helps to insure the right for parents to request an "opt out" for their children. The key word is "request." *Mozert* states that the request is not necessarily automatic. In this issue, it is very important for public school administrators, teachers, parents, and students to communicate about these matters should they surface and to deal with them as openly and as early as possible. While the public school administrator has discretion in making the decision as to the disposition of a request to "opt out," the PPRA and various court decisions other than *Mozert* give parents and students some legal grounds for their request.

Certainly, *Zorach v. Clauson* (1952) is relevant to the discussion of the right to "opt out" of public school functions. The Supreme Court ruled in *Zorach* that students could receive "released time" from their public schools to receive religious instruction off of the public school campus.[61] Though this is not the same as opting out of a particular assignment in a particular class, it does set the stage for the basic idea of students leaving the public school for religious reasons. Hence, the idea of "opting out" has a long constitutional history dating back over fifty years. To avoid litigation for all parties involved, an understanding needs to be reached in this area of student and parental religious rights. This will require parents, students, teachers, and administrators to sit down and to attempt to reach an understanding that is both respectful to free exercise rights and to the public school's charge to produce well-informed and critical thinkers.

THE PUBLIC SCHOOL ADMINISTRATOR'S CHALLENGES

The public school administrator deals with numerous challenges when it comes to questions of religion within the public school environment. The public school serves as a major crossroads for many of the nation's ideas and ideals. Various societal viewpoints—and often clashing viewpoints—meet at the schoolhouse door. Indeed, it is more than just a clash of ideas and ideals that take place at the schoolhouse door; rather, these ideas and ideals actually enter the schoolhouse in the form of America's children who come from and represent the varied groups in American society. Is it any wonder that when religion in public schools is brought up, it evokes intense passion and debate? After all, we are talking about our children and a place (the public school) that will deeply impact who they are and who they will become.

As stated earlier in this chapter, much has been settled about free exercise and establishment in the public schools. Basically (and succinctly), we have come to the conclusion through the courts and legislation that the public schools cannot coerce their captive student audiences to engage in religious activity or to sponsor religious activity. This could change with future legislation, amendments, and/or court decisions. However, for now, it seems to be where we have settled as a people. The public school administrator needs to respect and be cognizant of these decisions made by legislators and the courts. Constitutional literacy is a must for the public school administrator when dealing with these issues.

Nonetheless, there remains confusion about where the lines are drawn when it comes to religious expression. While people and groups outside of a public school may not use the public school to push their religious agendas, the Supreme Court has ruled that public schools are also not religion-free zones. Students, who are required to attend school under compulsory education laws, may enter the public school with their constitutional rights intact. Granted, minor students do not have equivalent constitutional rights to adults, but they do retain a large measure of these rights as explained by the Supreme Court in various decisions. This large measure of constitutional protection certainly applies to student rights to religious expression as well. Students may pray, organize with others for religious expression, and operate within the public school environment alongside every other group or person as long as they do so without disruption to school order or discipline. Religious students cannot be discriminated against because their speech is religious or because their groups are religious. Anyone objecting to their speech or groups, including public school administrators, must exercise toleration.

A difficulty arises for public school administrators when diverse student groups come into conflict while operating as a proxy for outside forces within the school system. For instance, a group of students (often but not always acting at the behest of adults from beyond the schoolhouse gates) may not like that a Christian school group actively evangelizes classmates during non-instructional time. They may find the viewpoints of the Christian group offensive. However, the Christian student group's right to existence and to expression is not defined by the opinions of others. Likewise, under these rules of engagement within public schools, non-Christian religious groups can form as well and attempt to exercise persuasion. Student religious-based and student secular groups all possess this right to association and free expression. Fundamental issues of free exercise, free expression, and freedom of association must be respected as these public school students become adults who we expect to function as literate and active citizens in a democratic republic. In *Keyishian v. Board of Regents* (1967), Justice William J. Brennan writes that "the classroom is peculiarly the 'marketplace of ideas.' The Nation's future depends upon leaders trained through wide exposure to that robust exchange of ideas which discovers truth 'out of a multitude of tongues, [rather] than through any kind of authoritative selection.'"[62] This statement by Justice Brennan sums up the importance of allowing students to have robust free exercise and free speech rights on the public school campus.

With the public schools providing a forum for much of a community's interaction, these issues of student religious expression and freedom of association have deeper meanings that extend beyond the schoolhouse gate. Indeed, the policies implemented and the decisions arrived at in the courts can be used by different societal groups in order to make their points about the exclusion or integration of religious practice and dialogue in the larger public forum. Where are boundaries drawn between one person's free exercise rights in the public sphere and another person's right to be free from coercion? Is there a right to be free from coercion in a public space? Can government ever accommodate religious practice as separationists would espouse—do government and religion need to be wholly separate? Though many of these groups have antipathy for each other on the public stage, this cannot be done in the nation's public schools.

The compulsory nature of American public school attendance means that all of these groups and individuals meet in the public school environment. Majority and minority groups and the individuals that make up these groups all have constitutional protection in the public school. In some ways, it is a microcosm of the larger society. And how appropriate it is that learning to live together and even how to disagree takes place within the public school setting. These are certainly skills necessary to the functioning of a healthy democratic republic. A dialogue that excludes religious expression from its environment would miss important parts of our society. Hence, the law and the courts have come down on the side of allowing a great deal of student religious expression. This expression aids in teaching and fostering civil discourse.

Yet it is the fluid environment of the courts that bring a good deal of ambiguity to these issues. Many of the decisions that have been handed down by the courts, and particularly by the Supreme Court, could change as the Court itself changes membership. Also, there remains real ambiguity like that found between the *Mozert* decision and PPRA, which was discussed earlier. One of the public school administrator's primary tasks related to student religious expression is to stay abreast of the legislative changes and current court decisions regarding these matters and to not show favoritism to any particular group. Even with the ever-present ambiguity surrounding this issue, it seems to have lessened somewhat over the years. In some ways, we seem to have adopted the old saying "Let a thousand flowers bloom" when it comes to student religious expression within the American public school system.

NOTES

1. For a solid overview of the separationist perspective see Leo Pfeffer, *Religion, State, and the Burger Court* (Buffalo, NY: Prometheus, 1984).
2. Kent Greenwalt, *Does God Belong In Public Schools* (Princeton, NJ: Princeton University Press, 2004), 8.
3. Robert Booth Fowler, Allen D. Hertzke, Laura R. Olson, and Kevin R. Den Dulk, *Religion and Politics in America*, 3rd ed. (Boulder, CO: Westview Press, 2004), 239.
4. Ibid., 208.
5. Paul J. Weber, "Neutrality and First Amendment Interpretation," in *Equal Separation: Understanding the Religious Clauses of the First Amendment*, ed. Paul J. Weber (Westport, CT: Greenwood, 1990), 9.
6. Fowler et al., *Religion and Politics in America*, 209.
7. Jesse H. Choper, "A Century of Religious Freedom" *California Law Review* 88, 6 (2000), 1736.
8. See for example Burt Rieff, "Conflicting Rights and Religious Liberty: The School-Prayer Controversy in Alabama, 1962–1985," *Alabama Review*, July (2001).
9. See for example Clarke Cochran, *Religion In Public and Private Life* (New York: Routledge, 1990).
10. Ibid., 81–88.
11. *U.S. Constitution.* Amendment 1.
12. Jesse H. Choper, Richard H. Fallon, Jr., Yale Kamisar, and Steven H. Shiffrin, *Constitutional Law: Cases & Comments, 10th edition* (St. Paul, MN: Thomson/West, 2006), 896, 1072, 1099–1100, 1129.
13. Ronald B. Flowers, *That Godless Court* (Louisville, KY: Westminster John Knox Press, 2007), 103.
14. Ibid.
15. Ibid., 106.
16. Ibid., 106–107.
17. Choper et al., *Constitutional Law: Cases & Comments*, 939–944.
18. Ibid.
19. Abigail Thernstrom, "Courting Disorder in the Schools," *Public Interest* 136, Summer (1999), 21–24.
20. Choper et al., *Constitutional Law: Cases & Comments*, 581, 945.
21. Ibid., 944–948.
22. Charles C. Haynes and Oliver Thomas, *Finding Common Ground: A Guide to Religious Liberty in Public Schools* (Nashville, TN: First Amendment Center, 2002), 118–124.

23. "Overcoming Opposition to Student Religious Clubs in Public Schools," http://www.religioustolerance.org/chr_club.htm (accessed January 15, 2007).

24. David Limbaugh, *Persecution: How Liberals Are Waging War Against Christianity* (Washington, D.C.: Regnery Publishing, 2003), ix.

25. Choper et al., *Constitutional Law: Cases & Comments*, 1098, 1129.

26. "Overcoming Opposition to Student Religious Clubs in Public Schools," http://www.religioustolerance.org/chr_club.htm (accessed January 15, 2007).

27. Choper et al., *Constitutional Law: Cases & Comments*, 1097–1099.

28. See for example Benjamin Dowling-Sendor, "A Question of Equality," *American School Board* 190, no. 2, (February 2003), 46–51.

29. *Tinker v. Des Moines Independent Community School District*, 393 U.S. 503 (1969).

30. Ibid.

31. Ibid.

32. David H. Rosenbloom and Robert S. Kravchuk, *Public Administration: Understanding Management, Politics, and Law in the Public Sector* (New York: McGraw-Hill, 2005), 316.

33. U.S. Department of Education, "Guidance on Constitutionally Protected Prayer in Public Elementary and Secondary Schools," http://www.ed.gov/policy/gen/guid/religionandschools/prayer_guidance.html (accessed January 17, 2007).

34. Ibid.

35. Ibid.

36. Ibid.

37. Ibid.

38. Ibid.

39. "syatp '06 // Be still. Know God," http://www.syatp.com/media/journalists/pressrel/index.html (accessed January 18, 2007).

40. U.S. Department of Education, "Guidance on Constitutionally Protected Prayer in Public Elementary and Secondary Schools," http://www.ed.gov/policy/gen/guid/religionandschools/prayer_guidance.html (accessed January 18, 2007).

41. Ibid.

42. *Bown v. Gwinnett County School District*, 112 F.3d 1464, 1469 (11th Cir.1997).

43. U.S. Department of Education, "Guidance on Constitutionally Protected Prayer in Public Elementary and Secondary Schools," http://www.ed.gov/policy/gen/guid/religionandschools/prayer_guidance.html (accessed January 18, 2007).

44. Ibid.

45. U.S. Department of Education, "Religion In The Public Schools: A Joint Statement Of Current Law," http://www.ed.gov/Speeches/04–1995/prayer.html#5 (accessed January 20, 2007).

46. U.S. Department of Education, "Guidance on Constitutionally Protected Prayer in Public Elementary and Secondary Schools," http://www.ed.gov/policy/gen/guid/religionandschools/prayer_guidance.html (accessed January 17, 2007).

47. Choper et al., *Constitutional Law: Cases & Comments*, 1125–1127.

48. Ibid.
49. *Santa Fe Independent School District v. Doe*, 530 U.S. 290 (2000).
50. U.S. Department of Education, "Guidance on Constitutionally Protected Prayer in Public Elementary and Secondary Schools," http://www.ed.gov/policy/gen/guid/religionandschools/prayer_guidance.html (accessed January 18, 2007).
51. Choper et al., *Constitutional Law: Cases & Comments*, 1121–1124.
52. Ibid.
53. Michael J. Julka, Shana R. Lewis, and Richard F. Verstegen, "Student Dress Codes," *Inquiry & Analysis*, May 2004, http://www.nsba.org/site/doc_cosa.asp?TRACKID=&DID=33494&CID=164 (accessed January 18, 2007).
54. Ibid.
55. "Pupils Rights Law Allows Parents to Opt Students Out of Surveys," *Health and Health Care in Schools*, May 2003, http://www.healthinschools.org/ejournal/2003/may03_2.htm (accessed January 19, 2007).
56. Ibid.
57. Choper et al., *Constitutional Law: Cases & Comments*, 1133–1134, 1140, 1173.
58. *Mozert v. Hawkins County Board of Education*, 827 F.2d 1058 (6th Cir. 1987).
59. Ibid.
60. Ibid.
61. Choper et al., *Constitutional Law: Cases & Comments*, 1090–1092.
62. *Keyishian v. Board of Regents*, 385 U.S. 589 (1967).

FURTHER READING

Kent Greenwalt's *Does God Belong In Public Schools* (Princeton University Press, 2004) provides a solid overview of U.S. Supreme Court decisions regarding religion in public schools. Additionally, it dispels the idea that religion is banned from public schools altogether. Robert Booth Fowler, Allen D. Hertzke, Laura R. Olson, and Kevin R. Den Dulk in *Religion and Politics In America*, 3rd edition (Westview Press, 2004) present the historical and sociological context necessary to have a firm understanding of the larger societal forces operating on religion within the public school. Further, the authors provide material that deal specifically with the issue of student religious expression. *Equal Separation: Understanding the Religious Clauses of the First Amendment* (Greenwood Press, 1990) edited by Paul J. Weber brings some of the foremost scholars together, including himself, to examine the religion clauses of the First Amendment. This work exposes the reader to the ambiguity that often surrounds the jurisprudence on this issue. A fine overview of the basic issues surrounding religious expression in the public and private sphere is provided in Clarke Cochran's *Religion In Public and Private Life* (Routledge, 1990). Ronald B. Flowers' *That Godless Court* (Westminster John Knox Press, 2007) gives a good historical overview of the issues dealt with by the Supreme Court related to the religion clauses of the First Amendment.

5

Free Speech and the Protection of Children

Mark Edward Gammon

The First Amendment is a familiar battleground for issues of church and state, one where a long history of disagreement about the meaning and scope of the Establishment and Free Exercise Clauses has held the public's attention. When it comes to issues of free speech, religious groups typically have pushed to maintain a distinctly religious voice in the public square, especially legislatures and education. Generally, this agenda has led churches to push for broader free speech rights in light of the free exercise clause; however, developments in technology, coupled with a general loosening of public standards of decency, have lent a new urgency to the question of when it is appropriate to curtail speech, especially in the interest of protecting children from overtly sexual or violent cultural products.

The question of how and why to restrict free speech has come to the public's attention recently due to the easy availability of violent and pornographic materials on the Internet. Congress and state legislatures have recognized a need to shield children from exposure to obscene material, but all involved recognize the difficulty of regulating Internet content without inappropriately curtailing free speech. Christian political organizations have been among the most active in pushing for this legislation, making obscenity restrictions a complicated field for the encounter of church and state. This issue is fraught with complex questions about moral development, the legal status of children, distinctions among different types of speech, and community standards of decency.

This issue is particularly complicated because it requires an exploration of the murky area of civil society between legal issues on the one side and theological and moral questions on the other. Obscenity is a subjective term, and in order to regulate it, one must define it and clarify the grounds on which it should be restricted. The courts have wrestled with this problem for decades, but its task is complicated by the relationship between religious commitment and sexual morality. The state has struggled to determine its responsibilities in this regard as the church has exerted political pressure to legislate particular moral norms. The church's legal justification relies on the concept of harm, which itself is a subjective notion with both moral and spiritual dimensions, and community standards, a concept in continual flux thanks to cultural and technological change.

What follows is an exploration of the many dimensions of this problem. The legal history of obscenity shows how the courts have struggled to understand the state's responsibilities in both defining and controlling obscene material. The contemporary debate has coalesced around the issue of Internet pornography, which complicates the question of how "community standards" can be used as a guideline. The theological side of the issue centers on the question of harm—namely, the degree to which the church's understanding of moral development in sexual matters can be justified objectively apart from its religious foundation. Here, one must ask questions about the relationship among religious faith, culture, and state power when it comes to children's moral development.

A LEGAL HISTORY OF OBSCENITY

Before the middle of the twentieth century, obscene material was limited largely to the underground and restrictions on such material could depend on cultural disapproval and the mostly uncontested common law tradition for support. At least as far back as ninth-century Carolingian Europe, government has recognized the need to suppress certain types of "blasphemous" speech, which could include sexually explicit material.[1] Even as the Western legal tradition became increasingly secular in the wake of the Enlightenment, the condemnation of sexually explicit material detached from its religious moorings and restrictions survived based on cultural standards of common decency.

This practice was reaffirmed in the English common law tradition by *Regina v. Hicklin* (1868). The "Bookseller's Row" on Holywell Street in London was the subject of an exposé in *The Daily Telegraph* in which it was revealed to the wider public that dozens of shops sold erotic novels, prints, and even prostitution catalogs. Concerned that the area was attracting both sexual thrill-seekers and curiously impressionable onlookers, Parliament passed the Obscene Publications Act in 1857, though there was considerable debate in the House of Commons as to the definition of obscenity. The test case dealt with the publication of an anti-Catholic pamphlet titled *The Confessional Unmasked: Shewing the Depravity of the Romanish Priesthood, the Iniquity of the Confessional, and the Questions Put to Females in Confession.* The author Henry Scott expressed outrage at the types of lewd conversations likely to be held between priests and young women in the confessional, though somewhat ironically, the pamphlet itself was deemed pornographic. This case directly tied obscenity restrictions to the potential for such material to "deprave and corrupt those whose minds are open to such immoral influences," meaning the relevant passages could be declared objectively obscene when considered out of context. With this case, a standard for punishable obscenity was established.[2]

The broader rights of speech guaranteed by the U.S. Constitution were not seriously tested with regard to obscenity until *Roth v. United States* (1957), which tested the so-called "Comstock Law." Although the United States had become increasingly pluralistic, the legacy of the moral hegemony of earlier periods assured general agreement about standards of decency. There were always people who sought to push the boundaries of etiquette, but the legal relationship between free-speech guarantees and obscenity took some time to coalesce. Immigration introduced more moral and religious pluralism, but western expansion pushed many "disreputable" endeavors to the frontier. In the middle of the nineteenth century, federal customs officials had been charged with the responsibility to confiscate sexually explicit pictures, but the statutes were not expanded and substantively enforced until the 1870s with the deputizing of Anthony Comstock as a special agent for the U.S. Postal Service.

Comstock (1844–1915), the son of a well-to-do Connecticut farmer, was a Civil War veteran who settled in New York City. There he saw the effects of rapid industrialization on urban life, as horrid working conditions fostered the growth of tenements, slums, taverns, and brothels. He became an active worker in the YMCA, one of the organizations that sought to combat unhealthy social conditions—including moral conditions—as part of the early stages of the Social Gospel movement. Comstock founded the New York Society for the Suppression of Vice and proved to be an able moral crusader, adept at political maneuvering. Though he had many enemies, he managed to convince Congress to support his cause with legislation.

The Comstock Law of 1873 prohibited the use of the mail to disseminate "obscene, lewd, or lascivious" materials, including pamphlets dealing with contraception and abortion.[3] The courts batted the issue around for the next eighty years, with some jurists questioning whether the underlying logic of *Regina v. Hicklin* meant that such restrictions applied only to children. Eventually, the courts relaxed standards even for children, having to admit that materials intended for sex education could be appropriate[4] and that sexuality had a legitimate place in literature as long as the intention of the work was not to create libidinous impulses.

The latter point was established by the famous outcry over James Joyce's *Ulysses*. In 1920, a magazine serialized an excerpt from the novel, including a portion dealing with the main character masturbating. The New York Society for the Suppression of Vice took action and in 1921 got the magazine declared obscene, effectively banning the novel's publication in the United States. Random House decided to test the issue by importing the French edition and arranging to have it seized by customs; in 1933, the district court ruled that the novel's sexual content served its larger literary purposes, and therefore was not pornographic.[5] Still, while the *definition* of obscenity was at issue, the larger question of the legal status of obscene material was not yet seriously questioned in the courts.

Ultimately, the constitutionality of the Comstock Law was tested by Samuel Roth, who had been convicted for publishing a magazine of erotica. The *Roth* case (1957) tested the limits of First Amendment guarantees for speech, with the court determining that obscenity did not have constitutional protection. The decision was reaffirmed by *Jacobellis v. Ohio* (1964), in which the manager of a movie theater had been convicted for showing a pornographic film. In the majority opinion, Justice Brennan cited *Roth*, with unprotected material being determined by questioning "whether to the average person, applying contemporary community standards, the dominant theme of the material taken as a whole appeals to prurient interest."[6] In *Jacobellis*, the Court clarified that the "contemporary community standards" in question were not those of the local legislative jurisdiction, but those of the nation considered as a whole. As to how these vague phrases were to be applied, Justice Stewart, in a concurring opinion, concluded that such restrictions could apply only to "hard-core pornography," which he famously defined by stating, "I know it when I see it."[7]

Jacobellis moved the issue from printed material to film, essentially broadening the *Roth* test in response to a different type of media environment. The Court later determined that the making and possessing of obscene material were constitutionally protected, even if viewing such material may lead to "antisocial conduct."[8] The issue then became a question about the public dissemination of obscene material, and as time went on, legislatures therefore softened restrictions on printed matter, which could be viewed in the privacy of the home. Public showings of pornographic films were another matter, and the Court revisited *Jacobellis* in a pair of 1973 cases.

With the legal definition of obscenity based on the *Roth* test hopelessly vague, the members of the Court found themselves reviewing pornographic films almost weekly to determine whether they were constitutionally protected, though Justices Black and Douglas, believing all such films protected, refused to weigh in.[9] Justice Stewart apparently having seen enough, the Court refined the obscenity test in *Miller v. California* (1973):

The basic guidelines for the trier of fact must be: (a) whether "the average person, applying contemporary community standards" would find that the work, taken as a whole, appeals to the prurient interest, *Roth, supra,* at 489, (b) whether the work depicts or describes, in a patently offensive way, sexual conduct specifically defined by the applicable state law, and (c) whether the work, taken as a whole, lacks serious literary, artistic, political, or scientific value. If a state obscenity law is thus limited, First Amendment values are adequately protected by ultimate independent appellate review of constitutional claims when necessary.[10]

The new *Miller* test got its first application in a decision issued the same day, *Paris Adult Theatre I v. Slaton* (1973). Here the Court addressed the question of whether sexually explicit material should be restricted in the first place. Deciding that the social-scientific evidence was inconclusive, Chief Justice Burger lamely deferred to Justice Cardozo's statement that "all laws in Western civilization are 'guided by a robust common sense.'" Here, reasoning based on common law precedent gave way to the flimsy assertion that this is the way things have always been:

The sum of experience, including that of the past two decades, affords an ample basis for legislatures to conclude that a sensitive, key relationship of human existence, central to family life, community welfare, and the development of human personality, can be debased and distorted by crass commercial exploitation of sex. Nothing in the Constitution prohibits a State from reaching such a conclusion and acting on it legislatively simply because there is no conclusive evidence or empirical data.[11]

In a telling dissent, Justice Brennan, with Justices Stewart and Marshall joining in, seemed to give up on the issue, questioning the very idea of legal restrictions on obscenity:

Our experience since *Roth* requires us not only to abandon the effort to pick out obscene materials on a case-by-case basis, but also to reconsider a fundamental postulate of *Roth*: that there exists a definable class of sexually oriented expression that may be suppressed by the Federal and State Governments. Assuming that such a class of expression does in fact exist, I am forced to conclude that the concept of 'obscenity' cannot be defined with sufficient specificity and clarity to provide fair notice to persons who create and distribute sexually oriented materials, to prevent substantial erosion of protected speech as a byproduct of the attempt to suppress unprotected speech, and to avoid very costly institutional harms.[12]

Brennan recognized that the obscenity test, even as refined by *Miller*, remained hopelessly vague. While the precedent stayed on the books, cultural changes coupled with legal uncertainty narrowed the judicial understanding of obscenity subject to controls. By the 1980s, the question was not *whether* pornographic films could be shown publicly, but *where* they could be shown—that is, it came down to a zoning question.[13]

WHICH COMMUNITY'S STANDARDS?

The legal language used to define obscenity repeatedly turns on the idea of "community standards," raising the question of what exactly this vague phrase means. Each person is simultaneously a member of several communities, each with its own set of ethical standards. Market trends and state-sponsored education complicate this picture considerably, for if every local community has more or less the same set of shops, restaurants, media outlets, and educational priorities, the moral relevance of local community identity is severely mitigated.

Legally speaking, the Court decided in *Jacobellis* that community standards meant the *national* community.[14] However, as restrictions on obscene material loosened in the wake of ongoing confusion about just what that national standard should be, the issue was relegated to zoning cases; morally and legally speaking, this development essentially returns the authority to local governments.

Relying on the principle of subsidiarity seems appropriate given the state's morally pluralistic character in a liberal polity, but local governments have their own problems in zoning decisions of this sort. Here the locality must make a moral distinction, something that is considerably more complicated constitutionally than making the distinction between commercial and residential zones. There is a clear problem with allowing only certain *kinds* of commercial establishments within a defined area, though there is certainly precedent in the prevalence of liquor boards. The courts have generally accepted the idea of "secondary effects" as legal justification for such restrictions—that is, certain types of commercial establishments could devalue other businesses. In the past, localities could, if nothing else, rely on the "shame factor" to relegate adult bookstores and theaters to the outskirts. Even if zoning laws could not keep the establishment out of the center of town, owners had to take patrons' fears of being seen entering or leaving into consideration when choosing a location. In general, both legal and cultural factors created a situation where patrons would have to seek out the store.

Technological and cultural developments have interdependently worked to alter this situation, however. More and more, the seedy adult bookstore on the edge of town has been supplanted by the clean, well-lit sex boutique in commercial centers, as both a factor in and a response to the mainstreaming of pornography and so-called marital aids. It is difficult to appeal to "community standards" to restrict minors' access to such material when mothers are introducing their daughters to sex toys as part of normal adolescent sex education.

Proponents of obscenity restrictions are wise to focus on the Internet as an important agent of change. It brings sexually explicit material into the home quickly, conveniently, and oftentimes unintentionally. This method of delivery removes the shame factor entirely from the picture—one can view or purchase such material relatively anonymously. In this way, the Internet mitigates the importance of community standards of morality, at least when we consider community in terms of locality. The Internet is arguably a community itself, with its own standards of morality and etiquette. It also is a home to thousands of subsets—virtual communities fostering connections among groups dedicated to sexual fetishes, fundamentalist Christianity, and everything in between. While one could argue that the Internet is a factor in the collapse of community and the radical individualization of American culture, there is no doubt that these virtual communities have an impact on identity formation and moral education.[15]

Again, the state's interest is a complicated question. While the state has some stake in the cultivation of national identity and in relegating obscenity matters to localities, the courts have suggested that the state's role is limited to enabling local communities to self-define—a legal conundrum stirred up over and over in religious cases, from public education to the displays of holiday crèches on public property. In entering the discussion about community standards, the church is caught between the Scylla of demanding its own free speech rights and the Charybdis of relying on state power to restrict the rights of others in accordance with Christian standards of decency.

PROTECTING CHILDREN FROM OBSCENITY

While the right to produce, own, and disseminate obscene material has broadened in scope, the Court has nonetheless recognized a key limit on this right—reasonable precautions can be taken to restrict the access to such material by minors. The *Hicklin* test referenced the need to protect "those whose minds were open to such immoral influences," which in its particular context likely included women and so-called "weak-minded" adult men in addition to children. Both changes in attitudes toward women and technological developments in media have shifted the focus to those more clearly developmentally vulnerable. That is, the speech rights of adults may be limited in order to protect children.

This limit on free speech is assumed in many of the obscenity cases prior to *Ginsburg v. New York* (1968), in which the owner of a shop, who had been convicted for selling "girlie" magazines to a sixteen-year-old boy, appealed, thus forcing the Court to distinguish between the First Amendment rights of children and adults when it comes to access to certain types of material. In *Ginsburg,* the Court determined that the state could apply a flexible standard of obscenity and further restrict the access of children to materials that should be available to adults.

The Court's reasoning hinged on two key ideas, which on examination do not appear to be readily compatible. First, the primary responsibility for the well-being of children falls to parents, and to a lesser degree to teachers and others charged with the care and rearing of children, who "are entitled to the support of laws designed to aid discharge of that responsibility." At the same time, the state has an independent interest in the well-being of children, and though sexually explicit material may or may not be harmful to the "ethical and moral development of our youth," the legislature could reasonably assume that it is, even in the absence of proof.[16] Note that according to the first argument, there is nothing to prevent parents from purchasing obscene material and giving it to their children should they choose to do so. The second argument, however, suggests that the state may have the right to impinge on parents' rights to expose their children to what they see fit. While the state historically has been content to act as *parens patriae* (literally "parent of his or her country") as a last resort, this right could theoretically be asserted in the absolute, as with Plato's guardians in *The Republic.*[17]

The constitutionality of broadcast decency standards for radio and television also turned on the problem of potential harm to children, as determined in *Federal Communications Commission v. Pacifica Foundation* (1978). At 2:00 p.m., a New York radio station broadcast a recording of George

Carlin's routine about "filthy words" banned from the public airwaves. A parent complained to the FCC that he had heard the recording while driving with his young son. The FCC notified Pacifica Foundation, the owner of the station, that it was within the Commission's rights to sanction or fine for such broadcasts, though no fine was issued at the time. Upon being challenged to clarify its standards, the FCC claimed that it did not seek to ban the use of such language from the airwaves entirely, but only to restrict it to hours when children were much less likely to be listening.

In its decision, the Burger Court backed away from *Roth*, stating, "the fact that society may find speech offensive is not a sufficient reason for suppressing it. Indeed, if it is the speaker's opinion that gives offense, that consequence is a reason for according it constitutional protection. For it is a central tenet of the First Amendment that the government must remain neutral in the marketplace of ideas." Nevertheless, the Court recognized the new challenges presented by broadcast media, which are uniquely present in the home, where a person's right to be left alone trumps an "intruder's" right to be heard. To a large degree, this restriction is justified because broadcast media are "uniquely accessible" to children, and in the case in question, "Pacifica's broadcast could have enlarged a child's vocabulary in an instant." While other media, such as magazines, can be controlled without restrictions at the source, broadcast media are unique and are thus subject to tighter controls. The Court was careful to note the narrowness of its finding, suggesting that different forms of media may require examination to determine appropriate restrictions. Recognizing that obscenity is largely a question of appropriateness to the particular audience and setting, the Court nonetheless concluded, "We simply hold that when the Commission finds that a pig has entered the parlor, the exercise of its regulatory power does not depend on proof that the pig is obscene."[18]

The Internet, of course, offers the proverbial pig a new doorway. Over the course of the last three decades, the FCC and the traditional broadcast media have reached a more-or-less stable understanding about standards, although Janet Jackson's infamous "wardrobe malfunction" during the halftime of the Super Bowl in 2004 has prompted the FCC to begin fining with renewed vigilance. The Internet presents a new challenge, however, insofar as this medium has so far resisted attempts to restrict it. Internet content is delivered in such a way that it cannot be restricted to appropriate times of day, and the fact that children's technological aptitude often is superior to that of their parents make filters and locks moderately effective at best. Congress has moved to address the problem, but with limited success.

The Communications Decency Act (CDA) (1996) was a bipartisan effort by Congress to address the problem that new technologies, including the Internet and cable television, presented in protecting children from harmful material. The American Civil Liberties Union (ACLU) challenged the constitutionality of the legislation, objecting in particular to the following language:

Whoever (1) in interstate or foreign communications knowingly (A) uses an interactive computer service to send to a specific person or persons under 18 years of age, or (B) uses any interactive computer service to display in a manner available to a person under 18 years of age, any comment, request, suggestion, proposal, image, or other communication that, in context, depicts or describes, in terms patently offensive as measured by contemporary community standards, sexual or excretory activities or organs, regardless of whether the user of such service placed the call or initiated the communication; or (2) knowingly permits any telecommunications facility under such person's control to be used for an activity prohibited by paragraph (1) with the intent that it be used for such activity, shall be fined under title 18, United States Code, or imprisoned not more than two years, or both.[19]

The Supreme Court unanimously decided that this language was far too broad and struck down the CDA, with Chief Justice Rehnquist joining Justice O'Connor in a concurring decision, dissenting only in part and in essence proposing the restriction of some Internet content to "adult zones," a solution which, depending on the details of implementation, may be constitutional.[20] The board of the Internet Corporation for Assigned Names and Numbers, which regulates domain names, recently voted 9–5 to reject a proposed "xxx" domain, in part due to concerns about its being called upon to regulate content.[21]

Congress tried again with the Child Online Protection Act (COPA) (1998), stating that "the protection of the physical and psychological well-being of minors by shielding them from materials that are harmful to them is a compelling governmental interest." The COPA was narrower than the CDA, applying only to commercial materials, but its scope included not only obscenity, but also "any material harmful to minors," with the specifying definitions doing little to rule out "soft-core" sexual content. Ultimately, what constituted harmful material was left up to "community standards."[22] The ACLU challenged the law, getting a preliminary injunction to prevent enforcement. The Supreme Court reviewed the law in *Ashcroft v. ACLU* (2004), finding only that the reliance on community standards as a measure did not itself render the act unconstitutional. The Court sent the case back to the Third Circuit for further review, however, suspecting that the act's language was too broad, as in the CDA.[23] The circuit court in

Philadelphia heard arguments in October and November 2006, and on March 22, 2007, Judge Lowell Reed agreed that the act was too broad and made the injunction against enforcement permanent; Reed also noted that filters and parental controls were both more effective and more constitutionally acceptable.[24]

Congress tried a third time, though with considerably narrower scope, by passing the Children's Internet Protection Act (CIPA) (2000). With CIPA, the federal government acted to limit minors' access to "harmful" sexual material on computers located in libraries and schools. Libraries and schools were ordered to install software filters on all computers accessible to minors or lose all federal funding. The American Library Association challenged the law, arguing that such filters were too blunt an instrument, unacceptably limiting access to legitimate information related to health care, sexuality, and public policy. In *U.S. v. American Library Association* (2003), the Supreme Court upheld the law, though in the grand scheme of things, this measure is largely symbolic.[25]

As seen above, the legal restrictions on obscene material are generally justified by concern about the well-being of children. Christians and other religious persons, however, must ask what kind of danger children are in. What, exactly, is the risk in children being exposed to certain cultural products? Are the government's interests in restricting free speech consonant with the church's? How are we to understand "well-being" absent a particular community's definition of health and welfare? Religious organizations have weighed in on the latest round of legal wrangling, namely those cases having to do with the Internet, generally endorsing the legislative language that sets the obscenity measure according to community standards. Beyond satisfying the religious constituency, however, it is unclear precisely what the state's interests are and if, theologically speaking, they are shared by the church.

HARM: PSYCHOLOGICAL, MORAL, AND SPIRITUAL

When Congress' attempts to regulate access to obscene material on the Internet have been challenged in the courts, religious organizations have weighed in to support the legislation. For instance, *Ashcroft v. ACLU* (2004) saw the Court entertaining *amicus* briefs in support of the COPA from the Family Research Council, which is affiliated with James Dobson's evangelical "family values" organization, Focus on the Family; Morality in Media, an interfaith anti-obscenity group founded by the late Rev. Morton A. Hill, a Jesuit priest; and the American Center for Law and Justice, the First Amendment law center affiliated with Pat Robertson's Regent University.

Unlike the progressive Protestant activism of the early Social Gospel over a century ago, the mainstream liberal Christian denominations have been relatively silent about obscenity questions. Non-Christian religious groups also have not visibly entered the debate; worries about the dangers of Christian cultural establishment likely override any shared concerns about exposure to sexually explicit material. In recent years, evangelical Protestant and some conservative Catholic groups have led the political and legal charge to regulate sexually explicit media. These groups unanimously supported the COPA's use of "community standards" as a measure for obscenity, though none directly addressed the question of whether the Christian community's standards necessarily reflected those of the nation at large. Insofar as regulation depends upon protecting children, a key church-state question is to what degree some objective understanding of harm can hold up outside of a specifically theological worldview.

The interested groups support broad definitions of "harm" and "wellbeing," but they typically have not distinguished among psychological, moral, and spiritual understandings of the terms. The *amicus* brief filed by the American Center for Law and Justice (ACLJ) in support of the COPA is a useful case in point.[26] The brief references several psychological and sociological studies describing a link between pornography and "harm" to children, though the scope of researchers is limited. Some studies suggest that pornography is a danger for its addictive potential, which results in desensitization to the material and eventually modeling what is viewed.[27] One study, in which male subjects were exposed to "hardcore non-violent adult pornography" over the course of six weeks, concluded that such exposure led subjects to:

- develop an increased callousness toward women;
- trivialize rape as a criminal offense;
- develop distorted perceptions about sexuality;
- develop an appetite for more deviant, bizarre, or violent types of pornography;
- devalue the importance of monogamy; and
- view non-monogamous relationships as normal and natural behavior.[28]

Another study of child molesters and rapists suggested that as many as one third of those studied claimed to have been incited to commit an offense by viewing pornography.[29] Some research suggests that exposure to pornography during childhood is connected to the likelihood of sexually transmitted disease, unplanned pregnancy, and sexual addiction later in life.[30]

These studies suggest that pornography serves as a form of destructive sex education, but Judith Levine, Marjorie Heins, and other civil libertarian social activists have argued that they are not without methodological problems. Importantly, links do not imply causation, and the long-term studies here are limited insofar as they study those already affected, thus inviting the chicken-or-egg question: do sexual deviants like pornography, or does pornography create sexual deviants? Also, there is reason to believe that sexual identity is a product of a complex web of influences, including family life, education, and involvement in various types of communities. This is to say that even prolonged exposure to pornography is certainly one form of sex education among many, and though it has addictive potential, it cannot clearly be identified as a *primary* cause of sexual deviance.[31] Millions view pornography every day, but comparatively few commit acts of sexual assault as a result.

Also, beyond acts in which there is a clear victim such as sexual assault or child molestation, deviance is in the eye of the beholder; as with legal definitions of obscenity, the subjective nature of the claims are legally problematic. Not all of the behaviors noted above are recognized as disordered, even by many Christians. While monogamy is a generally recognized norm, and "bizarre" sexual activities are, by definition, unusual, absent a clear community standard, it is hard to say what contributes to overall well-being, sexually speaking. Until recently, homosexuality was a recognized psychological disorder, but it has been increasingly normalized to the point that even many churches are divided about its acceptability. While many would identify bondage and sado-masochism as "bizarre" behavior, there is little doubt that many otherwise "normal" monogamous married couples indulge in such practices now and then. It is telling that while the legislation in question has focused on *sexual* material, the intellectual debate about media effects on moral development has tended to focus more on the effects of media *violence,* where questions of right and wrong are much easier to address objectively. In other words, the widespread disagreement over sexual norms makes legislation controversial absent a clear, compelling state interest.

This disagreement may be why liberal Protestants have not been visibly active in obscenity issues, circumscribing sexual morality as a "private" matter, even as Catholics and evangelicals have argued for its public relevance. Those Christians who have supported restrictive legislation do not all think the same way about their endeavors, but generally speaking there are a couple of essential ecclesiological ideas in play. Some think of the church as an interest group—in this case, a group of people coming together to assert their right not to be exposed to certain things. Also involved are parents' expectations that the state will take reasonable measures to assist in fulfilling certain types of parental responsibilities. This is indirectly an educational issue, and just as the state provides schools, parents can expect that it will act to regulate potentially harmful educational influences, as discussed further below.

Slightly more complex, both legally and theologically, is the belief that the Christian tradition is the bearer of an objective moral truth that is publicly relevant, even separated from its moorings in faith. Since John Courtney Murray provided Catholicism with the theoretical resources to rethink its position in a secular democracy, American Catholics have relied on the natural law tradition to argue for universally relevant moral truths that can be advocated in the public square with nondoctrinal arguments. While Protestants do not tend to embrace natural law reasoning as often, they may nonetheless see Christian sexual ethics as a kind of moral wisdom relevant to family and community stability. In this regard, it is a cultural power that the state should value and support within certain limits.

The spiritual questions surrounding sexual morality, therefore, can be said to have public import, and as a spiritual question, sexual habituation has long been a concern for the Christian tradition. While the gospels have very little to say about sexual norms directly, Paul does display concern with sexual immorality. In the Corinthian correspondence, Paul addresses several issues facing the nascent church, and his responses at once show a pragmatic flexibility and a keen concern that sexuality is a phenomenon with the peculiar power to destabilize a community (1 Cor. 5–7). Paul clearly prefers celibacy above even marriage, but he knows that very few are recipients of such a gift (1 Cor. 7:1–6). Therefore, he sees the value of channeling and disciplining sexual appetites with marriage. Here, as with other issues, Paul does not produce a rule-based ethic; he instead approaches sexual ethics with an eye toward the edification of community. Implicit in this approach is the recognition that satisfaction of sexual desires is not, theologically speaking, a right, and that those desires have a power, perhaps unique, to turn one away from God, to the detriment of the relationships with one's brothers and sisters in the church. In his letter to the Romans, Paul recognizes certain sexual appetites as themselves the consequence of idolatry, the disordered desires that result from worshiping some aspect of creation rather than the Creator (Romans 1:18–32).

Augustine schematizes this insight from Paul, recognizing sexuality as a lesser good, though one that Augustine himself struggles mightily with, to the point that it prolongs the "birth pangs" of his conversion, and he famously prays, "Grant me chastity and continence, but not yet."[32] Oddly, it never seems to occur to Augustine upon his conversion to marry his son's mother, to whom he seems to have been faithful as a concubine for over ten years. As with Paul, Augustine recognizes celibacy as the highest calling of a Christian, with marriage a lesser good through which God transforms the evil of lust through procreation, friendship, and the sacramental bond.[33] Ultimately Augustine appears unable to reconcile a deep spiritual commitment to God with sexual pleasure; "original sin" is to a large extent the taint of sexual desire passed on to every person. Sexual immorality, therefore, can be said to hinder the development of harmoniously functioning community unless disciplined and sublimated to a higher good.

While this is not the place for an elaborate history of Christian sexual ethics, a review of these two foundational thinkers provides a useful baseline from which to address the contemporary American church's interest in restricting access to obscene material. Of course, relatively few contemporary American Christians point directly to Augustine as an authority for sexual ethics; nonetheless, his formulation of the tradition was tremendously influential, and his concerns and language continue to be the lenses through which we view the New Testament. Protestant Christians expressly rely on the biblical texts, particularly Paul, as an authority on sexual matters, and Augustine's influence cannot be ignored, even in contemporary critical scholarship.

Catholic sexual ethics rely on scripture, but they are more expressly grounded in natural law. The most important statement has been *Humanae Vitae,* Pope Paul VI's 1968 encyclical, which identifies two inseparable purposes for human sexuality—procreation and unitive intimacy. By centering on procreation, the Magisterium ties sexual expression to marriage and argues that disciplined, monogamous sexuality is key to full human flourishing. The Catholic position also ties sexual ethics to social stability, arguing that governing authorities should act to support the strength of the family unit. Such support includes the restriction of pornography, which inhibits proper habituation to virtuous sexual practices.[34]

Whatever one may think of its particular conclusions, the Christian tradition makes a connection between the sexual and political, and Augustine's influence on the later scholastics and established Christianity shows his importance to the very concept of public regulation of sexuality. So when the church enters the public sphere to advocate for a particular vision of well-being, it brings together sexual morality, state power, and religious devotion in a potent amalgamation—one that at times makes it difficult to discern exactly whose interests are being served.

STATE, CHURCH, AND PARENTAL INTERESTS

The contemporary American Christian agenda regarding "family values," typically understood, finds support in the classical Christian theological tradition, albeit ambiguously. Paul and Augustine privilege celibacy over marriage, and both view marriage as an arrangement for the control of lust. Whether premarital sex is expressly forbidden by following this logic is open to debate. Sexual norms certainly were prescribed by the medieval church, which used natural law to complement the biblical asceticism of the ancient tradition; while the Protestant traditions largely rejected scholastic theology, its sexual norms remained influential even as their natural law foundations were dismissed.

Nonetheless, the tradition does not speak as unanimously about sexuality and the family as is often presumed by many American Christians. Prior to the Victorian period, the Anglo-American norm was a progressive commitment in stages, often featuring sexual consummation at a "betrothal" stage before marriage.[35] The recognized norm for family life—"the nuclear mother-father team in intact first marriages"—is relatively new, even as it is changing rapidly in response to economic and cultural forces.[36] It is worth considering to what degree the norm itself was the product of non-religious influences, and to what degree Christians' evolving moral standards surrounding sexuality and family life are the product of "colonization" by state and market forces.[37]

Therefore, for Christians and other interested religious persons, "traditional" sexual and family values demand evaluation in their own right in advance of deciding how the widespread availability of obscene material may serve to degrade those values. Certainly much of the confusion and disagreement in the church over issues of sexual morality originate in the tradition's failure to articulate a coherent theological understanding of physical pleasure. Sexuality has remained inextricably bound to procreation—a connection better supported by natural law than by the New Testament—and Christians have failed to make sense of purely erotic pleasures.[38] Despite a recent evangelical emphasis on sexual satisfaction in marriage, there is reason to believe that the church's longtime stigmatization of sexuality is itself a factor in the cultivation of sexual disorders and the transmission of sexually transmitted diseases. Some have argued that the church's failure to educate its children adequately about sexuality means other influences, including illicit and pornographic material, are left to fill the vacuum. As noted above, pornography is at most one source of sexual education among many; from a theological point of view, its detrimental influences may be exacerbated by the church's failure to marshal its own disciplinary resources in support of a spiritually healthy appreciation of the erotic.

From the "church" side of the church-state issue, therefore, there is a key ecclesiological question that involves layers of complexity. Whether Christians can use their political influence to harness state power in support of an essentially spiritual matter is a theological question as much as a legal one. Some Christians argue that it is up to the tradition to make its way in the marketplace of ideas, suggesting that using state power in this way taints the spiritual enterprise. If there is a Christian understanding of moral harm that holds up objectively in the public sphere, however, the church could be offering a public service to civil society by encouraging media restrictions. The state's interest may be more indirect. The Christian vision of sexual and family morality could ultimately promote social stability, to the state's benefit. However, it may be that the state's responsibility here is to protect free exercise of religion—if free exercise can be said to include the religious person's right not to see certain types of cultural products or to protect his or her children from exposure to the same. Even the free-exercise case for protecting children hinges on making a theological case against pornography.

Insofar as the issue of restricting access to obscene material is a matter of protecting children, the question is how such material may impede the cultivation of Christian character. Speaking generally, it is in the church's interest to educate children to be members of the body of Christ, participants in the holy community of God. Following Paul, the community is edified to the degree that its members embody the way of the cross, which is mutual self-sacrifice. The question, then, is what pornography may teach contrary to this end. There are three obvious conflicts.

First, pornography reinforces an assumption common to contemporary American society, namely that there is a right to sexual satisfaction. Disagreements over homosexuality often turn on just this question—whether the "natural" existence of a desire implies the right to pursue its fulfillment. Recognizing the power of consumptive desire, pornography contributes to the commodification of sexuality, reducing to a product what should be, theologically speaking, a gift subject to stewardship. This transformation is the logic of the market, but it is problematic for the edification of the Christian community, which relies on the sublimation of desire to sacrifice. The pursuit of sexual satisfaction in this way reinforces selfishness and jealousy in members of the community, and children learn that their identities as consumers are prior to their spiritual commitments.

Related to the first issue are the problematic implications for the status of women. The commodification, objectification, and degradation of women, which is common in pornography, if sometimes only implicitly, is unacceptable to Christians across the theological spectrum. One could argue that detaching sexuality from personal identity, male or female, is to do violence to the integrity of the creature, but given the historical oppression of women, pornography is even more threatening to their status, both as persons worthy of virtue and respect and as sexual beings.

Finally, pornography also encourages viewers to detach sexual activity from its moral consequences. Sex carries with it a relational vulnerability that implies responsibility for both the body and the spirit of one's partner. Although the tradition has not done much to integrate the idea of non-procreative erotic pleasure, it is wise to have recognized that the possibility of creating children remains the most serious potential moral consequence of sexual activity. To this end, the recent evangelical campaigns promoting sexual satisfaction within marriage serve to strengthen families and thus support the welfare of children. While absolute rules about premarital sex may or may not be integral to discipleship, the habitual detachment of sexual activity from interpersonal commitment, as modeled by pornography, certainly is not countenanced by the church.

Taking these issues into consideration, the church still must consider what exactly is the state's interest in supplementing the church's internal disciplinary resources by limiting the promulgation of certain types of cultural products. Do church and state seek to create the same kind of person? How does children's exposure to certain types of cultural materials bear on this question? Here an important observation requires us to shift the terms of the debate: while both legislation and the political muscle of the church have been focused on sexually explicit material, the academic debate surrounding the potential harm to children focuses on violence.

One certainly could argue that the state has a legitimate interest in promoting a certain vision of sexual morality and that its ends comport well with the church's in some ways. Still, while the promotion of stable families and the control of the spread of disease are in the interest of the state, the demands of a free market economy encourage liberal divorce laws, two-career families, and the sexualization of the entertainment and advertising industries. It could be argued that the state's disproportionate interest in sex over violence reflects the church's priorities, if not the New Testament's, but it is worth wondering if this is an area where Christian ethics has been colonized by state interests.

In discussing the conflict between free speech and the protection of children, the academic argument shifts away from pornography to the effects of media violence on child development, despite the fact that the legislative history of the issue and its attendant religious support clearly focus on sexual material. Even the media outlets that have successfully avoided state regulation by adopting voluntary ratings and control systems tend to take sexual content more seriously than violence. The best known—and arguably most successful—of these systems, the Motion Picture Association of America's voluntary ratings system, includes violence as a factor, but is much more restrictive toward sexual content.[39]

When legislatures *have* moved to restrict minors' access to media depicting violence, the courts have held that unlike sexual obscenity, violent expression *is* protected by the First Amendment. The legal definition of obscenity encompasses only sexually explicit material, while attempted legislation with almost exactly the same standards of judgment about violence has been struck down. Missouri's 1993 law restricting violent movie rentals to minors appealed to "contemporary community standards" as a measure, and it restricted violent material lacking "serious literary, artistic, political, or scientific value."[40] The courts overturned the law, however, expressly disagreeing with Missouri's attempt to connect violence with previous legal restrictions on obscenity: "Obscenity, however, encompasses only expression that 'depicts or describes sexual conduct.' Material that contains violence but not depictions or descriptions of sexual conduct cannot be obscene."[41] While First Amendment protection of violent speech is not absolute,[42] there are certainly fewer restrictions, meaning easier access for children.[43]

This situation is all the more astounding given that there is far more evidence to suggest media violence is harmful to children than there is suggesting pornography is harmful. While many of these studies only show short-term connections, several have attempted to overcome the logistical obstacles to make a long-term connection between media violence viewed by children and aggressive or criminal behavior in late adolescence and adulthood.[44] Longitudinal studies on the issue are particularly difficult to construct, however, leading some to challenge the methodologies of the most influential studies and describe their claims of proven harm to children as "bogus."[45] Nonetheless, there are many more studies and many more connections, however tenuous, suggesting violent material is objectively harmful to children, yet such material receives constitutional protections not afforded to sexual expression.

Even if the long-term harmful effects of violent media cannot be definitively demonstrated, the church does have something at stake in the normalization of violence. For most of its history, Christianity has not embraced pacifism, though even at the height of religious establishment, the church put a check on violent power, including that of the state. To some degree, however, the legacy of the Reformation is the division of the self into public and private spheres, and while the church may be free to hold sway in the latter, the state has set the terms of participation in the former. Caesar holds his office by virtue of the sword, and the only true "public" is a sphere where an institutional body claims a monopoly on the legitimate use of violence.[46] The peace prescribed by the Gospel is therefore only a private peace, one enabled and protected by the threat of violence standing behind public order.

Normalized violence, in other words, speaks to the privatization of religious identity. For the church, what is at stake is not so much the potential that the child viewing violent films or playing first-person shooter games will show notable short-term aggressiveness, or even eventual sociopathic tendencies as an adult; rather, the church's concern is the way violent media serve as a form of moral education. The Hollywood action hero often teaches the child that violence is the answer to any of a number of dilemmas, a moral lesson that stands in striking contrast to the New Testament.[47]

This issue of course stirs up broader ecclesiological concerns about Christian participation in governance and the church's attempting to influence or co-opt state power for moral ends, but perhaps the theological danger here is subtler. It could be that the state has allowed the media restrictions in question because it has some stake in normalizing some broadly drawn picture of sexual well-being, but it also could be that the state has allowed the church a degree of power in defining and controlling sexually explicit media to prevent Christians from turning their gaze on the state's stake in perpetuating the connection between moral authority and violent power. A child habituated to killing aliens in *Halo* is of more potential use to the state than a child who models Jesus' apparent pacifism.

This disproportionate concern with sex over violence casts doubt on the suggestion that the state's role in obscenity restrictions is really limited to supporting parents in their freedom to raise children as they see fit. In some sense, it is the state's mission in a liberal polity to *inhibit* the parents' rights in this regard. While the purveyors of sexually explicit or violent media products may not have absolute First Amendment rights to distribute, children may have "developmental" rights to view some material. While the political reality is that very few politicians would openly challenge parental rights to raise children in a particular moral or religious way, it is certainly an open legal question to what degree children have a say in their own moral and religious growth. This is to say that as far as the state is concerned, parents' rights to raise their children may be only "rights-in-trust"—children's own rights legally entrusted to another agent who is ultimately subject to review by the state.[48] The legal history of the matter centers on the producers' rights to create and distribute the material, but comparatively little attention has been paid to whether children have a right to view it. Therefore, the state's mandate is unclear, as it must weigh its involvement with respect to the parent's right to raise a child a certain way, the child's right to have a say in what kind of adult he or she will become, and the state's interest in self-perpetuating its authority to decide. The church's legal status is dependent upon its persuasive power over these other entities, and as such it faces the danger of being morally colonized by any of them.

CONCLUSIONS

The church of course is a community with its own standards, though its identity with regard to sexual mores and its relationship with the state are both highly contentious matters. Using the state apparatus to shield children from exposure to sexually explicit material is a complex issue in part because sexual morality is itself a divisive issue for the church. The internal ecclesiological tensions wrought by the lingering effects of religious establishment, however unofficial in the American context, deepen the complexity further still. Both sexual morality and the relation of the church to the state have to account for the ambiguity of the New Testament witness, especially the problem of how a collection of writings produced from a position of political weakness translates to a contemporary democratic polity.

Culturally speaking, disestablishment is not a complete process in America, and it likely never will be. This is especially true now in the midst of an American evangelical revival, which like other revivals tends to identify the church closely with American national identity. If America is a "Christian nation," as many would like to think of it, then it is easier to direct the resources of the state to aid in the cultivation of Christian character. When it comes to children, it may be reasonable for the church to ask the state to regulate certain types of material. What should be clear, however, is that there is a price to be paid in doing so, and the state may be more willing to aid the church in some areas than others, perhaps in part to preserve its own interests.

The recent defeat of the Child Online Protection Act certainly will not be the end of the issue. The mainstreaming of pornography in American culture continues, helped along by technological developments, and the largely libertarian ethos of the Internet is coming under increasing scrutiny by advocates of "common decency" in public discourse. America's appetite for sex and violence is matched by its need to protect the welfare of its children, and both church and state strive to determine their role in shaping the future of American culture.

NOTES

1. Thomas P. Oakley, "The Cooperation of Mediaeval Penance and Secular Law," *Speculum* 7, no. 4 (1932): 515–24; Floyd Seyward Lear, "Blasphemy in the Lex Romana Curiensis," *Speculum* 6:3 (1931): 445–59.
2. *Regina v. Hicklin*, 3 Queens Bench 360, 362 (1868).
3. *An Act for the Suppression of Trade in, and Circulation of, Obscene Literature and Articles of Immoral Use*, c. 258, §2, 17 Stat. 598, 599 (1873).
4. *United States v. Dennett*, 39 F.2d 564, 568 (2d Cir. 1930).
5. *United States v. One Book Called "Ulysses,"* 5 F. Supp. 182, 183–185 (S.D.N.Y. 1933), affirmed, *United States v. One Book Entitled Ulysses by James Joyce*, 72 F.2d 705 (2d Cir. 1934).
6. *Roth v. United States*, 354 U.S. 476, 487 (1957).
7. *Jacobellis v. Ohio*, 378 U.S. 184, 192–195, 197 (1964).
8. *Stanley v. Georgia*, 394 U.S. 557, 566–568 (1969).
9. Bob Woodward and Scott Armstrong, *The Brethren* (New York: Simon & Schuster, 1979), 193–200.
10. *Miller v. California*, 413 U.S. 15, 24–25 (1973).
11. *Paris Adult Theatre I v. Slaton*, 413 U.S. 49, 57–63 (1973); citing *Steward Machine Co. v. Davis*, 301 U.S. 548, 590 (1937).
12. *Paris Adult Theatre I v. Slaton*, 413 U.S. 49, 103 (1973).
13. *City of Renton v. Playtime Theatres*, 475 U.S. 41 (1986).
14. *Jacobellis v. Ohio*, 378 U.S. 184, 192–95 (1964).
15. Robert D. Putnam, *Bowling Alone: The Collapse and Revival of American Community* (New York: Simon & Schuster, 2000), 148–180.
16. *Ginsburg v. New York*, 390 U.S. 629, 639–643 (1968).
17. David Archard, "Free Speech and Children's Interests," *Chicago-Kent Law Review* 79, no. 1 (2004): 83–102.
18. *FCC v. Pacifica Foundation*, 438 U.S. 726, 746–751 (1978).
19. *Communications Act of 1996*, 110 Stat. 133, 47 U.S.C.A. (Supp. 1997).
20. *Reno v. ACLU*, 521 U.S. 844 (1997).
21. Matt Moore, "Construction on Online Back Alley Halted," http://www.boston.com/business/articles/2007/03/30/icann_set_to_vote_on_xxx_domain/.
22. 47 U.S.C. 231.
23. *Ashcroft v. ACLU*, 542 U.S. 656 (2004).
24. *ACLU v. Gonzalez*, F3d. (2007).
25. *U.S. v. American Library Association*, 539 U.S. 194 (2003).
26. Following references to the brief may be found at www.aclj.org/Cases.
27. Victor B. Cline, "The Effects of Pornography on Behaviour," http://www.c-a-s-e.net/The%20Effects%20of%20Porn.htm.
28. D. Zillman and J. Bryant, "Pornography's Impact on Sexual Satisfaction," *Journal of Applied Sociology* 18, no. 5 (1988): 438–453; D. Zillman and J. Bryant, "Effect of Prolonged Consumption of Pornography on Family Values," *Journal of Family Issues* 9, no. 4 (1988): 518–544.

29. W. L. Marshall, "The Use of Sexually Explicit Stimuli by Rapists, Child Molesters, and Nonoffenders," *The Journal of Sex Research* 25, no. 2 (May 1988): 267–288.

30. Donna Rice Hughes, "How Pornography Harms Children," available at www.protectkids.com/effects/harms.htm.

31. For a controversial treatment of the issue, see Judith Levine, *Harmful to Minors: The Perils of Protecting Children from Sex* (Minneapolis, MN: University of Minnesota Press, 2002); also Marjorie Heins, *Not In Front of the Children: "Indecency," Censorship, and the Innocence of Youth* (New York: Hill and Wang, 2001), 243–253.

32. Augustine, *Confessions,* trans. Henry Chadwick (New York: Oxford University Press, 1991), 145.

33. Augustine, *St. Augustine on Marriage and Sexuality,* ed. Elizabeth Clark (Washington, D.C.: The Catholic University of America Press, 1996), 45–55.

34. Paul VI, *Humanae Vitae* (1968), http://www.papalencyclicals.net/Paul06/p6humana.htm. For a more recent Catholic warning of the dangers of pornography, see Bishop Robert W. Finn's pastoral letter *Blessed Are The Pure In Heart* (2007), http://www.catholicculture.org/docs/doc_view.cfm?recnum=7438.

35. Adrian Thatcher, "When Does Christian Marriage Begin? Before or after the Wedding?" *The Witness* 83, no. 4 (April 2000): 20–22.

36. Don S. Browning and Carol Browning, "The Church and the Family Crisis: A New Love Ethic," *Christian Century* 108 (August 7–14, 1991): 746–749.

37. Don S. Browning, *Christian Ethics and the Moral Psychologies* (Grand Rapids, MI: Eerdmans, 2006), 222–225; see also Alan Wolfe, *Whose Keeper? Social Science and Moral Obligation* (Berkeley: University of California Press, 1989).

38. Mark D. Jordan, *The Invention of Sodomy in Christian Theology* (Chicago: University of Chicago Press, 1997), 166–176.

39. Kirby Dick, Director, *This Film Is Not Yet Rated* (2006).

40. *Mo. Rev. Stat.* § 573.090 (2003).

41. *Video Software Dealers Ass'n v. Webster,* 773 F. Supp. 1275 (W.D. Mo. 1991), aff'd 968 F.2d 684 (8th Cir. 1992).

42. Gloria Tristani, "On Children and Television: Keynote Address, Annenberg Public Policy Center's 5th Annual Conference on Children & Media, Washington, D.C., June 26, 2000," http://www.fcc.gov/Speeches/Tristani/2000/spgt009.html.

43. See also Jessalyn Hershinger, "State Restrictions on Violent Expression," *Vanderbilt Law Review* 46, no. 2 (1993): 473; Kevin W. Saunders, *Violence as Obscenity: Limiting the Media's First Amendment Protection* (Durham, NC: Duke University Press, 1996).

44. Amitai Etzioni, "On Protecting Children from Speech," *Chicago-Kent Law Review* 79, no. 1 (2004): 34–39.

45. Marjorie Heins, "On Protecting Children—From Censorship," *Chicago-Kent Law Review* 79, no. 1 (2004): 239–249.

46. William T. Cavanaugh, "'A Fire Strong Enough to Consume the House': The Wars of Religion and the Rise of the State," *Modern Theology* 11, no. 4 (October 1995): 397–420.

47. Richard B. Hays, *The Moral Vision of the New Testament: Community, Cross, New Creation* (San Francisco: Harper San Francisco, 1996), 317–346.

48. See Joel Feinberg, "The Child's Right to an Open Future," in *Whose Child?: Children's Rights, Parental Authority, and State Power,* ed. William Aiken and Hugh La Follette (Totowa, NJ: Rowman & Littlefield, 1980); see also Archard (2004).

FURTHER READING

The legal and social issues surrounding obscenity restrictions are debated in the *Chicago-Kent Law Review* 79:1 (2004) in a symposium somewhat inaccurately named "Do Children Have the Same First Amendment Rights as Adults?" Guest editor Amitai Etzioni makes a communitarian proposal for restrictions, and a number of scholars respond in an effort to tease out the various legal and philosophical issues at play, including the legal status of children as compared to adults. The symposium is somewhat limited to the Internet questions, and it is notably lacking an explicitly religious voice. One of the participants is Marjorie Heins, director of the Free Expression Policy Project at the National Coalition Against Censorship. Heins' book, *Not In Front of the Children: "Indecency," Censorship, and the Innocence of Youth* (New York: Hill and Wang, 2001), is an argument against restrictions. Heins includes a legal history and a thorough review of the sociological and psychological studies used by those who have wished to regulate speech in the interest of protecting children. Judith Levine's *Harmful to Minors: The Perils of Protecting Children from Sex* (Minneapolis, MN: University of Minnesota Press, 2002) is a controversial argument about the need to recognize the realities of children's sexuality; she suggests that the Christian Right promulgates fear and misinformation in an effort to force its morality on others through state power. The opposite point of view is ably presented by the Family Research Council (www.frc.org) in a number of pamphlets and position papers. The relevant Supreme Court cases have been collected in *Obscenity and Pornography Decisions of the United States Supreme Court* (San Diego: Excellent Books, 2000). For an in-depth examination of moral education and state power as related to theological concerns, see Don S. Browning, *Christian Ethics and Moral Psychologies* (Grand Rapids, MI: Eerdmans, 2006).

6

School Vouchers in America

Michael Coulter

In recent decades, some religious leaders, economists, activists, and politicians—mostly associated with the conservative movement—have promoted the idea that parents should be given some financial assistance in placing their children in the school—public or private—of their choice. Often, the assistance advocated is a voucher given to parents that could be redeemed at a school of their choosing. Some advocates urge that vouchers should be made available for all children while others only promote the idea in areas with troubled public school districts or limit vouchers to those of modest means. Some suggest that the assistance to parents should take the form of a tax credit. That is, parents would get some reduction of their tax liability (either state or federal) because they have paid private school tuition. There have only been a few school voucher programs and a few tuition tax credit programs enacted in the United States, and in comparison to the total number of students they have affected only a small portion of school-age children. However, as a political and social issue, vouchers have been greatly significant in the past few decades, generating controversial court decisions and political battles in legislatures as well as mobilizing interest groups and voters concerning the issue.

There are several issues involved in the school choice debate. Some proponents of school choice argue that the current system of delivering education, in which most students attend the government school to which they are assigned because of their residence, leads to schools functioning like a monopoly. There is little competition between schools and therefore little incentive to provide quality service. The central premise of this argument is that competition will lead to greater quality. Other school choice proponents argue that religious parents should be able to choose schools for their children that reflect and reinforce the religious beliefs of their children rather than sending their children to public schools that have come to be regarded as, at least in some instances, hostile to religion. Both sets of proponents assert that choice programs should permit parents to choose private schools, and in the United States the vast majority of private schools are either operated by a church or by those with strong religious commitments. Because choice proponents want vouchers or tax credits to assist those choosing religious schools, this has generated opposition to school choice on the grounds that aid to private religious schools would violate the First Amendment's Establishment Clause because the state would be supporting religious organizations. Rather than focusing on economic theory or the impact of choice on academic performance, this essay will focus on the intersection of the school choice debate and church-state issues. Instead of interpreting vouchers as a violation of the Establishment Clause, as many legal observers would have reasonably anticipated, the U.S. Supreme Court and some state courts have accepted vouchers and tax credits as being consistent with constitutional precepts separating church and state. The debate over the practicality of school vouchers continues because powerful interests argue that it is not a good use of public money or that choice programs will harm public schools.

BACKGROUND

Elementary and secondary public education in the United States developed around "common schools" that were largely supported with local tax revenues. These schools, as they evolved in the nineteenth century, were largely supportive of the Protestant culture of which they were a part.[1] During the latter half of that same century, American Catholics developed an extensive parochial school system that educated many Catholics. Other groups with strong identities such as Jews, Lutherans, and Dutch Calvinists also developed systems of private education, although these systems were often limited to particular areas and educated fewer children than those in Catholic schools. These schools were strongly supported by their sponsoring religious organizations, and adherents of those religious groups were strongly encouraged to enroll their children in those schools. While there were many private schools—both religious and non-religious—most children in the United States were educated in public schools.

There was intermittent pressure in the late-nineteenth and early-twentieth centuries for state support of religiously-affiliated schools, because during this same time period there was increasing financial support for public education. In response to the possibility of public support for religious schools, there was a movement to enact legal provisions, generally known as "Blaine Amendments," prohibiting public funds for sectarian schools. These were named after Maine politician James G. Blaine, who as Speaker of the House proposed in 1875 an amendment that would have prohibited any federal funds from going to sectarian schools.[2] The proposed amendment passed the House of Representatives 180–7, but it failed in the Senate. States then considered their own Blaine Amendments and 37 states have since incorporated some form of the provision into their state constitution.[3] At that time, the Blaine Amendments were directed against attempts for the direct support of religious schools; these amendments became important in the later political battles over school voucher programs.

The US Supreme Court addressed the constitutionality of prohibiting religious schools altogether in *Pierce v. Society of Sisters* (1925) when it overturned a 1922 Oregon law that required all 8- to 16-year-olds to attend a public school. This decision thus established the right of non-public schools to exist. The Supreme Court later entered the fray over support of private religious schools in its *Everson v. Board of Education* (1947) case. In this case the Supreme Court determined that reimbursing parents who paid for transportation for their children who were attending Catholic schools was constitutional. The Court stated that "the First Amendment has erected a wall of separation between church and state . . . that wall must be high and impregnable . . . [but] New Jersey has not breached it here." The court compares this support of parents to the general protection provided to the citizens by policemen and firemen. During the first half of the twentieth century, any attempt to assist parents who have chosen private schools was usually in some form of direct government assistance to the school or provisions of services, such as busing, to parents. Vouchers were not part of the political debate.

Vouchers first were promoted not by someone operating private religious schools, but by an economist. Milton Friedman, a professor at the University of Chicago from 1946 to 1976 and a recipient of the Nobel Memorial Prize in Economics in 1976, suggested the development of voucher programs in his 1955 essay, "The Role of Government in Education."[4] According to Friedman, a voucher system "would bring a healthy increase in the variety of educational institutions available and in competition among them."[5] There is little evidence that the argument attracted much attention at the time. Friedman republished with only slight revision the 1955 piece in his 1962 work, *Capitalism and Freedom*. This work was widely read and discussed at the time in publications associated with the conservative and libertarian movements, such as the *National Review*.

In 1957, Virgil Blum, S.J., a professor of political science at Marquette University, began promoting vouchers when he founded Citizens for Educational Freedom. He is the first to initiate a public campaign for vouchers. He published *Freedom of Choice in Education* in 1958, wherein he argues on both religious and civil liberty grounds that parents should have assistance in choosing schools for their children. In 1973, Blum founded the Catholic League for Religious and Civil Rights, and until the time of his death in 1990 that organization actively promoted vouchers.

During the 1960s, the U.S. Supreme Court made some important decisions affecting public schools which, while not directly regarding school vouchers or tax credits, are important for the emerging voucher movement. In *Engel v. Vitale* (1962) and in *Abington v. Schempp* (1963), the U.S. Supreme Court ruled, respectively, that compulsory Bible reading and prayers led by teachers were violations of the First Amendment's Establishment Clause. Some critics of these decisions directed political activism towards re-establishing prayer and other forms of religious expression in public schools. Other conservative Protestants—many of whom could be characterized as members of the New Right—began establishing new networks of private religious schools, so that their children would have an education that is integrated with religious belief.[6] Some supporters of these new religious schools joined Catholics in supporting vouchers.

In the 1970s vouchers developed a growing following. The White House's Office of Economic Opportunity sponsored a voucher program (which did not include sectarian schools) for a brief period beginning in 1970. In 1972, New York established the Elementary and Secondary Education Opportunity Program. This provided per-pupil grants to private schools that primarily served low-income populations, and it provided a partial tuition reimbursement to low-income parents who sent their children to those schools. In *Committee for Public Education v. Nyquist* (1973), the U.S. Supreme Court struck down this New York law as violating the First Amendment's Establishment Clause. In 1972, some California parents filed suit against the State of California for not having a voucher program. They claimed that the lack of such a program constituted a violation of free exercise and equal protection rights. This suit was rejected by the Ninth Circuit Court of Appeals. Michigan voters placed a voucher initiative on the ballot in 1978. California placed a voucher question on the ballot in both 1980 and 1982. All three of those ballot questions failed, however.

Senators Robert Packwood (R-Oregon) and Daniel Patrick Moynihan (D-New York) introduced a tuition tax credit bill in 1977 at the urging of Blum and other Catholic leaders, but it failed to become law.

REAGAN'S ADVOCACY OF SCHOOL CHOICE

In his 1980 campaign for the presidency, Ronald Reagan expressed support for vouchers and tuition tax credits, positions he continued to endorse, and even legislate, while in office. Reagan supported vouchers because it was important to both religious conservatives and to economists, two groups that were an important part of the Reagan coalition. According to *Congressional Quarterly*, Reagan pushed for voucher and tax credit measures in each Congress from 1981 to 1986. In 1983 he gave the most attention to vouchers and tax credits with several public statements in support of them. On March 12, 1983, Reagan devoted his weekly radio address to improving education, touting a forthcoming "education package" that contained several proposals. Reagan endorsed tax credits, which would have allowed a reduction in tax liability for those who paid local school taxes and who paid for private school tuition. He then added: "Second, we're proposing a voucher system to help parents of disadvantaged children."[7] The program would have allowed parents in poorer school districts to make use of federal funds sent to their district to pay for tuition at private schools in their area. On April 7 of that year, Reagan offered brief remarks at a meeting of the National Catholic Educational Association where he spoke of the voucher proposal for disadvantaged parents. He added that "if anyone realizes the need for free parental choice, it is the Catholic community."[8] On April 26, 1983, upon receiving the report, *A Nation At Risk*, which was produced by the National Commission on Excellence in Education in 1983, Reagan reiterated his call for vouchers and tuition tax credits so that parents would have choices; he also believed that competition would lead to improvement in schools.[9] In another radio address just a few days later, April 30, 1983, Reagan once again repeated his call for vouchers and tax credits.

For what were likely both policy and political reasons, he strongly supported means to enable parents to send their children to non-public schools. In no public comment does Reagan seek to explain how programs that would have supported students attending private religious schools were not a violation of Establishment Clause, even though others, such as Americans United for Separation of Church and State, asserted such programs to be violation of the Constitution. The proposals were not passed out of Congress during Reagan's time in office.[10]

Tax credits and vouchers remained important for the Republican coalition as those issues were included as part of the Republican platform throughout the 1980s and 1990s. For example, in the 1984 Republican Platform, it is stated: "We offer hope, not despair; more opportunities for education through vouchers and tuition tax relief." The 1988 Platform statement also strongly supports vouchers, saying that "choice and competition in education foster quality and protect consumers' rights" and that "states should consider enacting voucher systems or other means of encouraging competition among public schools."

THE MILWAUKEE PARENTAL CHOICE PROGRAM (MPCP)

While vouchers had been proposed at the state level during the 1970s and 1980s, both in legislatures and before voters in the form of initiatives, no program had been enacted during that time. Wisconsin became the first to do so with the enactment of the Milwaukee Parental Choice Program in 1989. As first established by the Wisconsin legislature, the program permitted those attending Milwaukee Public Schools (MPS) to attend another public school or a private non-sectarian school. Eligible students, who could comprise no more than one percent of the total students in the MPS, had to be members of families whose household income was less than 1.75 times the federal poverty level. The program was framed as means of helping poorer families rather than helping religious families choose religious schools. As first enacted, students could choose to attend only a non-sectarian private school. When a student chose to attend a private school, the school received the per-student state aid that would have otherwise gone to the MPS. Participating schools had to accept this amount as the total tuition charge for each student. During the 1990–1991 school year, 334 students participated in the program, attending eleven non-sectarian private schools. In 1993, the cap was increased to 1.5 percent of the total students in the MPS. In 1995–1996 nearly 1,600 students participated, attending seventeen schools. There were a number of legal challenges to the program during these years, including one arguing that the exclusion of sectarian private schools was a violation of the Equal Protection Clause of the Fourteenth Amendment, but these challenges had no impact on the law.

In 1995, as part of the budget bill, the MPCP was significantly revised by the Wisconsin General Assembly. The most important change was that sectarian schools could participate in the program and the cap on participation was raised to fifteen percent of the students in the MPS. Furthermore, the State Superintendent had previously conducted investigations of participating private schools, and this supervisory role was limited in the 1995 revision of the law. There was also a change in the mechanism of payment to private schools. Under the amended law, payments from the state to the private schools would be sent to the private school, but issued in the name of the parent(s) or guardian of the child attending that school. Those checks would be "restrictively endorsed" to the school, which meant that parents had to sign them over to the school. This method of payment was devised so that funds would not go directly to the school from the state treasury. Finally, the amount paid to private schools would be the lesser of the per-pupil grant or the per-student cost at the private school. For example, in 2006–2007 eligible students could receive up to $6,501 dollars to spend at a participating school. These changes led to a dramatic expansion of this program. In 2006–2007, over 17,000 students chose to make use of the program, and they attended 124 different schools.[11]

When the law was changed to allow students to attend private sectarian schools, there were new legal challenges to the program. On January 15, 1997, Dane County (the county that includes Milwaukee) Circuit Court Judge Paul Higginbotham ruled that the newly revised MPCP was unconstitutional because it violated a provision of the Wisconsin Constitution which states that no "money shall be drawn from the treasury for the benefit of religious societies or religious or theological seminaries."[12] Higginbotham further argued that the schools which were operated by religious organizations and participated in the MPCP were an integral part of the religious mission of those churches. Supporting those schools would be supporting those churches. Higginbotham maintained that the religious organizations, not the students, would be the primary beneficiaries of the program. Moreover, even though the checks for tuition were written out to the parents, Higginbotham ruled that this still constituted direct aid to private religious schools.

Higginbotham's decision was affirmed by a Wisconsin appellate court in a 2–1 decision later in 1997. The Wisconsin Court of Appeals ruled that the MPCP violated the Wisconsin "Blaine Amendment" cited in Higginbotham's decision, but they did not issue as part of their ruling a determination of whether the MPCP was a violation of the U.S. Constitution's First Amendment. The dissenting judge in this case, Pat Roggensack, argued that the program violated neither the state for the U.S. Constitution with respect to church-state grounds.

The state of Wisconsin, as then led by pro-voucher Governor Tommy Thompson, appealed the decision to the Wisconsin Supreme Court. This court case attracted significant attention as a major voucher program hung in the balance. Arguing the case were some of the most vocal opponents and supporters of school voucher programs. The legal team defending the

MPCP included Kenneth Starr of the Washington law firm of Kirkland and Ellis and Clint Bolick of the Institute for Justice, a Washington, D.C., public interest law firm that has devoted significant resources to defending voucher programs. The legal team challenging the statute included counsel from the American Civil Liberties Union and Americans United for the Separation of Church and State. There were several *amicus curiae* (friend of the court) briefs submitted as attempts to influence the determination of the Wisconsin Supreme Court justices. For example, People for the American Way, a liberal advocacy group submitted a brief arguing that the MPCP was unconstitutional. There were several briefs submitted in favor of the program from groups such as the National Association of Evangelicals, the Christian Legal Society, Liberty Counsel, Focus on the Family, the Lutheran Church (Missouri Synod), and the Ethics and Religious Liberty Commission of the Southern Baptist Convention.

The Court ruled 4–2 in *Jackson v. Benson* (one justice did not participate in the decision) to uphold the MPCP. The majority opinion was aware of the many arguments for and against vouchers, but Justice Donald Steinmetz, who was elected to the Wisconsin Supreme Court in 1980 and again in 1990, asserted that the Court would focus only on constitutional issues. The majority opinion first addresses whether the MPCP violates the Establishment Clause. Applying the three-pronged constitutionality test established in the U.S. Supreme Court's decision in *Lemon v. Kurtzman* (1971), the high court in Wisconsin ruled that the MPCP has a secular purpose, namely improved educational performance, satisfying the first of *Lemon's* requirements.

Another prong of the *Lemon* Test regards whether a law has a primary effect of advancing religion. There have been some post-*Lemon* cases in which the U.S. Supreme Court has ruled that programs which distribute educational assistance to a wide range of parents and to both sectarian and non-sectarian schools are not seen as primarily advancing religion. Following these cases, the Wisconsin Supreme Court characterized the MPCP as having "neutral, secular criteria that neither favor nor disfavor religion" for those who can participate. The majority opinion states that parents have many options under this program, including other public schools and non-sectarian private schools. Here the opinion cites the *Everson* opinion when Justice Hugo Black states that "a policeman protects a Catholic, but not because he is a Catholic . . . [and] the fireman protects the church-school, but not because it is a church-school." The majority further states that money only reaches a school "as a result of the numerous private choices of the individual parents of school-age children." The majority opinion cites as significant the process whereby the voucher payments are made out in the names of the parents and must be signed over to the school of choice. The Wisconsin Supreme Court held that the process of funding is "not some type of 'sham' to funnel public funds to sectarian private schools."

The final part of the *Lemon* Test concerns excessive entanglement of the state with religion. Excessive entanglement includes not only involvement in decision-making, but even close supervision of religious organizations that is likely to the change the behavior of those organizations. The Wisconsin Supreme Court ruled that there is not excessive entanglement because the reporting and auditing requirements of participating schools are minimal. The health and safety requirements for participating schools do not constitute excessive entanglement as they already exist for private schools in Wisconsin. The Court then ruled that the MPCP was consistent with the federal *Lemon* Test.

The Court then addressed whether the MPCP was a violation of the state constitution, which was at the heart of Higginbotham's ruling. The opinion states that the "no money from the treasury" clause, cited above, should be understood in a manner similar to the U.S. Constitution's Establishment Clause. In this sense, the majority asserted that previous Wisconsin Supreme Court rulings on its Establishment Clause did not erect a greater wall of separation than that found in the U.S. Constitution. The opinion then asked whether the MPCP primarily benefits religious institutions. The majority found "that the Supreme Court's primary effect test, focusing on the neutrality and indirection of state aid, is well-reasoned." The majority also found that there have been previous programs in Wisconsin where some educational assistance helped those at private sectarian educational institutions and that those have been accepted as constitutional. In sum, the MPCP's primary effect was not advancing a particular religion.

The Wisconsin Supreme Court considered some other constitutional issues—such as whether the clause calling for uniform public education was violated, whether the bill serves a public purpose which is not a specific passage of the constitution but rather a doctrine utilized by the Court, and whether the MPCP violates the Equal Protection Clause of the Fourteenth Amendment. None of these measures relates to church-state issues and on none of these grounds was the MPCP in violation of the state or federal constitutions.

At this point, *Jackson v. Benson* was the most important court decision in favor of a voucher program. Those who lost this case immediately appealed to the U.S. Supreme Court. On November 9, 1998, the U.S. Supreme Court announced that they would not hear an appeal of the case. This meant that only three or fewer of justices of the Supreme Court wanted to grant a Writ of Certiorari to those challenging the case.

THE OHIO PILOT PROJECT SCHOLARSHIP PROGRAM

After the MPCP was started and while it was being litigated, Ohio started a voucher program that would result in a significant U.S. Supreme Court decision. On June 28, 1995, the Ohio General Assembly adopted the Ohio Pilot Project Scholarship Program as part of a biennial budget bill for fiscal years 1996 and 1997. This program established a voucher program in any district under the direct management and supervision of the State Superintendent of Public Instruction due to mismanagement at the local level. In Ohio at that the time (and since), only one district has been subject to this law: the Cleveland Public School District, which was so designated because of an order by the United States District Court for Northern Ohio on March 5, 1995.

The Cleveland voucher program offered scholarships to anyone living in the district, regardless of income, but it gave preference to those whose income was 200 percent or less of the poverty level. That is, if those below twice the poverty level filled all available spots at participating private schools, there would be no scholarships for those families above twice the poverty level. The total number of scholarships offered was based on the specific amount appropriated for the program. It was estimated at the time that 60 percent of students in the Cleveland school system lived in a household that earned less than twice the poverty rate. At its inception, the program capped tuition charges at $2,500—the state of Ohio would offer a voucher to parents for 90 percent of that amount ($2,250) for low-income families and would pay 75 percent ($1,875) for other families. When a guardian chose a non-public school, the scholarship checks were to be made payable to the families choosing the voucher, but it would be mailed to the school. Students could attend a public school in a neighboring district if any bordering districts were willing to accept students, and in those cases the check would be made out to the school receiving the student. Since the inception of the program, no neighboring public school was willing to take students from Cleveland. Many students participated in the tutoring programs funded by the legislation, but the controversial element was not the options for public schools or the tutoring program (both of which were never legally challenged). It was, most certainly, the program of scholarships to private schools.

There were two challenges to the legislation in the Ohio court system in January 1996. Those cases were consolidated and the case became known as *Simmons-Harris v. Goff* (Simmons-Harris was a parent of a child in the Cleveland Public School System and John Goff was the Superintendent of Public Instruction for the State of Ohio). Those challenging the law asked a local court for summary judgment (a trial without extensive testimony because it was assumed that the outcome would be appealed, regardless of who prevailed). Next an intermediary appellate court in Ohio heard the case and declared the program to be unconstitutional, asserting that the program violated the Establishment Clause of the First Amendment and the Establishment Clause of the Ohio Constitution, as well as two sections of the Ohio Constitution that relate to schools (a funding clause and the uniformity clause). That appellate court held that the statute did not violate the state's constitutional clause requiring "a thorough and efficient system of public education" and Ohio Constitution's clause requiring legislation to be about a single subject.

The case was appealed to the Ohio Supreme Court, which heard the case in September 1998 and issued a ruling on May 27, 1999. This case, like the Wisconsin case heard the year before, attracted national attention, and lawyers specializing in school choice argued the case on behalf of the parties to the case. The case also attracted several significant *amicus curiae* briefs from groups either advocating or opposing school choice. The Ohio Supreme Court almost completely reversed the holding of the appellate court. It upheld the law as being in conformity with state and federal constitutional law, except for the state provision directing that legislation concern a single subject.

The Court's majority opinion devoted much attention to the question of whether this program constituted a violation of the Establishment Clause of the First Amendment. Like the Wisconsin Supreme Court, the Ohio Supreme Court used the three-prong test from *Lemon*. Concerning the purpose of the program, the court quickly agreed that it had a recognizable secular purpose. The Court considered whether the law would have the effect advancing or inhibiting religion. Here the Ohio Court rejected the notion than any money assisting the educational function of a religious organization would be ipso facto invalid. The Ohio Supreme Court relied primarily on two cases, *Agostini v. Felton* (1997) and *Zobrest v. Catalina Foothills School District* (1993), both of which concerned special services being provided to students at private schools and which held that such a provision of services did not violate the Establishment Clause. In both of these cases, the U.S. Supreme Court held that the because the services were distributed in a neutral fashion—that is, without respect to a religious organization—aid in and of itself cannot be said to be advancing religion as such, even though the ability to receive specialized services might encourage more students to attend private sectarian schools.

The Court was troubled by a provision in the law that gave priority among those attending a private sectarian school to the members of the sponsoring religious organization. Since public money was involved, this seemed to give members of religious groups a privileged position and thus to violate the principle of neutral distribution of a public good. The court ruled, however, that the section of the statute giving priority to the members of the church or religious group operating a school could be struck and the remainder of the program could remain in tact. Finally, they addressed the final prong of the *Lemon* Test: excessive entanglement. They held that the program did not violate this element of the text because the requirements for registering for the program were "not onerous and failure to comply is punished by no more than a revocation of the school's registration in the school voucher program."[13]

The Ohio Supreme Court then addressed whether the statute violated the Establishment Clause of the Ohio Constitution, which states that "no person shall be compelled to attend, erect, or support any place of worship, or maintain any form or worship, against his consent; and no preferences shall be given, by law to any religious society; nor shall any interference with the rights of conscience be permitted" (Section 7, Article I). The Court then said that there is no lengthy jurisprudence from the Ohio Supreme Court on the meaning of those Constitutional passages, and so they should apply the *Lemon–Agostini* framework to those passages. They conclude that there is no violation of the state's "Establishment Clause."

There is another passage in the Ohio Constitution regarding the state and religious education, which is the Blaine Amendment language. It states that "no religious or other sect, or sects, shall ever have any exclusive right to, or control of, any part of the school funds of this state" (Section 2, Article VI). The Court stated that "no money flows directly from the state to a sectarian school and no money can reach a sectarian school based solely on the efforts of the state." Because the money did not go directly to the school, the voucher program withstood constitutional scrutiny.

The Court also ruled on constitutional provisions which do not relate to church-state issues, such as the constitutional requirement for a "thorough and efficient system" of funding schools and the requirement that schools operate uniformly throughout the state. They recognized that the program operates only in Cleveland, but could exist in other districts if those districts were put under the control of State Superintendent. There was one remaining issue to be considered by the Court, which was the constitutional requirement that bills should have a single subject. In this decision, the Court ruled that the Ohio General Assembly violated the constitutional provision in Section 15, Article 2, that every piece of legislation must have a single subject. On this basis, the Court struck down the law.

But this was not the end of the voucher program in Ohio. The Ohio

General Assembly in June 1999 passed legislation in re-enacting the voucher program in substantially the same form as it was originally passed. Simmons-Harris and others challenged the law again, but this time in Federal court, rather than state court. On December 20, 1999—after a period of legal wrangling—the U.S. District Court for the Northern District of Ohio ruled that the program violated the Establishment Clause. The State of Ohio immediately appealed that decision. The appeal was argued before the Sixth District Court of Appeals on June 20, 2000. That court rendered a 2–1 decision on December 11, 2000, thereby affirming the decision of the U.S. District Court that the Ohio Pilot Project Scholarship Program violated the Establishment Clause of the First Amendment. It did not consider other merits (or demerits) of voucher programs.

The Court of Appeals, too, considered the *Lemon* Test and gave special attention to *Committee for Public Education v. Nyquist* (1973), a case involving a New York law that provided for partial tuition reimbursement for low-income parents whose children attended private schools. The decision gave significant attention to the fact that 85 percent of the children receiving some form of assistance were attending a sectarian private school. The Court of Appeals reviewed other cases involving aid, either direct or indirect to private religious schools, but came back to *Nyquist* as being essential. The Court of Appeals said that "we find that *Nyquist* governs our result" and that "the program at hand is a tuition grant program for low-income parents whose children attend private school parallel to the tuition reimbursement program found impermissible in *Nyquist*." The Court of Appeals said that there was no way to guarantee that the funds would only be used for "secular, neutral, and non-ideological purposes." The Court of Appeals considered it significant that 96 percent of the students using the voucher for a private school attended sectarian schools. The Court of Appeals further stated that the program as it was constructed discouraged non-sectarian private schools, which generally charged more than sectarian schools, as well as neighboring public school districts from participating because those districts would receive only $2,250 for each student that they enrolled—an amount significantly less than the amount public schools in suburban districts spent per student. The program, the Court held, would only be a true program of choice if there were many choices, rather than just choices among religious schools.

The dissenting judge, James Ryan, argued that the statute was "essentially different" than the New York statute considered in *Nyquist* because that statute gave direct and indirect aid to schools. The New York law, Ryan asserted, was intended to help financially impoverished schools, while the Cleveland voucher program was intended to help parents and children. Furthermore, Ryan argued that recent U.S. Supreme Court jurisprudence permitted some benefits to go to private sectarian schools as a result of parental choices.

The State of Ohio then appealed the U.S. Court of Appeals decision to the U.S. Supreme Court. When the Supreme Court is considering whether to hear a case (grant "certiorari"), interested parties can submit briefs to encourage the Supreme Court to take or not take the case. Twenty-two parties submitted briefs asking the Supreme Court to hear the case and uphold the statute. Among those petitioners included those who had advocated vouchers as a means of improving educational quality. There were also several religious organizations that filed briefs indicating that in their understanding such a program did not violate the Establishment Clause. Among these groups were the Christian Legal Society, the Beckett Fund for Religious Liberty, and the United States Conference of Catholic Bishops.[14] Regarding the latter group, the USCCB did not call for direct funding of Catholics schools or even a broad program of vouchers. Instead, the USCCB brief asserts that the Ohio program is constitutional when one considers the recent jurisprudence of the Supreme Court.

The Court agreed to hear the case during its 2001–2002 term and issued its ruling in *Zelman v. Simmons-Harris* on June 27, 2002. The Supreme Court in a 5–4 decision upheld the program, holding that the program and the vouchers are not automatically a violation of the Establishment Clause. Chief Justice Rehnquist issued the opinion of the Court and was joined by Justices Antonin Scalia, Sandra Day O'Connor, Clarence Thomas, and Anthony Kennedy. Rehnquist gave greater attention to the failing status of the school district than did the appeals court. He cited an Ohio state auditor's report that said that the district was experiencing a "crisis that is perhaps unprecedented in the history of American education." Rehnquist also cited a state report that the district did not meet performance standards and that it had extremely high drop-out rates. He also noted the availability of "community" schools (often called "charter schools" in other states) and the availability of magnet schools within the Cleveland district.

In the majority opinion, Rehnquist asserted that there is no doubt that the program had a secular purpose. The more difficult issue, according to Rehnquist, was whether the program advanced religion. Because the program depended on the choices of parents, Rehnquist wrote for the majority that "it [is] irrelevant to the constitutional inquiry that the vast majority of beneficiaries were parents of children in religious schools." During the 1999–2000 school year, there were nearly 4,000 children who received vouchers, and 96 percent of those students attended sectarian schools, which comprised 46 of the 56 private schools that agreed to take students.

(During the 2006–2007 school year there were nearly 6,000 students using a voucher to attend a private school.) Rehnquist later referred to the program as one of "true private choice." Therefore, the program cannot be seen as a means by which the state was advancing religion. Rehnquist suggested that the case was not a break with previous cases but rather was "in keeping with an unbroken line of decisions rejecting challenges to similar programs."

The decision in this case may not lead to many new voucher programs because public opinion may not support such programs, and, even if it did, powerful groups such as teacher unions will likely continue to oppose such programs. However, one of the main objections to vouchers—that they would always constitute a violation of the First Amendment's Establishment Clause—is no longer a significant hurdle for voucher proponents. While the U.S. Supreme Court could revisit this issue—perhaps in a slightly different program—it is unlikely, at least in the near term, that the court would see a similar program as a violation of the Establishment Clause.

STATEWIDE VOUCHER PROGRAMS

While the two most prominent vouchers programs have been the Milwaukee and Cleveland programs, there been some other vouchers programs implemented at the state level. These programs have likely been adopted in the states described below because of strong gubernatorial support, strong support from legislative leaders, or some combination of the two. These programs have not led to significant court cases where religion clauses have been crucial to the outcome. This has largely been the case because the voucher programs were either challenged on other grounds or the voucher programs were approved after *Zelman*.

There have been three states that have enacted statewide voucher programs. Florida, with the strong support of Governor Jeb Bush, enacted in 1999 the Opportunity Scholarhip Program as part of the A+ Educational Plan. As the program was established, students could receive vouchers to attend another public school or a private school if the public school where they lived received a failing grade by not meeting state standards in two out of four years. The program led to only a small number of students attending private schools with a voucher. In 1999–2000, only 56 students attended a private school through the program. In 2005–2006, that number rose to 734 students. For the 2005–2006 school year, 56 private schools accepted students, and most of those schools (63 percent) were sectarian.[15] The private school option was struck down as unconstitutional by the Florida Supreme Court in a 5–2 decision on January 5, 2006, not because the program violated the state or federal Establishment Clauses, or even a Blaine Amendment clause, although a state appellate court did rule that the program violated a "no-aid" to private schools clause (Article I, Section 3). Rather, the Florida Supreme Court ruled that the program violated a clause requiring a uniform system of public education which guarantees all Florida students a "uniform, efficient, safe, secure and high quality system of public education" (Article IX, Section 5).

On April 16, 2003, the Colorado legislature, with the strong support of Governor Bill Owens, enacted the Colorado Opportunity Contract Pilot Program. This program would have allowed students from low-performing schools with a significant number of students from low-income families to attend a participating private school. In the first year of operation, only one percent of students in the targeted school districts were permitted to obtain a voucher. By the fifth year of the program, as many as 20,000 students could have sought a voucher. In the first year of the program, students in eleven districts would have been eligible for a voucher. The program was short-lived, as the Colorado Supreme Court struck down the program on June 28, 2004, because it violated a state constitutional provision regarding school finance.[16] The Colorado Supreme Court did not rule on whether the program violated the Blaine Amendment language or the 'compelled support of religion clause' of the Colorado Constitution. Because the Colorado and Florida Supreme Courts ruled on state constitutional provisions, these cases cannot be appealed to the U.S. Supreme Court.

Ohio also established a statewide voucher program in July 2005. During the spring of 2006, Ohio's EdChoice program enrolled about 2,600 students in private schools. Under the legislation, up to 14,000 students who attended schools that have been graded by the Ohio Department of Education (ODE) as being either in academic emergency or on academic watch could receive scholarships to attend private schools. If more than 14,000 students apply, priority is given to families at or below 200 percent of the poverty level.

Students in kindergarten through eighth grade can receive vouchers for up to $4,250, while high school students can receive up to $5,000—though if a school charges less than those amounts, the state will pay only the tuition amount. Schools cannot charge families at or below 200 percent of the poverty level more than $4,250 for K–8 students, or more than $5,000 for high school students. Once a student receives a scholarship, he will have priority for a scholarship in future years. The participating student will continue to be eligible, even if the public school he or she previously attended is no longer on the academic watch or academic emergency lists. By the summer of 2006, approximately 300 private schools had chosen to participate—including Catholic schools, Protestant and Jewish religious schools, and nonreligious schools.[17]

Two other states, Maine and Vermont, have also attempted to enact voucher programs, both of which have resulted in litigation. The social circumstances in these two cases were unique in that both Maine and Vermont practice 'tuitioning,' which occurs when a local school district that is too sparsely populated to operate a high school pays for tuition at another public or private school. According to the Institute for Justice, both Vermont and Maine had paid tuition for students at private religious schools for a long period of time beginning in the late-nineteenth century. Vermont stopped paying for tuition at private religious schools in 1961 and Maine stopped doing so in 1980 after the state Attorney General issued an advisory opinion to the state Department of Education. The Maine legislature ratified that decision with law in 1982. Families in both Maine and Vermont challenged the statute as being a violation of the Free Exercise Clause of the First Amendment and the Equal Protection Clause of the Fourteenth Amendment. In 1999, the Vermont Supreme Court upheld the prohibition on paying for tuition at religious schools, because to do so would violate the "compelled support" clause of the Vermont Constitution. The Maine case made it to the Maine Supreme Judicial Court, which ruled on April 26, 2006, that the Maine statute was constitutional. The case was appealed to the U.S. Supreme Court, which declined to hear an appeal of the case.

TAX CREDITS INSTEAD OF VOUCHERS

Tuition tax credits have been promoted and enacted in a few states to support students attending religious elementary and secondary schools. The same groups who have supported vouchers have also supported tax credits as a means of helping parents send their children to private schools. It is likely these tax credit programs have been adopted as an alternative to a voucher program and that this alternative route has been chosen because of insufficient political support for vouchers or concern about a voucher program being challenged in court. Some tax credit programs have directly supported parents or guardians who pay for private education. Some states, beginning in the late 1990s, have enacted programs that give a credit to qualifying taxpayers who contribute to a non-profit organization that provides scholarships to those attending private schools.

Minnesota made an education tax credit available in 1998. The tax credit does not cover private school tuition per se, but it does pay for education-related expenses at public or private schools. The credit is limited to $1,000 per student and $2,000 per family. The credit is means tested, so it only applies to those at lower income levels. Expenses that qualify for the tax credit include tutoring, fees for after school programs, non-religious academic books, and software used for educational expenses. Minnesota has also had a tax deduction for private school tuition since 1955. The tax deduction only reduces the amount of taxable income. The tuition tax deduction was challenged as being a violation of the First Amendment's Establishment Clause. The U.S. Supreme Court in *Mueller v. Allen* (1983) ruled that the tax deduction had a secular purpose and did not create excessive church-state entanglement.

In 1998, the amount that could be deducted from taxable income increased to $1,625 from $650 for K–6th grade students and to $2,500 from $1,000 for 7th–12th grade students. Parents can deduct private school tuition, tuition for college courses taken to satisfy high school requirements, tutoring by a qualified person, nonreligious books purchased for instruction, as well as fees that were used to pay for transportation and educational software.[18]

Illinois enacted the Educational Expenses Tax Credit in 1999. It became effective in 2000. The law permits parents to claim a non-refundable credit of up to $500 per family for tuition, books, and lab fees at any public, private nonreligious, or private religious school. The credit covers 25 percent of educational expenses after $250, up to $2,250. The law was challenged in Illinois state courts, but it was upheld.

Arizona enacted the School Tuition Organization Tax Credit education tax credit. The law provides for a dollar-for-dollar credit for contributions of up to $200 per household for donations to public schools for extracurricular activities and up to $500 for donations to school tuition organizations (STOs) that provide scholarships to students who wish to attend private schools. The STOs must distribute nearly all of their revenue in the form of tuition scholarships. There is no state-mandated income test for those receiving scholarships. In 1999, STOs in Arizona awarded 3,800 scholarships, with an average award of $637. On September 29, 1997, the Arizona Education Association, the Arizona School Boards Association, the Arizona Federation of Teachers, and the ACLU filed a lawsuit challenging the tax credit program as a violation of both the U.S. and Arizona Constitutions' Establishment Clauses.

On January 26, 1999, the Arizona Supreme Court in *Kotterman v. Killian* upheld the tuition tax credit law in a 3–2 ruling. The decision cited the Wisconsin Supreme Court's ruling on the Milwaukee choice program (*Jackson v. Benson*) and the U.S. Supreme Court's ruling in *Mueller v. Allen* (1983), which upheld tax deductions for school expenses. In *Mueller v. Allen*, the Court ruled that the tax deductions have a secular purpose, that they do not have a primary effect of advancing religion, and that they do not create excessive church-state entanglement, thus satisfying the *Lemon* Test. The Arizona Supreme Court held that private schools are "at best only incidental beneficiaries" and that the "primary beneficiaries of this credit are taxpayers who contribute, parents who might otherwise be deprived of an opportunity to make meaningful decisions about their children's educations and the children themselves."

The Arizona Supreme Court also agreed with the respondent's assertions that the legislature enacted the tuition tax credit law to improve academic achievement and increase parental choice. The Court held that the tax credit funds are not public funds at all and therefore cannot be public funds in aid of religious schools, nor is the statutory language a "Blaine Amendment." This is especially important, because if Arizona's language was a Blaine Amendment, the Court held that they would be "hard pressed to divorce the amendment's language from the insidious discriminatory intent that prompted it."[19] In February 2000, a group of Arizona taxpayers filed a federal court challenge to the Arizona School Tuition Organization Tax Credit, but in 2005 a federal district court in Arizona ruled that the program was constitutional.

In 2001, Pennsylvania adopted an education tax credit program similar to the Arizona program. The legislation came after several attempts by Governor Thomas Ridge to have the legislature enact a voucher program in the 1990s. In Pennsylvania, corporations (but not individuals) would be eligible for a 75 percent tax credit (i.e., a 75 cent reduction in taxes owed for each dollar contributed) for a donation given within a single year to an organization that gives scholarships to students attending a private school or for a donation given to a public school improvement organization. A two-year financial pledge to a scholarship or school improvement organization would make the corporation eligible for a 90 percent tax credit. The legislation placed a cap on total tax credits given to corporations. Corporations within the state could get credits for donations of up to $200,000 annually, and the total for all corporations was capped at $20 million. In 2003 these caps were increased to $26.7 million for scholarship organizations. According to the Reach Foundation, corporate contributions have reached the level of caps in every year of the program and they estimate that as many as 20,000 children have been assisted in attending a private school through this program.[20] This tax credit program has not faced serious legal challenge in either state or federal courts.

CONCLUSION

The desire for public assistance for those attending or wishing to attend private schools has led to much public controversy and many court challenges, most of which have concerned constitutional doctrines regarding church-state relations. The U.S. Supreme Court addressed these issues in a momentous, and to some surprising decision in *Zelman v. Simmons-Harris* in 2002, wherein they ruled that the voucher program did not violate the Establishment Clause. Several state supreme courts—for example, in Wisconsin, Ohio, Arizona, and Maine—have also considered school choice issues and in doing so considered both state and federal provisions regarding church-state relations. The state court decisions have been mixed with some states permitting school choice programs, while others have rejected attempts at vouchers. In some states, when vouchers proponents were thwarted in their attempts to establish a voucher program, those same proponents have promoted tax credit programs to assist those seeking to attend private schools. Even though court cases have permitted some voucher programs, it is likely that the battle over voucher and other school choice programs will remain intense—although the public dispute will generally focus on the use of vouchers as a means of improving education, rather than on church-state issues.

NOTES

1. R. Freeman Wells and Lawrence A Cremin, *A History of Education in American Culture* (New York: Holt, Rinehart and Winston, 1961), 376–377.

2. See http://www.blaineamendments.org/Intro/whatis.html.

3. Kyle Duncan, "Secularism's Laws: State Blaine Amendments and Religious Persecution," *Fordham Law Review* 72 (December 2003): 493.

4. *Economics and the Public Interest*, ed. Robert A. Solo (New Brunswick, NJ: Rutgers University Press, 1955).

5. Milton Friedman, "The Role of Government in Education," reprinted at www.schoolchoices.org/roo/fried1.htm (accessed April 4, 2007).

6. James Carper, "The Christian Day School," in *Religious Schooling in America*, ed. James C. Carper and Thomas C. Hunt (Birmingham, AL: Religious Education Press, 1984), 110–129.

7. Ronald Reagan, "Radio Address to the Nation on Education," http://www.reagan.utexas.edu/archives/speeches/1983/31283a.htm (accessed April 4, 2007).

8. Ronald Reagan, "Remarks to Members of the National Catholic Educational Association," http://www.reagan.utexas.edu/archives/speeches/1983/40783b.htm (accessed April 4, 2007).

9. Ronald Reagan, "Remarks on Receiving the Final Report of the National Commission on Excellence in Education," in John Woolley and Gerhard Peters, The American Presidency Project [online], Santa Barbara, CA: University of California (hosted), Gerhard Peters (database). http://www.presidency.ucsb.edu/ws/?pid=41239.

10. In 1982, the Senate Finance Committee reported the tax credit legislation

to the full Senate, which never took action on the measure, and the measure died when the Senate adjourned. See "Tuition Tax Credit, 1982 Legislative Chonology" and "Tuition Tax Credit, 1983 Legislative Chronology." CQ Electronic Library, CQ Congress and the Nation Online Edition, catn81–0011175583. Originally published in *Congress and the Nation, 1981–1984*, vol. 6 (Washington, D.C.: CQ Press, 1985).

11. See http://schoolchoicewi.org/k12/detail.cfm?id=4 and Supreme Court of WI opinion.

12. The decision is printed in its entirety at http://ffrf.org/fttoday/1997/jan_feb97/higginbotham.html.

13. *Simmons-Harris v. Goff*, Ohio Supreme Court, http://www.sconet.state.oh.us/rod/newpdf/0/1999/1999-Ohio-77.pdf.

14. These briefs are collected at http://www.ij.org/schoolchoice/ohio_ussc/OH-USSC-amicus.html.

15. See http://www.floridaschoolchoice.org/Information/OSP/files/Fast_Facts_OSP.pdf.

16. *Owens v. Colorado Congress of Parents*, http://www.courts.state.co.us/supct/opinions2003/03SA364.doc.

17. Michael Coulter, "Thousands Use Ohio EdChoice Vouchers," *School Reform News* (September 1, 2006). http://www.heartland.org/Article.cfm?artId=19610.

18. For information on education tax credits, see http://www.heritage.org/Research/Education/SchoolChoice/schoolchoice.cfm#map.

19. *Kotterman v. Killian* 193 Ariz. 273, 972 P.2d 606 (Ariz. 1999). http://lw.bna.com/lw/19990209/970412.htm.

20. Information about the Pennsylvania tax credit can be found at http://www.paschoolchoice.org/reach/cwp/view.asp?a=1367&Q=568487&reachNav=.

FURTHER READING

To examine the intersection of school choice and church/state issues, one should examine relevant Supreme Court decisions. The Institute for Justice has collected on its website—www.ij.org—court decisions, both state and federal, related to school choice cases. For example, regarding the Cleveland school choice program, one can find all the relevant state and federal court decisions. There are also copies of articles and press releases related to the cases. This site also has copies of *amicus curiae* briefs filed in support of the Cleveland school voucher program for the *Zelman v. Simmons-Harris* cause. Another useful website is that of the Americans United for the Separation of Church and State, a group which opposes vouchers, in part because they understand such programs to constitute an improper establishment of religion. This site (www.au.org) has discussions of relevant court cases as well as a lengthy analysis of the *Zelman* case. The Beckett Fund for Religious Liberty sponsors a website (www.blaineamendments.org) that provides text of state Blaine Amendment provisions and citations, summaries, and in some cases the full text of scholarly articles examining Blaine Amendment provision.

For other sources on school choice, one should consider Milton Friedman's argument for vouchers that is found in *Capitalism and Freedom*, which was originally published in 1962 but remains in print. Two recent works have examined several dimensions of the school choice debate. For an activist's account in defense of school vouchers as well as a description of the campaign for school choice in California, see *School Choice: Why You Need It—How You Get It* (Cato Institute, 1994) by David Harmer. In *School Choice: The Struggle for the Soul of America's Schools* (Yale University Press, 1995), Peter Cookson is largely critical of most school choice programs and proposals, arguing that they would lead to increased social stratification, but he does offer a 'managed' choice proposal.

The Future of the School Choice, ed. Paul Peterson (Hoover Institution Press, 2003) contains ten essays by legal scholars, political scientists, and education policy analysts that examine the *Zelman v. Simmons-Harris* ruling on both legal and philosophical grounds. There are five essays that consider the policy implications for the ruling as it regards all forms of school choice, including charter schools, tax credits, and school vouchers. Peterson, along with Bryan C. Hassel, also edited *Learning from School Choice* (Brookings Institution Press, 1998), which contains essays examining some early choice programs. A product of the National Working Commission on Choice in K–12 Education, *Getting Choice Right: Ensuring Equity and Efficiency in Education Policy* (Brookings Institution Press, 2005) contains ten essays examining questions related to school choice programs. A couple of the essays examine economic questions related to school choice, while others review existing research regarding the social impact of school choice.

7

Religion and Higher Education

J. David Holcomb

Educational institutions have proven to be fertile ground for church-state controversy. Indeed, some of the most significant church-state disputes in the history of the United States have involved either the role of religion in public educational institutions or public financial support for religious schools. Many of the famous controversies over school prayer, Bible clubs, and vouchers have taken place at the elementary and secondary levels. Nonetheless, colleges and universities continue to provide the context for significant church-state conflicts as well. For instance, a recent decision by the president of the College of William and Mary to remove a bronze cross from the historic Wren Chapel because it was deemed "unwelcoming" to non-Christians led to a firestorm of controversy. One prominent donor withdrew a twelve million dollar pledge in protest while more than seventeen thousand people signed a petition calling for the college to reverse its policy. Upon the recommendation of a committee made up of students, alumni, and faculty, the president restored the cross, but in a glass case with citations noting the historic relationship of the college to the Anglican Church. While the controversy was resolved without litigation, the debate illustrates the tensions over religion at taxpayer-supported public universities.[1]

Another conflict recently emerged at the University of Missouri, where a Christian fraternity sought an exemption from the university's nondiscrimination policy that prohibited discrimination based upon religion. The "Brothers Under Christ" or BYX fraternity required that pledges confess a relationship with Jesus Christ. In ultimately granting an exemption to BYX, the University of Missouri was forced to wrestle with several seemingly conflicting constitutional values. BYX claimed freedom of association and free exercise of religion rights, while the university not only had nondiscrimination goals it sought to advance but also feared violating the separation of church and state if it were to provide recognition, access, and potentially funding to a distinctly religious organization. In the end, the university determined the free exercise and association rights of the fraternity outweighed the university's nondiscrimination and Establishment Clause concerns.[2]

The university's constitutional instincts on this issue were well-founded, as the tradition of the U.S. Supreme Court has been to allow for greater accommodation of religious groups, exercises, and instruction at public, tax-supported universities than at public elementary and secondary schools. Generally, the Court has reasoned that college students are less impressionable than their elementary and secondary school counterparts. Furthermore, other constitutional scholars have argued that colleges and universities are more insulated from violations of the separation of church and state, as attendance is voluntary, principles of academic freedom and critical inquiry tend to characterize their atmospheres, and the size and diversity of the student bodies mitigate against religious indoctrination or endorsement.[3] Moreover, the Court has determined that free speech principles apply broadly to college and university settings. Public colleges and universities that create open forums by allowing various student organizations to meet and express their viewpoints on campus are prohibited by the free speech clause from discriminating against student religious groups' use of their facilities and even the funding of their publications. This is true despite concerns they may be aiding them in advancing a religious message.

These same distinctions between public college and elementary/secondary schools have also been used to allow for greater aid from the state to private religious colleges and universities. Thus, state and federal financial aid may be used by college students to attend a religiously affiliated university, while vouchers remain a highly contested issue at the elementary and secondary school level. Even more direct forms of aid, such as construction grants and loans, can be received by church-related colleges as long as they are not used for religious purposes. With aid, however, has come government regulation of private colleges and universities. A steady stream of litigation has resulted from attempts by religiously affiliated colleges to retain their autonomy in light of challenges to their religion-based discriminatory policies in hiring or treatment of student organizations.

Considering that most of the oldest colleges and universities founded in America were directed under the auspices of religious groups, it is not surprising that the place of religion in higher education has provided the context for some of the key controversies over the meaning of religious freedom and the separation of church and state. Whether settling disputes concerning public financing and government regulation of religious colleges or the accommodation of religious groups and practices in public universities, the U.S. Supreme Court has been forced to grapple with the meaning and application of the First Amendment's religion clauses. As the following discussion suggests, issues of funding, accommodation, and regulation will continue to appear on the courts' First Amendment agenda.

RELIGION AND HIGHER EDUCATION IN HISTORICAL CONTEXT

The first colleges founded in colonial America were sponsored by the Protestant-established churches of the day. Harvard (1636) and Yale (1701) were founded by the Puritan Congregationalists, and the College of William and Mary (1693) was formed under the guidance of the Anglican Church in Virginia. Although under the control of the established churches of their colonies, these colleges had a broader educational mission than the training of future ministers. Both church and state were to be served by these institutions as they endeavored to prepare future colonial leaders "disciplined by knowledge and learning."[4]

By the early eighteenth century, the growing pluralism and religious divisions fostered by the Great Awakening led to the creation of colleges that were to serve the new and disenfranchised religious voices of the day. For instance, Princeton was established by New Light Presbyterians that sought an institution of higher education more accepting of the theology and practice of the Great Awakening.[5] No matter what their origin, however, colonial colleges and universities were seen as crucial enterprises demanding sacrificial financial support. According to one study, as much as 65 percent of private college funds came from public tax support during the colonial era. Other state benefits included tax exemptions, gifts of lands and buildings, as well as exemptions from public duties for students and faculty.[6] As the eighteenth century progressed, however, a greater variety of relationships emerged between the colleges and their churches. The state-church college formula under which Harvard was birthed gave way to emphases on diversity and toleration.[7]

As with elementary and secondary education, the provision for higher education remained a state issue after the adoption of the U.S. Constitution. As a result, many of the colonial patterns of education, with the requisite religious influences, remained into the early national period. Yet the ideological emphases of the Revolutionary and Early National eras facilitated new developments in both private and public education. Several states established nondenominational institutions, such as the University of North Carolina (1789), South Carolina College (1801), and Thomas Jefferson's University of Virginia (1819). Jefferson's opposition to established churches and "narrow sectarianism" certainly informed his plans for the University of Virginia. He nonetheless accommodated religious worship on campus and provided resources for the study of Christianity. He even encouraged the creation of theological schools near the university campus.[8] Generally, though, the University of Virginia became an elite regional institution aimed at educating the sons of wealthy southern planters.[9]

The primary story of higher education in America during the first half of the nineteenth century was the rapid growth of church-related colleges. These often fledgling schools littered the western landscape as the growing evangelical denominations such as the Methodists and Baptists joined the more established denominations in creating institutions of higher education. Consequently, these institutions were often more sectarian and dependent upon local churches for financial support. The insecurity of these colleges was witnessed by the fact that they were "small in enrollments, lean in operations, and poor in endowment."[10]

The proliferation of small denominational schools did not satisfy the quest for more democratic and comprehensive experiments in higher education. Spurred in part by the Morrill Act of 1862, a resurgence of state-supported universities took place after the Civil War. The Morrill "Land Grant" Act provided a state an allotment of western lands based upon its congressional representation. The proceeds from the sale of these lands were to go to higher education programs in the "useful arts," such as agriculture, mining, and military instruction.[11] The relationship of religion to the growing land grant and other state-funded institutions became a complex if not paradoxical one. The second half of the nineteenth century witnessed what has been called the "high water mark of church-state separation," exemplified in part through the passage of state constitutional amendments banning public funding of religious activities and institutions. These so-called "Blaine Amendments" often prohibited both direct and indirect support for religious educational institutions.[12] Yet at the same time, many of the state universities reflected the pan-Protestant ethos of the day. As George Marsden has observed, most of the state colleges and universities had required chapel and church attendance policies, and faculty were given the liberty to express their Christian perspectives in the classrooms.[13]

While state universities were often located in smaller towns and rural areas that maintained a distinctly Protestant ethos, many of the urban universities that sprang up during the late-nineteenth and early-twentieth centuries were Catholic. This was a natural development, as much of the new immigration from the period was Catholic and tended to settle in urban areas. Eventually, an extensive network of Catholic higher educational institutions would be created around the country. And in the future, these institutions would serve as the battlegrounds of church-state disputes over state aid to and regulation of religiously affiliated colleges and universities.[14]

The last several decades of the nineteenth century also witnessed the emergence of private universities funded by wealthy industrialists. Stanford, Chicago, Johns Hopkins, and Vanderbilt were each either launched or enhanced through gifts by major benefactors. Each embraced over time the emphasis on the German educational approach of the primacy of research rooted in science within a context of academic freedom. Several of these philanthropic progeny were church-related, but their administrations and governing bodies saw little conflict between their denominational ties and quests to embrace the latest in more secular and scientific approaches to knowledge. As John Thelin has argued, "'Science' as it was invoked in American institutions—government, business, and education—was less a value system at odds with religion than an organizational ethos that prized order and efficiency."[15] Thus, the growth of public universities and well-funded private institutions had a significant impact of democratizing education. Yet it also contributed to the diminishing role of religion in higher education. According to Stephen Haynes, "both the liberal arts ideal and the influence of denominational colleges was eroded" due to the emphases on science, democratization, and the marginalization of clerical influences.[16]

The general growth in higher education at the turn of the century was in the direction of the comprehensive state university. The shift of emphasis away from denominational and other private liberal arts colleges to more comprehensive universities was driven by the growing emphases upon science, research, and academic specialization. This development was furthered by the creation of philanthropic foundations that would become major players in the shaping of higher education. These included the Rockefeller Foundation, the General Education Board, and the Carnegie Foundation for the Advancement of Teaching. The financial power these foundations possessed was used to move higher education in the direction of greater standardization, as well as "coherence and efficiency." The pursuit of these goals would have a profound impact upon the role of religion in university life. Colleges that sought to participate in the Carnegie Foundation's pension plan, for example, had to standardize their admissions requirements and remove from their undergraduate curriculum any sectarian teachings or emphases.[17] Chapel witnessed a steady decline at both state and some denominational colleges. As a result, religious practices lost their centrality in the life of many institutions.[18] With the seeming secularization of both public universities and some prominent church-related institutions, some people began to question the future of church-related colleges. They persisted, however, and have remained a key element of the American higher education landscape—today they comprise approximately one-third of the institutions of higher education in America.

The post–World War II era would present new challenges and a number of legal controversies involving religion and higher education, however. Key to these developments was the significant increase in the federal government's role in higher education. As colleges grew in number and size, so did their programs and curricula, creating a costly venture for leaders in higher education. And in post–World War II America, the government understood the wide expansion and availability of higher education to be crucial for the development of a workforce in an increasingly technological and competitive world. A number of government programs aimed at making college education affordable for the masses were initiated. Perhaps the most famous of these was the Serviceman's Readjustment Act, more commonly known as the G.I. Bill. This 1944 bill provided financial aid to former soldiers and allowed them the freedom to attend the college or university of their choice. Other congressional funding plans followed that provided more direct forms of aid to higher educational institutions. The 1963 Higher Education Facilities Act provided tax funds for the construction of various buildings on public and private school campuses. And the Elementary and Secondary Education Act of 1965 allowed for grants to colleges and universities to aid in the training of teachers, although no funds could go toward religious education.

Greater federal regulation of higher education naturally followed the funding. The Civil Rights Act of 1964 and the 1972 Education Amendments banned, among other things, discrimination in higher education based upon race, gender, and national origin. Since religiously affiliated colleges and universities were frequently the beneficiaries of both federal and state student aid and other forms of more direct aid, controversies naturally followed over the constitutionality of taxpayer support for religious institutions and whether they should enjoy constitutional immunity from governmental regulations.[19]

AID TO RELIGIOUSLY AFFILIATED HIGHER EDUCATION

With the second half of the twentieth century witnessing a dramatic growth in the level of both federal and state financial aid for college students, the government has become, through Pell Grants, Supplemental Educational Opportunity Grants, and various loan programs, the largest source of financial aid and, with the rising costs of higher education, an absolutely essential source of funding for most colleges, including religiously affiliated colleges and universities. As new forms of public support become available to institutions of higher education, however, church-state disputes have arisen.

In determining violations of the Establishment Clause of the First Amendment, the U.S. Supreme Court has traditionally made a clear distinction between the constitutionality of aid to elementary and secondary schools and aid to colleges and universities. The Court has been more willing to allow aid to flow from the federal government to religious colleges and universities than to elementary and secondary schools because college students are perceived to be "less susceptible" to indoctrination, college courses tend to be less sectarian, and academic freedom prevails more readily at the collegiate level.[20] Stephen Monsma has argued that the Court's greater willingness to uphold aid to church-related colleges and universities than to elementary and secondary schools is rooted in two fundamental legal principles. First, the Court has found that the sacred and secular aspects of religiously-based colleges are more separable and distinct than in elementary and secondary schools. Second, the Court has concluded that church-related elementary and secondary schools are more likely to be "pervasively sectarian" than their higher education counterparts.[21] Moreover, federally-funded student financial aid used at church-related colleges and universities has never been successfully challenged as a violation of the Establishment Clause.[22] While federal aid to students attending religiously affiliated colleges has not faced a serious constitutional challenge, other forms of more direct aid, such as federal- or state-funded construction grants or loans, have led to numerous court challenges over their permissibility.[23]

The Pervasively Sectarian Test

The key test the U.S. Supreme Court has used to determine violations of the Establishment Clause in aid cases has been called the pervasively sectarian test. When weighing the constitutional implications of an aid program, the Court has frequently attempted to determine if these institutions "are not so pervasively religious that their secular activities cannot be separated from their sectarian ones."[24] The issue of religious indoctrination permeating the atmosphere of educational institutions goes back at least to the landmark case of *Lemon v. Kurtzman* in 1971.[25] Here the U.S. Supreme Court struck down a Pennsylvania statute that provided the "purchasing" of secular educational services from nonprofit elementary and secondary schools, including religiously affiliated schools. Essentially, the state paid parochial schools for the costs of teachers' salaries, textbooks, and instructional materials for teaching secular subjects. The decision in *Lemon* codified the controversial tripartite "Lemon Test" the Court would subsequently use in Establishment Clause cases. According to the *Lemon* Test, for a statute to satisfy constitutional muster, it must have a secular purpose, a primary effect that neither advances nor inhibits religion, and may not foster an excessive entanglement between church and state. In holding the statute unconstitutional, the Court determined that the religious nature of the school would make it difficult if not impossible to ensure that state aid would not be going to support religious instruction or indoctrination. The "Handbook of School Regulations" governing one of the schools in question stated that "religious formation is not confined to formal courses; nor is it restricted to a single subject."[26] "We simply recognize that a dedicated religious person, teaching in a school affiliated with his or her own faith and operated to inculcate its tenets," the Court concluded, "will inevitably experience great difficulty in remaining religiously neutral."[27] The Court further held that to ensure tax funds were not going to subsidize religious instruction, "a comprehensive, discriminating, and continuing state surveillance" would result. This ongoing surveillance would lead to unconstitutional excessive entanglement between church and state.[28]

In subsequent cases involving church-related elementary and secondary schools, the Court held that the provision of instructional materials, auxiliary services, and the retaining of public school teachers to assist in secular educational instruction on a part-time basis was unconstitutional. In *Meek v. Pittenger*, for example, the Court struck down several forms of direct aid because of the sectarian nature of the school.[29] Church governance, required religious exercises, and religious preference in hiring and admissions were key factors in the Court's assessment of the sectarian nature of the schools.[30] Since religion permeated the atmosphere of these institutions, a "symbolic link between religion and government" would result, leading to the unconstitutional advancement of religion.[31] Due to the pervasively sectarian nature of the schools, then, most any form of direct aid would run afoul of the Establishment Clause, despite attempts to utilize only secular aid for secular instruction.

Lemon and subsequent cases provided the contours of the pervasively sectarian test. Yet it was more fully developed in several higher education decisions of the 1970s. In the 1971 case of *Tilton v. Richardson*, the U.S. Supreme Court upheld the constitutionality of federal grants used for the construction or renovation of buildings at four church-related colleges in Connecticut.[32] At issue was Title I of the Higher Education Facilities Act of 1963 that provided federal grants for construction of college facilities as long as the funded buildings were not used for sectarian instruction or worship. Moreover, a twenty-year period had to elapse before the building could be used for religious purposes.

Those challenging the constitutionality of the act established a "composite profile" of the "typical sectarian" institution. Key characteristics included religious restrictions on hiring and admissions, compulsory attendance at religious exercises, obedience to church doctrine, and continual propagation of the faith. Noting the church sponsorship of the college and the fact that doctrine was taught in some of the classes at the university in question, the opponents of the funding argued that the Title I funds had the primary effect of advancing religion.[33]

The Supreme Court disagreed, holding that the statute in question did not have a primary effect of advancing religion because it barred the religious instruction, worship, or symbols in the buildings funded by federal grants. The Court rejected the contention that religion "so permeated" the educational environment of the church-related college that one could not distinguish between the secular and religious education provided.[34] This was particularly true since "the schools were characterized by an atmosphere of academic freedom" where faculty taught according to the "academic requirements intrinsic in the subject matter."[35] Since the construction grants were to be used to build libraries, a language laboratory, and a science building, the Court further concluded that "there is no evidence that religion seeps into the use of those facilities."[36]

Despite its ruling in *Lemon*, the Court in *Tilton* drew a constitutional distinction between church-related colleges and their elementary and secondary counterparts. In particular, the Court argued that college students were less impressionable and subject to religious indoctrination. In addition, the Catholic colleges in question admitted non-Catholic students, hired non-Catholic faculty, and taught religious courses other than those of the Catholic religion. Fundamentally, the Court determined that the religious schools that received the funds did not have religious indoctrination as a substantial purpose or activity. "In short," the court asserted, "the evidence shows institutions with admittedly religious functions but whose predominant higher education mission is to provide their students with a secular education."[37]

The threat of excessive entanglement was further diminished by the "nonideological character of the aid." Unlike the instructional subsidies in *Lemon*, the aid in *Tilton* was a "one-time, single-purpose construction grant" that mitigated the need for an ongoing or continual oversight by the government.[38] At the same time, the Court struck down the twenty-year time limit for the restricted use of the facilities, finding that the possible future use of the buildings for religious purposes could lead to the impermissible advancement of religion.

In his dissenting opinion, Justice William O. Douglas challenged the majority's arguments that distinguished *Tilton* from *Lemon*. For Douglas, the grants represented a direct subsidy from the state to a religious institution contrary to the no-aid principle established in the landmark Establishment Clause case *Everson v. Board of Education*.[39] Douglas further rejected the distinctions the majority sought to make between church-related higher and lower educational institutions. Significantly, Douglas argued that at church-related schools religious and secular teaching are "enmeshed" and that they are "unitary institutions with subtle blending of sectarian and secular instruction." Consequently, continual surveillance by the state would necessarily result.[40]

Two years after *Tilton*, the Court upheld the South Carolina Educational Facilities Act, which authorized tax-exempt revenue bonds to be issued to assist in the financing of college facilities. While the act did not exclude religiously affiliated institutions, it expressly prohibited the use of bond financed facilities for sectarian purposes. At the center of the legal dispute was the Baptist College at Charleston, which had requested nearly 2 million dollars for a variety of capital projects. Basing its decision on the majority opinion in the *Tilton* case, the U.S. Supreme Court upheld the Baptist College's use of the bonds. Despite the close denominational control of the college, the Court determined that the school was not pervasively sectarian due to the fact non-Baptists served on the faculty and that there was not a religious requirement for admission to the school. The Baptist College at Charleston was comparable to the Catholic colleges in *Tilton* leading the Court to decide that "there is no basis to conclude that the College's operations are oriented significantly towards sectarian rather than secular education."[41]

The Court's most extensive effort at defining a pervasively sectarian institution came in the 1976 case of *Roemer v. Board of Public Works*.[42] Here, the State of Maryland authorized payments of non-categorical grants to qualifying institutions of higher education provided the money was not used for sectarian purposes. In addition, institutions that exclusively awarded theological degrees were not eligible to receive funds through the program. Administrators at the recipient schools were required to file annual reports attesting to the secular use of the funds. After five church-related institutions of higher education received approximately $525,000 from the program, a group of Maryland taxpayers challenged the constitutionality of the Maryland program stating that the limited regulation of the non-stipulated funds violated the Establishment Clause of the First Amendment.[43]

Justice Harry Blackmun wrote the plurality opinion of the Court upholding the Maryland program. "To answer the question whether an institution is so 'pervasively sectarian' that it may not receive direct state aid of any kind," Blackmun opined, "it is necessary to paint a general picture of the institution, composed of many elements." The key elements on which the plurality relied in determining that the Catholic colleges in question were not pervasively sectarian were: a) the colleges enjoyed a significant amount of institutional autonomy from the Catholic church; b) religious indoctrination was not a primary purpose of any of the institutions because attendance at religious exercises was not required; c) while mandatory religion and theology courses were taught by Roman Catholic clergy, they were supplementary to a broader liberal arts curriculum that was governed by the canons of academic freedom; d) classroom prayers were practiced in only a small percentage of classes and were not officially sanctioned; e) faculty hiring decisions outside of the religion department were not made on a religious basis, nor were student admissions religiously discriminatory. As a result, Blackmun concluded that the religious functions of the school could be sufficiently distinguished from the secular ones. In fact, the schools claimed on their own behalf that spiritual concerns were merely a "secondary objective."[44]

Admitting that the question of excessive entanglement between church and state was a difficult one in this case, particularly since the aid was less restricted than in *Tilton*, the Court nevertheless concluded that the nature of the institutions receiving the aid minimized the need for ongoing and pervasive surveillance from the state. Relying on the District Court's findings, the plurality asserted that the colleges in question performed "essentially secular educational functions." As a result, "there is no danger, or at least only a substantially reduced danger, that an ostensibly secular activity—the study of biology, the learning of a foreign language, an athletic event—will actually be infused with religious content or significance."[45]

The second-half of the twentieth century witnessed many colleges and universities loosening their denominational ties or changing their missions in part to receive such funding and/or to avoid costly litigation, despite the Court's unwillingness to strike down most forms of aid. According to Kent

Weeks, "The secularization of mainline colleges and restructuring of organizational and governance systems by Catholic universities during the last thirty years of the twentieth century created a more favorable climate for public funds and diminished the likelihood of a successful constitutional attack on these institutions' receipt of public benefits."[46] Even Jerry Falwell's Liberty University made policy adjustments in light of its desire to receive $60,000,000 in tax-exempt municipal bonds to refinance its debts. A legal challenge was raised to its request, due to the pervasively sectarian nature of the school. Consequently, Liberty eliminated chapel requirements, diluted the references to its religious mission in university publications, relaxed religious requirements for admissions, and eliminated some of the required religion courses from its curriculum.[47]

The Neutrality Test

While many colleges and universities have loosened their religious ties to avoid constitutional conflicts, the Court in the last two decades has moved toward a more accommodationist approach to aid cases. The *Lemon* Test, particularly its excessive entanglement prong that proved to be a key barrier regarding state aid to religious institutions in the past, has largely been replaced by what has been called a neutrality or equal treatment test. The neutrality test essentially holds that public funding of religious institutions is constitutionally satisfactory as long as "neutral criteria" are used in determining eligibility for the aid. For instance, in *Witters v. Washington Department of Services for the Blind*, the Court ruled that a visually impaired person could not be denied a state vocational rehabilitation grant because he was studying at a Bible college with the ultimate goal of serving in the ministry. Utilizing the neutrality theory, the Court held that "any aid provided under Washington's program that ultimately flows to religious institutions does so only as a result of the genuinely independent and private choices of individuals."[48]

Following the trend of these higher education cases, the Court has utilized the neutrality test to allow direct aid at the elementary and secondary level as well. For instance, in *Agostini v. Felton*,[49] the Court specifically overturned its 1985 decisions in *Aguilar v. Felton* and *Grand Rapids v. Ball*. In upholding the provision of part-time public education teachers and other instructional aid to parochial schools, the Court concluded that "we have departed from the rule relied on in Ball that all government aid that directly aids the educational function of religious schools is invalid."[50]

Perhaps the most significant blow to the pervasively sectarian test and *Lemon* Test came in the 2000 decision in *Mitchell v. Helms*.[51] Here the

Court upheld a federally-funded aid program in which state and local agencies purchased educational materials and equipment for public and private elementary and secondary (including religious) schools. While the vote of the Court was 6–3, there was no majority opinion as Justice Sandra Day O'Connor wrote a separate concurring opinion joined by Justice Stephen Breyer. Nonetheless, the plurality opinion emphasized the "neutrality-of-aid" doctrine in addressing whether governmental aid to religious schools necessarily leads to religious indoctrination attributable to the state. At the same time, the plurality attacked the pervasively sectarian test and called for its abandonment by the Court. Since the "religious nature of the recipient should not matter to the constitutional analysis," the pervasively sectarian test led to the "offensive . . . trolling through a person's or institution's religious beliefs." Moreover, the plurality asserted that the pervasively sectarian test conflicted with other decisions that banned discrimination in the distribution of public benefits based upon religious status or sincerity." Consequently, the Court concluded that "nothing in the Establishment Clause requires the exclusion of pervasively sectarian schools from otherwise permissible aid programs . . . This doctrine, born of bigotry, should be buried now."[52]

Justices O'Connor and Breyer concurred in the holding of the Court but were not willing to accept that neutrality alone was sufficient to satisfy Establishment Clause concerns in aid cases. Rather, neutrality was one of several factors that the Court should consider, as was the ability to divert funds to religious purposes. While O'Connor avoided calling for the burial of the pervasively sectarian test, she too admitted that its presumption of religious inculcation or indoctrination in religious schools had become problematic for Establishment Clause cases. Instead, O'Connor said the emphasis should be on whether aid has been actually diverted to religious purposes leading to the unconstitutional advancement of religion.[53]

Locke v. Davey and State Constitutional Prohibitions

Mitchell v. Helms essentially overturned several prior cases that had ruled as unconstitutional aid to parochial schools. If under the neutrality theory even more forms of direct aid to elementary and secondary church-related schools were being upheld, then surely the death knell had been sounded for the pervasively sectarian test at the collegiate level. Yet, as the recent decision in *Locke v. Davey*[54] suggests, religious schools may find their state constitutions more prohibitive of funds than the current U.S. Supreme Court's interpretation of the Establishment Clause. The *Locke v. Davey* case involved a Washington State scholarship program that was established to assist academically gifted students with higher education expenses. The regulations of the scholarship program, however, prohibited funds to be used toward the obtaining of a "devotional theology" degree. This was stipulated in light of the Washington State constitution's prohibition of even indirect funding of religious instruction. Joshua Davey, a student at the Assembly of God-related Northwest College, was awarded a "Promise Scholarship," but was subsequently told he could not use it to pursue a degree in pastoral ministries. While not disputing that the pastoral ministries degree was "devotional," Davey filed suit arguing that it violated his free exercise rights since the law was not facially neutral with regard to religion.

Writing for a six-member majority, Chief Justice Rehnquist rejected Davey's claim that his free exercise rights were violated. According to Rehnquist, the case involved a "play in the joints" between the two religion clauses in that it "concerns a state action that is permitted by the Establishment Clause but not required by the Free Exercise Clause." Affirming the Court's previous decisions upholding indirect aid to religious institutions, particularly when the "link between government funds and religious training is broken by the private choice of recipients," Rehnquist conceded that Washington could allow scholarship funds to go to the study of devotional theology. However, he concluded that the Free Exercise Clause did not require the state to do so in light of its own constitutional prohibitions.[55]

Locke v. Davey offers a mixed bag for aid to religiously affiliated higher education. On the one hand, a state may very well restrict the type of aid, both direct and indirect, that goes to religious institutions. On the other hand, the decision affirms that indirect aid may go to pervasively sectarian colleges. According to the majority, Northwest College was clearly a pervasively sectarian school. Yet, theoretically, Davey could have used the Promise Scholarship there if he had chosen a course of study other than pastoral ministries. Although Washington's constitution would no doubt prohibit more direct forms of aid, such as was in question in *Tilton* and *Roemer*, the Court's current philosophy suggests that such aid would not be prohibited under the Establishment Clause of the First Amendment.

Indicative of this interpretation was a U.S. Fourth Circuit decision in 2001 involving the Seventh-Day Adventist-affiliated Columbia Union College in Maryland. Columbia Union had been denied a grant from the state's Sellinger Program, which provided public aid to accredited private colleges in the state as long as the money was not used for sectarian purposes. Despite the fact that several Roman Catholic schools had received funds, Columbia Union's request was denied, as the Maryland Higher Education

Commission determined that the school was pervasively sectarian. Columbia Union filed suit challenging the Commission's decision. The Fourth Circuit ruled in favor of Columbia Union, arguing that the school was not pervasively sectarian. It further declared that since the aid was dispersed based upon neutral criteria, "the government risks discriminating against a class of citizens solely because of faith" if it were to deny the aid to Columbia Union.[56]

The appellate court's decision in the Columbia Union case is a detailed analysis of the pervasively sectarian test as it has been applied in higher education cases. According to the decision, Columbia Union was first denied Sellinger Funds in 1990, then was denied funding again in 1992 despite the fact that it satisfied the six criteria laid out by the state for eligibility.[57] In 1995, Columbia Union requested reconsideration in light of the U.S. Supreme Court's greater emphasis on neutrality in aid cases. Nonetheless, the Commission determined that Columbia Union's "nature and practices" had not changed substantially and denied the funds again in 1996. Columbia Union's initial legal challenge was a losing effort in the District Court, but the Fourth Circuit remanded the case in order for the pervasively sectarian nature of the college to be investigated further.[58]

After holding a bench trial and reviewing thousands of pages of evidence, the District Court ruled that Columbia Union was not pervasively sectarian. Relying upon the *Roemer* precedent, the court looked to four key criteria in determining the religious nature of the college. First, while mandatory worship was a practice at the college, the policy only applied to a minority of the students. Second, in reviewing course syllabi, catalogs, and other documents, the court determined that the primary purpose of the curriculum was not religious indoctrination. Third, while a preference was given to Seventh-day Adventists in admissions and hiring, this factor alone did not rise to the level of making Columbia Union a pervasively sectarian institution. Fourth, the denominational control over the governance of the institution did not meet the pervasively sectarian threshold.[59]

In affirming the district court's findings, the Fourth Circuit reasserted the fact that the U.S. Supreme Court had never found a college to be pervasively sectarian. In looking back at the *Tilton*, *Roemer*, and *Hunt* cases, the court suggested that the colleges in question were similar in many ways to Columbia Union. In *Tilton* and *Roemer*, for example, the Catholic Colleges revealed a preference for Catholics in hiring and admission, there were certain religious restrictions on the curriculum, and there were required theology classes. Likewise, in *Hunt*, the South Carolina Baptist Convention closely governed the institution, and the "advancement of a particular religion" was a purpose of the Baptist College at Charleston. Thus, the court concluded that "looking at all the evidence, we fail to see any disqualifying differences between Columbia Union and the colleges in *Roemer, Hunt* and *Tilton*."[60]

Despite this assessment of the pervasively sectarian test, the circuit court concluded that Columbia Union was entitled to the Sellinger funds without having to consider the pervasively sectarian nature of the school. Utilizing the secular purpose and primary effect portions of the *Lemon* Test, the court ruled that the secular purpose of the Sellinger program is clear and that the neutral criteria used in distributing the aid avoided any unconstitutional advancement of religion. Further arguments for constitutionality included the safeguards used to insure funds were not being diverted for religious purposes and that the funds were going to institutions of higher education rather than to secondary schools. Thus, the court concluded that "Columbia Union's receipt of Sellinger funds is not only consistent with the 'neutrality plus' formula of Justice O'Connor's concurrence, it is a stronger case than *Mitchell* due to the fact that Columbia Union is a college."[61]

The Future of Aid to Religiously Affiliated Higher Education

The trends on the Court seemingly bode well for proponents of religious colleges and universities that seek government funding for their institutions. With the pervasively sectarian test virtually laid to rest and at least a plurality of the nation's highest court accepting the direct funding of religious institutions (provided the aid was based upon neutral criteria), it would seem that a church-related college could enhance its religious distinctiveness while receiving grants, loans, and other forms of public aid. The rationale for this development is that now religious institutions will be treated equally with their secular counterparts and, with barriers to public aid removed, will be able to flourish economically without having to marginalize their religious identities or practices.

The emergence of the neutrality test notwithstanding, a number of the justices on the U.S. Supreme Court remain opposed to direct funding of religious activities as inconsistent with the fundamental principles of the Establishment Clause. Some have raised objections that a neutral aid program may allow for the diverting of funds for religious purposes. Moreover, as new and increasing funds find their way into the hands of church-related colleges and universities, conflicts over the accompanying federal regulations will follow.

GOVERNMENT REGULATION OF RELIGIOUSLY AFFILIATED COLLEGES AND UNIVERSITIES

Governmental regulation of private institutions has thus become an increasingly contentious issue in church-state relations. Religiously affiliated schools are subject to a wide array of regulations regarding employment, facilities, and finances. Disputes often arise, then, over what exemptions there might be for religious institutions from these government regulations based upon free exercise rights and the desire to minimize entanglements between church and state.

Employment and Discrimination

One of the primary sources of disputes has been in the area of employment and discrimination. Here the competing goals of ending discrimination and protecting the freedom and autonomy of religious institutions have come into conflict. Moreover, these disputes illustrate the consequences of accepting even indirect forms of government aid.[62] While the Civil Rights Act of 1964 banned discrimination based upon religion in hiring in both public and private facilities, Title VII of that same act allowed for exemptions for religious institutions. According to section 702 of Title VII, religious preference in hiring can be made if the institution is a religious "corporation, association, educational institution, or society." Section 703(e)(2) allows for religious preference in hiring in higher educational institutions that are religiously affiliated. Further, section 703(e)(1) permits employers to discriminate on the basis of religion, as well as gender and national origin, if it is "a bona fide occupational qualification reasonably necessary to the normal operation of that particular business or enterprise."[63]

Several federal and U.S. Supreme Court decisions have addressed the contours of these exemptions, particularly as they relate to employees that fulfill more secular functions at religious institutions. For instance, in the 1987 case of *Church of Jesus Christ of Latter-day Saints v. Amos*, Section 702 of the Title VII was challenged as a violation of the Establishment Clause if it allowed religious employers to discriminate on religious bases for nonreligious employees. At issue was the dismissal of an employee of a nonprofit gymnasium owned and operated by The Church of Jesus Christ of Latter-day Saints. A sixteen-year employee of the gym was dismissed because he failed to qualify for a "temple recommend." He challenged his dismissal by arguing that the Section 702 exemption that the Mormon

Church was claiming violated the Establishment Clause. In applying the *Lemon* Test, the U.S. Supreme Court essentially ruled that the exemptions allowed for religious corporations under Section 702 could be applied to all employees. It first determined that the required secular purpose of the law was satisfied because it would "alleviate significant governmental interference with the ability of religious organizations to define and carry out their religious missions."[64] Neither did the broad reading of the statute's exemptions result in the advancement or inhibition of religion. "A law is not unconstitutional simply because it *allows* churches to advance religion . . . For a law to have forbidden 'effects' under *Lemon*, it must be fair to say that the government *itself* has advanced religion through its own activities and influence," the Court concluded. Neither did the statute lead to an unconstitutional excessive entanglement between the religious institution and the state. Rather, "the status effectuates a more complete separation between the two."[65]

While the *Amos* case did not involve a college or university, its ruling reaffirmed what several federal appellate courts had concluded in employment discrimination cases at church-related colleges. *Prime v. Loyola University of Chicago*, for example, involved a challenge to Loyola University's practice of reserving a significant number of its faculty positions in its philosophy department for Jesuit priests. Emphasizing the bona fide occupational qualification of Section 703, the Seventh Circuit Court of Appeals allowed for the preference given Jesuits due to the longstanding relationship of the order to the school and the need to maintain that presence for the ongoing traditions and character of the school.[66] Similarly, the Seventh Circuit Court ruled in *Maguire v. Marquette University* that theology departments be given "broad latitude" in making preferential hiring practices.[67]

One exception to this trend came in 1993, when the Ninth Circuit Court ruled that the ownership, affiliation, purpose, and makeup of a private secondary school did not allow it Section 702 exemptions from religious discrimination in hiring despite the fact that the will establishing the school called for the hiring of only Protestants to the faculty and staff. Here the court ruled that the benefactor's provision was not enough to insulate the school from nondiscrimination laws. Rather, the court concluded that outside of the provisions in the will, the school's primary purpose was to provide education in secular subjects. Since there was no distinct relationship with a church, the school had failed to fulfill section 703's requirement that it be "owned, supported, controlled, or managed by a particular religion." Some commentators have suggested that this narrow reading of the religious exemptions statutes could have profound implications for religious higher education. If a school were to be required to provide evidence that it is "primarily religious" or that its relationship to a church or religious body is "clear and unmistakable," it may find itself open to more discrimination suits or challenges to its receipt of government aid.[68]

While the preceding cases have suggested that federal courts typically interpret the Title VII exemptions quite broadly in allowing for religious discrimination in hiring, another contentious area of litigation involves whether religious exemptions enable discrimination in the areas of gender or race. Two Baptist institutions provided the context of two Fifth Circuit Court decisions seeking to draw parameters around the ability of the government to monitor and regulate religious institutions' hiring practices. In *EEOC v. Mississippi College*,[69] the Fifth Circuit Court reversed a federal district court decision that upheld the school's refusal to turn over information regarding hiring practices to the EEOC, claiming that it would lead to an excessive entanglement between church and state and would violate the free exercise of the college to prefer Baptists for its faculty positions. The EEOC's investigation was instigated by a complaint filed by a part-time Presbyterian female faculty member who was passed over for a full-time faculty position that was given to a Baptist male. Her gender discrimination complaint further argued that Mississippi College had a history of discrimination. The Circuit Court held that if Mississippi College did indeed base its decision fundamentally upon the fact that the male candidate was of the preferred denomination, then it was covered by Title VII exemptions. However, the court affirmed the right of the EEOC to investigate charges of sexual and racial discrimination at church-related colleges and universities. That Title VII did not completely exempt such schools from EEOC jurisdiction was held in contradiction to the broad claim of Mississippi College that "the employment relationship between a church-related school and its faculty is not within the purview of Title VII." After claiming that the state had a "compelling interest in eradicating discrimination in all forms," the court concluded that "creating an exemption from the statutory enactment greater than that provided by section 702 would seriously undermine the means chosen by Congress to combat discrimination and is not constitutionally required."[70]

In *EEOC v. Southwestern Baptist Theological Seminary*,[71] the Seminary refused to submit an EEOC-6 form that provided data on race, sex, and national origin, as well as compensation and tenure of employees. The basis for the institution's refusal was that as a seminary, it was a "wholly religious" institution and thus was entitled to the same autonomy from regulation that a church enjoys. The circuit court agreed in part, ruling that the seminary had the essential status of a church and that any employee in a teaching or supervisory position had ministerial status. However, the court ruled that support personnel did not have the status of ministers and, as a result, the seminary would have to provide EEOC reports on those staff.[72]

As the preceding discussion reveals, Title VII exemptions provide religiously affiliated colleges and universities substantial freedom to practice religious preference in their hiring. And in part due to the fact that the Court has been unwilling to declare a school to be "pervasively sectarian," the ability of such schools to receive indirect student financial aid has not been compromised. Yet as the *Mississippi College* and *Southwestern Baptist Seminary* cases affirmed, religiously affiliated institutions are not completely immune, under Title VII guidelines, from EEOC jurisdiction. Nevertheless, courts have generally given religious institutions broad deference in claiming religiously based exemptions from government regulation in the area of employment.

Tax Exemption and Discrimination

The highly publicized case of *Bob Jones University v. United States* (1983) illustrates how the taxing power of government can be used to advance public policy goals such as nondiscrimination. While tax exemption for church property was affirmed by the U.S. Supreme Court in its 1970 decision of *Walz v. Tax Commission*,[73] subsequent controversies have arisen over the tax exemption for other religious institutions. Bob Jones University, a fundamentalist Christian school in South Carolina, had long asserted that the scriptures prohibited interracial dating and marriage. As a result, prior to 1971, the school did not accept blacks and for five subsequent years would only accept married African-Americans. Nevertheless, the school maintained a policy of no interracial dating or marriage upon punishment of being expelled.[74]

In 1976, IRS officials revoked the tax-exempt status of Bob Jones University due to its racially discriminatory policies. The university sued, seeking to recover its tax-exempt status, arguing that their policies were rooted in a deep and sincere religious belief and thus protected under the First Amendment. Integral to the debate over Bob Jones's tax-exempt status was a controversy over whether the IRS tax code section 501(c)(3), governing nonprofit organizations, embraced the common law concept of charity. If so, the institution in question could not engage in activities contrary to settled public policy. With only Justice Rehnquist dissenting, the U.S. Supreme Court ruled that the 501(c)(3) code did embrace the charity concept and thus Bob Jones's policies were contradictory to the requirement that "charitable exemptions are justified on the basis that the exempt entity confers a public benefit."[75] As a result, "the institution's purpose must not be so at odds with the common community conscience as to undermine any public benefit that might otherwise be conferred." The Court further rejected the free exercise claim of Bob Jones by contending that the government had an overriding state interest in eradicating racial discrimination. The Court thus concluded that the "governmental interest substantially outweighs whatever burden denied of tax benefits places on petitioners' exercise of their religious beliefs."[76]

As the previous discussion reveals, employment and discrimination issues represent a unique challenge, as the government seeks to respect the autonomy and freedom of religious institutions while at the same time furthering both public policy and the constitutional protections of equality and fairness. Indeed, some critics of the *Bob Jones* decision argue it could have a "devastating impact on educational institutions." Despite the compelling interest of the state to rid society of racial discrimination, its regulatory power through tax policies could either jeopardize the financial survival of some religious institutions or force them to alter their fundamental teachings.[77]

One of the newest and most emotionally charged areas of the law involves discrimination based upon sexual orientation. While the national debate rages, several states and local communities have passed laws aimed at protecting homosexuals from discrimination. In 1987, the Circuit Court of the District of Columbia was faced with determining whether D.C.'s Human Rights Act, which prohibited educational institutions from discrimination based upon sexual orientation, could be used to force Roman Catholic Georgetown University to recognize gay and lesbian student groups on its campus. While the groups enjoyed endorsement of the student body, they had not received formal university recognition that would provide them potential funding as well as access to campus mail services. Georgetown justified it refusal to recognize the groups by claiming that such an endorsement would conflict with Catholic teachings concerning homosexuality.[78]

Seven separate opinions were penned by a D.C. Court that skirted the fundamental constitutional issues by separating endorsement from the provision of funding and other resources. While contending that the university did not violate the statute by refusing recognition of the groups, it did run afoul of its intent by not allowing the groups equal access to benefits. The court further concluded that any burden upon the university's religious freedom by providing benefits to these organizations was overridden by the District of Columbia's compelling interest to eliminate discrimination based upon sexual orientation.[79]

ACCOMMODATION OF RELIGION IN PUBLIC UNIVERSITIES

While issues related to the funding and regulation of religiously affiliated higher educational institutions have generated significant First Amendment litigation, public colleges and universities have faced their own controversies over the role of religion on their campuses. In a number of cases, the U.S. Supreme Court has made a distinction between the permissibility of religious exercises at public elementary and secondary schools and public colleges and universities. And while university directed worship and proselytizing are prohibited in either context, state universities have been less reticent about offering courses in religious studies and even housing religious studies departments and programs. Ironically, during the twentieth century, when the last vestiges of the old Protestant ethos public institutions were becoming extinct, a number of schools began establishing departments and even schools of religion. Little headway was made when challenging these programs due to the fact that they embraced a more comparative approach to the study of religion. Plus, the U.S. Supreme Court had made explicit in *Abington v. Schempp* that the academic study of religion at all levels of public education was fully appropriate if not desirous. Justice Tom Clark, in his majority opinion in *Schempp*, declared:

> It might well be said that one's education is not complete without a study of comparative religion and its relationship to the advancement of civilization. It certainly may be said that the Bible is worthy of study for its literary and historic qualities. Nothing we have said here indicates that such study of the Bible or of religion, when presented objectively as part of a secular program of education, may not be effected consistently with the First Amendment.[80]

Use of Facilities

While instruction in religious studies has avoided any serious church-state challenge, other controversies have emerged over the use of public university facilities and student fees for religious exercises and programs. In 1981, the U.S. Supreme Court addressed the issue of whether the University of Missouri at Kansas City could forbid a Christian Bible study group called Cornerstone from using university facilities. The policy established by the university's Board of Curators held that as a public taxpayer-supported university, it was compelled to prohibit the use of campus facilities "for purposes of religious worship or teaching" by the Establishment Clause of the First Amendment. In bringing suit, the students countered that they had been discriminated against and that their free exercise and free speech rights had been violated.[81]

While the district court upheld the policy on Establishment Clause grounds, the court of appeals reversed, arguing that establishment concerns did not present a compelling enough interest to justify "a content based discrimination against religious speech." A majority of the U.S. Supreme Court agreed, concluding in *Widmar v. Vincent* that since the university had created an "open forum" for student groups, it could not engage in content-based discrimination of speech. In setting aside the Establishment Clause objections, the majority determined that the incidental benefits religion would receive from an open forum policy would not lead to its having the primary effect of advancing religion.[82]

The *Widmar* decision drew a great deal of attention from constitutional scholars—and church-state experts particularly—due to the fact that the Court utilized free speech public forum analyses to settle what was also a free exercise dispute. While the lopsided Supreme Court vote suggested a clear precedent, some commentators shared Justice White's concern of the implications of the Court's rationale. In his dissenting opinion, White warned that treating "religious worship *qua* speech . . . the Religion Clauses would be emptied of any independent meaning in circumstances in which religious practice took the form of speech."[83] Despite White's concerns, *Widmar* provided a constitutional rationale for allowing student-led religious clubs to meet at public secondary schools as well. With the passage of the Equal Access Act in 1984 and its constitutionality being upheld in the case of *Board of Education v. Mergens*, public secondary schools are prohibited from discriminating against student groups meeting in campus facilities based upon the religious, political, or philosophical content of their speech.[84]

Funding of Student Publications

Conflict between the Free Speech and Establishment Clauses would characterize another recent dispute over the funding of a religious newspaper at the University of Virginia. The University refused to use revenues from mandatory student fees to pay for the printing of an evangelical Christian student newspaper called *Wide Awake*. The university policy, challenged by a group of students as a violation of their free speech rights, prohibited the use of such funds for a publication that "primarily promotes or manifests a particular belief in or about a deity or an ultimate reality." In contrast, the students argued that since the university funded other student activities and publications, it had created a "limited open forum" and thus could not engage in viewpoint discrimination.[85]

The key question in *Rosenberger v. University of Virginia* (1995) was whether the Establishment Clause required the university to discriminate against religious publications. A narrowly divided U.S. Supreme Court ruled that it did not. Justice Anthony Kennedy, in writing for a 5–4 majority, argued that much like in *Widmar*, the university had created an open forum and in doing so could not engage in viewpoint discrimination. For Kennedy, if the funding had been distributed on a neutral basis, then the Establishment Clause concerns could be set aside. In other words, the policy was established to create an open forum "for speech and to support various student enterprises." Since the publication requested funding as a student journal, and not on the basis of its religious viewpoint, then the Court concluded that the principle of neutrality should prevail. "We have held that the guarantee of neutrality is respected, not offended," the Court asserted, "when the government extends benefits to recipients whose ideologies and viewpoints, including religious ones, are broad and diverse."[86] Kennedy further warned that by allowing the denial of funding, the Court would put state officials in a position of having to determine what constituted a legitimate religious message. Kennedy also argued that the direct payment from the university to a third party printer further insulated the university from Establishment Clause concerns.[87]

A lengthy dissent was penned by Justice David Souter declaring in part that "the Court today, for the first time, approves direct funding of core religious activities by an arm of the state."[88] In particular, Souter took issue with the Court's neutrality theory that removed any consideration of the effects of the policy. For Souter, the mandatory student fee was the equivalent of a tax that would, in this instance, go toward the publication of an evangelical and proselytizing publication. For the Establishment Clause to have much meaning, according to Souter, the effects of the law should trump the mere evenhandedness required by free speech guidelines.[89]

CONCLUSION

The *Rosenberger* decision was a victory for advocates of greater accommodation of religious practices in public universities and for those claiming the Court's past adherence to a strict no-aid or separationist approach to the Establishment Clause had led to the marginalization of religion in American public life. In contrast, critics of the decision bemoaned what they perceived to be a further watering down of the separationist principle underlying the Establishment Clause they deemed essential to the preservation of religious liberty. While a majority of the current U.S. Supreme Court has embraced the neutrality or equal treatment approach, leading many to see the opportunity for even greater partnerships between government and religion, not all religious practices at publicly-funded universities will be justified even under a less strict reading of the Establishment Clause. The *Mellen v. Bunting*[90] decision by the Fourth Circuit Court illustrates that even some longstanding religious practices are just too difficult to reconcile with the religion clauses of the First Amendment. Even though other circuit courts had upheld commencement prayers at state colleges and universities, the court found Virginia Military Institute's practice of daily mealtime prayers to be coercive and thus violative of the Establishment Clause.

In the area of aid to religiously affiliated colleges and universities, the recent *Locke v. Davey* decision revealed that state constitutions may have stricter barriers to aid than what the prevailing interpretation of the First Amendment allows. The relationship of aid to religious colleges and government regulation will no doubt continue to be a thorny area of the law as well. There certainly will be increased legal challenges due to the fact that aid has become more available to religious institutions (through the demise of the pervasively sectarian test and *Lemon* Test), while these same institutions are allowed to discriminate based upon religion in their hiring practices. One commentator has argued that this view of the Establishment Clause leads to "'equal' opportunities for funding on the one hand while providing for 'unequal' rights to discriminate and 'unequal' immunity from regulation on the other."[91] This apparent inconsistency has led others to conclude that religiously affiliated colleges and universities are "not out of the woods yet" with regard to church-state challenges to their funding and employment practices.[92] And as the *Gay Rights Coalition of the Georgetown University Law Center* case reveals, state and local antidiscrimination statutes may place a greater burden upon religious colleges and universities than do federal laws, particularly in the areas of gender or sexual orientation.

The past decade has witnessed a renewed interest in the study of religion and spirituality. Moreover, there has been growth in religiously-oriented student clubs and organizations on public university campuses. At the same time, some church-related institutions have sought to reinvigorate their religious identities by encouraging the "integration of faith and learning" in the classroom. In light of these trends, it may be safely assumed that religion and higher education will remain a key battleground over competing interpretations of religious freedom and the separation of church and state.

NOTES

1. Fredrick Kunkle, "Cross Returns to Chapel—But Not on the Alter," *Washington Post*, March 7, 2007.
2. Tim Townsend, "In Constitutional Clash, Christian Fraternity Wins Big," *St. Louis Post-Dispatch*, February 19, 2007.
3. David Fellman, "Religion, the State, and the Public University," in ed. James E. Wood, Jr., *Religion, the State, and Education* (Waco, TX: J.M. Dawson Institute of Church-State Studies, 1984), 79–80.
4. Frederick Rudolph, *The American College and University: A History* (New York: Knopf, 1962), 7.
5. John R. Thelin, *A History of American Higher Education* (Baltimore: Johns Hopkins University Press, 2004), 29.
6. F. King Alexander, "Issues in Higher Education: The Decline and Fall of the Wall of Separation Between Church and State and Its Consequences for the Funding of Public and Private Institutions of Higher Education," *Florida Journal of Law and Public Policy* 10 (Fall 1998), 107.
7. Rudolph, *The American College*, 16.
8. Anson Phelps Stokes and Leo Pfeffer, *Church and State in the United States* (New York: Harper and Row, 1964), 54.
9. Thelin, *A History of American Higher Education*, 51–52.
10. Thelin, *A History of American Higher Education*, 61; Stephen Haynes, "A Review of Research on Church-Related Higher Education" in *Professing in the Postmodern Academy: Faculty and the Future of the Church-Related College* (Waco, TX: Baylor University Press, 2002), 2–3.
11. Thelin, *A History of American Higher Education*, 76.
12. Fernand N. Dutile and Edward M. Gaffney, Jr., *State and Campus: State Regulation of Religiously-Affiliated Higher Education* (South Bend, IN: University of Notre Dame Press, 1984), 13.
13. George M. Marsden, *The Soul of the American University* (New York: Oxford University Press, 1994), 3.
14. Thelin, *A History of American Higher Education*, 141–142.
15. Ibid., 114.
16. Haynes, "A Review of Research," 3.
17. Thelin, *A History of Higher Education*, 146; Haynes, "A Review of Research," 4.
18. Thelin, *A History of Higher Education*, 148.
19. See Edward M. Gaffney, Jr. and Philip R. Moots, *Government and Campus: Federal Regulation of Religiously-Affiliated Higher Education* (Notre Dame, IN: University of Notre Dame Press, 1982).
20. Much of the material in this section is drawn from a previously published article; J. David Holcomb, "Financing Faith and Learning: Assessing the Constitutional Implications of Integrating Faith and Learning at the Church-Related College," *Journal of Church and State* 48 (Autumn 2006): 831–850.

21. Stephen V. Monsma, *When Sacred and Secular Mix: Religious Nonprofit Organizations and Public Money* (Lanham, MD: Rowman & Littlefield, 1996), 35–40.
22. Dutile and Gaffney, *State and Campus*, 11.
23. See also the Court's 2004 decision in *Locke* v. *Davey* 540 U.S. 712 upholding a Washington State constitutional ban on using a state-funded scholarship toward the obtaining of a degree in "devotional theology."
24. *Roemer v. Board of Public Works*, 426 U.S. 736 (1976) at 755.
25. *Lemon v. Kurtzman*, 403 U.S. 602 (1971).
26. 403 U.S. 602 at 618.
27. Ibid.
28. Ibid. at 619–20. The excessive entanglement prong became a particularly stiff barrier to aid. According to the *Lemon* majority decision, even if the sacred and secular functions of the aid could be separated, the state would still have to engage in continuous surveillance of the institution to ensure that no funds went to support religious indoctrination. See Monsma, *When Sacred and Secular Mix*, 32.
29. "The very purpose of many of those schools is to provide an integrated secular and religious education; the teaching process is, to a large extent devoted to the inculcation of religious values and belief. Substantial aid to the educational function of such schools, accordingly, necessarily results in aid to the sectarian school enterprise as a whole." 421 U.S. 349 (1975) at 366.
30. See *Aguilar v. Felton*, 473 U.S. 402 (1985) at 412.
31. Monsma, *When Sacred and Secular Mix*, 33.
32. The schools and facilities in question included Sacred Heart University (library); Annhurst College (music, drama, and arts building); Fairfield University (library and science building); Albertus Magnus College (language laboratory); see *Tilton v. Richardson*, 403 U.S. 672 (1971) at 690.
33. 403 U.S. 672 at 682.
34. Ibid. at 680.
35. Ibid. at 681.
36. Ibid.
37. Ibid. at 687.
38. Ibid. at 688.
39. *Everson v. Board of Education*, 330 U.S. 1 (1947).
40. 403 U.S. 672 at 693–94.
41. *Hunt v. McNair*, 413 U.S. 734 (1973) at 744.
42. *Roemer v. Board of Public Works*, 426 U.S. 736 (1976).
43. Ibid. at 742–44.
44. Ibid. at 755–59.
45. Ibid. at 762–64.
46. Kent Weeks, "State and Local Issues," in *The Future of Religious Colleges*, ed. Paul J. Dovre (Grand Rapids, MI: William B. Eerdmans Publishing Company, 2002), 333.
47. Ralph Mawdsley, "Government Aid and Regulation of Religious Colleges

and Universities," in *Religious Higher Education in the United States: A Source Book*, ed. Thomas C. Hunt and James C. Carper (New York: Garland, 1996), 6–7.

48. *Witters v. Washington Department of Services for the Blind*, 474 U.S. 481 (1986) at 487.

49. *Agostini v. Felton*, 521 U.S. 203 (1997).

50. Ibid. at 225.

51. *Mitchell v. Helms*, 530 U.S. 793 (2000).

52. Ibid. at 810–19.

53. Ibid. at 840–841; the neutrality theory was advanced even more clearly two years later in the decision of *Zelman v. Simmons-Harris* 536 U.S. 639 (2002). Here the Court upheld a Cleveland educational voucher program arguing that it offered assistance to a broad class of individuals without respect to religion and that both religious and non-religious schools could participate.

54. *Locke v. Davey*, 540 U.S. 712 (2004).

55. Ibid. at 712–15.

56. *Columbia Union College v. John J. Oliver*, 254 F. 3d 496 (2001) at 510.

57. The state required that: (1) The college must be a non-profit college or university established in the state of Maryland prior to July 1, 1970. (2) The institution must be approved by the Maryland Higher Education Commission. (3) The institution must be accredited. (4) The institution must have awarded the associate of arts or baccalaureate degrees to at least one graduating class. (5) The college must maintain one or more programs leading to such degrees other than seminarian or theological programs. (6) The institution must submit each new program or major modification of an existing program to the Commission for its approval; Ibid. at 499.

58. Ibid.

59. Ibid. at 508.

60. Ibid. at 510.

61. Ibid. at 507.

62. In the case of *Grove City College v. Bell*, 465 U.S. 555 (1984), the Court ruled that indirect federal tax support of religious colleges through student financial aid can subject the institution to federal anti-discrimination laws.

63. Kent M. Weeks and Derek Davis, eds., *Legal Deskbook for Adminstrators of Independent Colleges and Universities* 2nd ed. (Waco, TX: Baylor University, 1999), ix–3; William A. Kaplin and Barbara A. Lee, *The Law of Higher Education* 3rd ed. (San Francisco: Jossey-Bass Publishers, 1995), 726–727.

64. *Church of Jesus Christ of Latter-Day Saints v. Amos*, 483 U.S. 327 (1987) at 331–335.

65. Ibid. at 336–38.

66. *Prime v. Loyola University of Chicago*, 803 F.2d 351 (7th Cir. 1986); Weeks and Davis, *Legal Deskbook*, ix–4; Kaplin and Lee, *The Law of Higher Education*, 727.

67. *Maguire v. Marquette University*, 814 F.2d 1213 (7th Cir. 1987).

68. *EEOC v. Kamehameha Schools/Bishop Estate*, 990 F.2d 458 (9th Cir. 1993); Weeks and Davis, *Legal Deskbook*, ix, 5–6.

69. *EEOC v. Mississippi College*, 626 F.2d 477 (5th Cir. 1980).
70. Kaplin and Lee, *The Law of Higher Education*, 729–730.
71. 651 F.2d 277 (5th Cir. 1981).
72. According to the court, Title VII exemptions only applied to "traditionally ecclesiastical or ministerial" positions, such as the president, dean of the chapel, academic deans, and other administrators that would supervise faculty; Kaplin and Lee, *The Law of Higher Education*, 731.
73. *Walz v. Tax Commission of the City of New York*, 397 U.S. 664 (1970).
74. *Bob Jones University v. United States* (1983), 461 U.S. 574 at 580.
75. Ibid. at 591.
76. Ibid. at 604.
77. Mawdsley, "Government Aid and Regulation," 21.
78. *Gay Rights Coalition of Georgetown University Law Center v. Georgetown University*, 536 U.S. A.2d. 1 (D.C. 1987); Weeks, "State and Local Issues," 346–348; Kaplin and Lee, *The Law of Higher Education*, 519–520.
79. Ibid.
80. "Nothing we have said here indicates that such study of the Bible or of religion, when presented objectively as part of a secular program of education, may not be effected consistently with the First Amendment." *Abington Township School Board v. Schempp*, 374 U.S. 203 (1963) at 225.
81. *Widmar v. Vincent*, 454 U.S. 263 (1981).
82. Ibid. at 267.
83. Ibid. at 284.
84. *Board of Education v. Mergens*, 496 U.S. 226 (1990).
85. *Rosenberger v. University of Virginia*, 515 U.S. 819 (1995), 822–830.
86. Ibid. at 839.
87. Ibid. at 844.
88. Ibid. at 863.
89. Ibid. at 895–899.
90. *Mellen v. Bunting*, 327 F. 3d 355 (2003).
91. Alan Brownstein, "Constitutional Questions About Charitable Choice," in *Welfare Reform and Faith-Based Organizations*, eds. Derek Davis and Barry Hankins (Waco, TX: J.M. Dawson Institute of Church-State Studies, 1999), 246.
92. Naomi Schaefer, "Vulnerable Under God," 1.

FURTHER READING

For a history and analysis of church-state issues related to the funding of higher education, see F. King Alexander, "Issues in Higher Education: The Decline and Fall of the Wall of Separation Between Church and State and Its Consequences for the Funding of Public and Private Institutions of Higher Education," *Florida Journal of Law and Public Policy* 10 (Fall 1998). Derek H. Davis' "The Supreme Court as Moral Physician: *Mitchell v. Helms* and the Constitutional Revolution to

Reduce Restrictions on Governmental Aid to Religion," 43 *Journal of Church and State* (Spring 2001): 213–31 provides a critical analysis of the neutrality test and its implications for the funding of private religious institutions. Paul J. Dovre, ed., *The Future of Religious Colleges* (Grand Rapids, MI: William B. Eerdmans Publishing Company, 2002) is a wide ranging collection of essays addressing a number of contemporary issues facing religious colleges. See especially Kent Weeks' essay entitled "State and Local Issues," in which he provides a helpful overview and analysis of state and local legal considerations of religious colleges and universities. Although a bit dated, both Fernand N. Dutile and Edward M. Gaffney, Jr., *State and Campus: State Regulation of Religiously-Affiliated Higher Education* (South Bend, IN: University of Notre Dame Press, 1984) and Edward M. Gaffney, Jr., and Philip R. Moots, *Government and Campus: Federal Regulation of Religiously-Affiliated Higher Education* (Notre Dame, IN: University of Notre Dame Press, 1982) remain very helpful studies of both state and federal regulation of religiously affiliated higher education. State constitutional provisions, employment, student discipline, taxation, and many other issues are assessed in these substantive volumes. A standard education law text, William A. Kaplin and Barbara A. Lee's *The Law of Higher Education: A Comprehensive Guide to Legal Implications of Administrative Decision-Making*, 3rd ed. (San Francisco: Jossey-Bass, 1995) provides excellent summaries and analysis of many key decisions involving religion and higher education. A much discussed and debated work, George M. Marsden's *The Soul of the American University: From Protestant Establishment to Established Nonbelief* (New York: Oxford University Press, 1994) provides a history of the particularly Protestant influence on higher education that lasted until the twentieth century. Marsden argues that traditional religious beliefs belong again on college campuses alongside other perspectives such as feminism and multicultural studies. In her short essay, "Vulnerable Under God: Could Religious Colleges Be the Next Institutions Under Legal Attack?" *The American Enterprise* (September 2002), Naomi Shaeffer suggests that while the trends on the U.S. Supreme Court bode well for advocates of more public aid to religious colleges and universities, greater legal challenges may exist in the future, especially as some religious schools are seeking to strengthen their religious identities. For an extended analysis of these issues, see J. David Holcomb, "Financing Faith and Learning: Assessing the Constitutional Implications of Integrating Faith and Learning at the Church-Related College," *Journal of Church and State* 48 (Autumn 2006): 831–850.

Appendix: Selected Cases

The following cases are discussed or referenced by the chapters in this volume. Only precedent setting decisions or important clarifications are included in this appendix. Though not all the cases here are, strictly speaking, matters of church and state jurisprudence, all have important ramifications for the issues covered in the volume.

Abington Township v. Schempp (1963): The town of Abington, Pennsylvania, required public school students to recite ten verses from the Bible every day, followed by the Lord's prayer. Though students could be exempted with a note from parents, the Supreme Court disallowed this practice because it violated both the Free Exercise Clause and the Establishment Clause of the First Amendment.

Agostini v. Felton (1997): A parochial school teacher challenged an earlier decision by the Supreme Court regarding whether or not public school teachers could teach secular subjects at parochial schools. In *Agostini*, the Supreme Court reversed *Aguilar v. Felton* (1985). Not only can public school teachers enter parochial schools without necessarily violating the Establishment Clause, this decision means that not all entanglements of church and state should be assumed unconstitutional.

Aguilar v. Felton (1985): Since the 1960s, New York City had used public monies to pay teachers in parochial schools as a means of combating educational inequality. The Supreme Court found that the monitoring of publicly paid teachers that was necessary to ensure that they were not promoting religion amounted to excessive entanglement between church and state. The Supreme Court later overturned this ruling in *Agostini v. Felton* (1997).

Bethel School District No. 403 v. Fraser (1986): High school student Matthew Fraser was suspended for using lewd language at a school assembly as part of a nominating speech for an elected position. Fraser contended that this suspension violated his First Amendment rights to free speech. The Supreme Court determined that public schools have the right to restrict speech that contradicts "fundamental values of public school education."

Board of Education v. Allen (1968): The New York Education Law required the state to provide textbooks for both secular and parochial school children in grades seven through twelve. Several New York school boards challenged this law as unconstitutional under the First and Fourteenth Amendments. The Supreme Court cited the *Everson v. Board of Education* (1947) decision in finding this law to be constitutional. The state provided only secular textbooks on loan, without any religious interest and provided them equally to all schools.

Bob Jones University v. United States (1983): The IRS revoked the tax-exempt status of Bob Jones University due to its policy against interracial dating and marriage and of the Goldsboro Christian School due to its policy of admitting only Caucasian students, causing the schools to claim a violation of its religious liberty. The Supreme Court sided with the IRS, arguing that the schools' policies inhibited the government interest in ending racial discrimination and therefore did not fit the requirements for tax-exempt status. Thus, the court determined that some restrictions on religious liberty are constitutional.

BOE of Westside Community Schools v. Mergens (1990): The Nebraska Westside School District prohibited students from forming a Christian Club with a faculty sponsor at their high school. While the school district thought such a club would violate the Establishment Clause, the students charged the school with violating the Equal Access Act. The Supreme Court allowed the students to form their Christian Club, using the *Lemon* Test (*Lemon v. Kurtzman*) to determine the constitutionality of the Equal Access Act.

Brown v. Board of Education (1954): Addressing five separate cases and just under 200 plaintiffs from five states, this case addressed the constitutionality of racial segregation, particularly in public school settings. The Supreme Court found that despite best efforts at separate but equal schooling for different races, inequality persisted, thus having a negative effect on minority children. This decision effectively ended all state-sponsored racial segregation.

Committee for Public Education v. Nyquist (1973): In an attempt to avoid overcrowding in public schools, New York State passed a law allowing supplemental grants or tax-deductions to parents who sent their children to non-public schools. The Committee for Public Education and Religious Liberty filed suit, claiming this law constituted a violation of the Establishment Clause. The Supreme Court ruled that though the law had a secular purpose, it did have a primary effect of supporting religion since the actual beneficiaries of the funds were the private schools, not the parents.

Corporation of the Presiding Bishop v. Amos (1987): An individual was fired from a nonprofit facility run by the Church of Jesus Christ of Latter-day Saints because he was not a member of the Church. He and other individuals brought suit against the church, alleging religious discrimination in violation of Title VII of the Civil Rights Act. The Supreme Court found the policy unconstitutional because both the work of the facility and the job in question were secular activities.

Edwards v. Aguillard (1987): The State of Louisiana's "Balanced Treatment for Creation-Science and Evolution-Science in Public School Instruction Act" mandated that any public school teaching either creation science or evolution science must give equal time to the other as well. The Supreme Court found this law unconstitutional on all three parts of the test developed in 1971's *Lemon v. Kurtzman*. There was no clear secular purpose, the law was meant to advance a religious viewpoint, and it mandated inappropriate entanglement between religion and government by using government funds for a religious purpose.

Elk Grove Unified School District v. Newdow (2004): Michael Newdow sued the Elk Grove Unified School District on behalf of his daughter, who as a public school student was required to either recite or listen to the Pledge of Allegiance. According to Newdow, the inclusion of the phrase "under God" in the Pledge violated the Establishment Clause of the First Amendment. The Supreme Court did not decide on the constitutionality of this case due to the fact that as a divorced father without custody of his daughter, Newdow did not have proper standing to represent his daughter in the case.

Engel v. Vitale (1962): In an attempt to standardize practice and minimize local conflict, the Board of Regents for the State of New York instituted a nondenominational and voluntary prayer to be said at the beginning of each school day. The Supreme Court determined that the prayer was unconstitutional despite its nondenominational nature and the allowance for abstention.

Epperson v. Arkansas (1968): Public school teacher Epperson sued the State of Arkansas for prohibiting public schools from teaching human evolution. Epperson claimed this regulation both violated the Establishment Clause and limited her right to free speech. The Supreme Court concurred that this constituted an establishment of religion in its origination with a particular religious group and its objectionable nature to other religious and nonreligious individuals.

Everson v. Board of Education (1947): New Jersey instituted a law allowing for the reimbursement of funds to parents who sent their children to both religious and public schools on public transportation buses. Everson charged that this violated the Establishment Clause by enacting state support of religious schools. The Supreme Court upheld the constitutionality of the law by claiming the reimbursement was available to religious and non-religious individuals alike and did not constitute direct support of religious organizations.

Grand Rapids School District v. Ball (1985): The Grand Rapids School District offered two classes in leased private school classrooms. The first class was held during regular school hours and was taught by a public school teacher and the second was held after school by teachers otherwise employed by religious schools. Taxpayers sued, claiming a violation of the Establishment Clause, and the Supreme Court agreed that this program had the effect of supporting religion.

Grove City College v. Bell (1984): In an attempt to maintain particular standards without governmental regulations, Grove City College refused all state and federal funding. However, many of its students received Basic Educational Opportunity Grants (BEOG) through the Department of Education (DOE). The DOE claimed the College should be subject to government requirements such as Title IX if it accepted these funds. The Supreme Court determined that funding students amounted to funding an institution, thus, if the College accepted the BEOG funds, it must be held to the Title IX anti-discrimination standards.

Jacobellis v. Ohio (1964): The State of Ohio banned showings of a French film, *Les Amants*, due to obscenity. Nico Jacobellis, a theater owner, was convicted and fined for showing the movie. The Supreme Court overturned the conviction for varying reasons, concluding the movie was not obscene. The most famous opinion came from Justice Potter Stewart, who argued for the Constitutional protection of everything but "hard-core pornography" and defined pornography by concluding, "I know it when I see it."

Keyishian v. Board of Regents (1967): Faculty members of the State University of New York were threatened with termination for refusal to affirm a loyalty oath to the United States. The Supreme Court ruled that New York's requirement of a loyalty oath was a violation of the rights of political expression and that the university had failed to prove that faculty members had been actively trying to overthrow the government.

Kitzmiller v. Dover Area School District (2005): In 2004, the Dover Area

School Board in Pennsylvania authorized the teaching of intelligent design as part of the regular curriculum. A group of parents sued the district, arguing that this amounted to a violation of the Establishment Clause. After a bench trial, a U.S. District Court judge ruled against the school board, which had, by then, changed membership. No appeal was filed, thus the ruling against the teaching of intelligent design in Dover area schools stands.

Lamb's Chapel v. Center Moriches School District (1993): School officials refused permission for a church group to use their facilities after hours for a film series and discussion group because of religious content. The Supreme Court ruled against school officials on the grounds that they were discriminating against a religious group and that allowing use of the facilities did not amount to an establishment of religion.

Lee v. Weisman (1992): A Providence, Rhode Island, middle school principal, Robert E. Lee, invited a rabbi to speak and offer a prayer at the school's graduation. A father of a graduating student, Daniel Weisman, moved to prohibit this speech or the inviting of clergy to speak at any public school events. The Supreme Court held that Lee's invitation to the rabbi constituted a violation of the Establishment Clause because the ceremony amounted to state-sponsored and state-organized religious practice.

Lemon v. Kurtzman (1971): This case was heard with two other cases involving laws in Pennsylvania and Rhode Island that funded teacher salaries and instructional materials for secular subjects taught in non-public schools. The Supreme Court concluded that these policies violated the Establishment Clause and through this case developed the "Lemon Test" for determining whether a law violated the clause. This test requires that (1) the law must have "a secular legislative purpose," (2) the law must neither advance nor hinder religion, and (3) the law cannot lead to "an excessive government entanglement with religion."

Leoles v. Landers (1937): A Georgia school expelled students for refusing to recite the Pledge of Allegiance. A state court affirmed this policy, and this decision was appealed to the Supreme Court. Following its precedent in *Nicholls v. Mayor of Lynn* (1937), the Supreme Court affirmed the duty of schools to educate children in American ideals and traditions.

Locke v. Davey (2004): In 1999, Washington State established its Promise Scholarship to provide college scholarships to top students. The State limited these funds by disallowing their use for theology programs. Joshua Davey earned a Promise Scholarship but declined the money in order to pursue pastoral ministries at a Christian college. Davey sued, claiming a violation of his free exercise of religion. The Supreme Court denied Davey's suit, stating that government has a right to restrict its funding and only support non-religious programs of instruction as a means of avoiding state support of religious activity.

Loving v. Virginia (1967): The State of Virginia sentenced an interracial couple to jail for violating miscegenation laws. The Supreme Court ruled unanimously that the laws were unconstitutional and "odious" to a free people.

Lynch v. Donnelly (1982): Daniel Lynch charged that the annual Pawtucket, Rhode Island, Christmas display in the city's shopping district violated the Establishment Clause by including a nativity scene as well as a Christmas tree, a "Seasons Greetings" banner, and a Santa Clause house. The Supreme Court disagreed and held that this display did not have a specific religious purpose but rather represented the history of the Christmas holiday.

McCollum v. BOE (1948): A coalition of Jewish and Christian organizations sponsored a period of voluntary religious instruction to take place during the regular school day. The Supreme Court found that the use of tax-supported property and the working relationship between public school and church authorities violated the Establishment Clause.

Meek v. Pittenger (1975): This case found that textbooks could be loaned to students in non-public schools as part of a program to make textbooks available to all students. Other forms of aid, such as counseling, testing, and related services were found to further the aims of the parochial schools, which as "pervasively sectarian" institutions were not eligible for state support.

Minersville School District v. Gobitis (1940): The Gobitis children were members of Jehovah's Witnesses who were expelled for not saluting the flag, an act they found to be in conflict with Biblical command. The Supreme Court upheld the mandatory flag salute, arguing that national unity was an important consideration and that attempts to promote it did not automatically violate a citizen's freedom.

Mitchell v. Helms (2000): This case, like others, focuses on the use of public money in sectarian schools. At issue here was the provision of funds for library, computer, and other educational materials. The Supreme Court ruled that the fact that all schools, religious and secular alike, were eligible for such aid means that the government has been neutral in its services and has thus not violated the Establishment Clause.

Mueller v. Allen (1983): Minnesota law allowed parents to write off certain expenses pertaining to their children's schooling, regardless of what type of school, religious or public, their children attended. Applying the test from the *Lemon* case (*Lemon v. Kurtzman*), the Supreme Court ruled that this practice was permitted by the Constitution. Of particular importance was the idea that the benefits were available to all parents, and thus that the law was neutral with respect to religion.

Pierce v. Society of Sisters (1925): This landmark case established the right of church groups to build and maintain their own schools in the face of public education. The State of Oregon had passed a law in 1922 requiring all students to attend public institutions, but the Supreme Court found that "additional obligations" beyond national citizenship could not be denied and were best served by guaranteeing the possibility of parochial institutions.

Prince v. Jacoby (2002): Washington school officials refused to allow a student-led Bible study group equal privileges with other student groups. The Ninth Circuit found that the school district had violated student rights, and the Supreme Court declined to review the case. Thus, equal access must be given to religious groups in public schools.

Reynolds v. U.S. (1879): George Reynolds, a member of the Church of Jesus Christ of Latter-Day Saints, was charged with bigamy in Utah. Along with certain procedural arguments, Reynolds held that religious duty obligated him to marry more than one woman at a time. The Supreme Court upheld Reynolds' conviction and drew a distinction between what religious people might believe and what they can practice in the public sphere.

Roemer v. Maryland Public Works Board (1976): The State of Maryland offered monetary grants to private colleges and universities that did not exclusively offer theological or ministerial degrees. A suit was brought by taxpayers, claiming that the program violated the Establishment Clause since public money was going to sectarian schools. The Supreme Court found that grants to religious institutions were permissible and that religious institutions were eligible for public money as long as the funds were used for specifically religious purposes.

Rosenberger v. UVA (1995): University of Virginia student Ronald Rosenberger requested a disbursement from the student activities fund to subsidize the publication of a Christian newspaper. The university refused on the grounds that it could not promote any specific religious viewpoint. The Supreme Court held that the University had acted in such a way as to penalize Rosenberger's speech, and it further found that the university's publication policy was neutral toward religious content and did not therefore violate the Establishment Clause.

Santa Fe Independent School District v. Doe (2000): Two families brought a suit against the Santa Fe Independent School District's practice of allowing an overtly Christian prayer before home football games. While the case was pending, the school district changed the policy from requiring a prayer to permitting one. The Supreme Court held that the new policy violated the Establishment Clause because the prayer took place on school property at an official function and therefore could appear to endorse religious practice.

Tennessee v. John Scopes (1925): This is the famous case dramatized in the movie *Inherit the Wind*. John Scopes was a high school teacher convicted of violating Tennessee law for teaching about evolution in the classroom. Though the prosecution won the trial, Scopes' accusers were portrayed as backwoods fundamentalists out of step with modern thinking.

Tilton v. Richardson (1971): Federal law provided for grants to be given to church-sponsored colleges and universities for the construction of facilities that were not used to advance religion, but it also provided a sunset clause to the effect that twenty years after construction, the building could be used for any purchase. The Supreme Court struck down the twenty-year limitation, arguing that the buildings were indistinguishable from other facilities and did not require excessive monitoring.

Tinker v. Des Moines Independent Community School District (1969): Three public school students were suspended for refusing to remove black armbands in protest of the Vietnam War. The Supreme Court ruled that although schools could impose certain restrictions on speech, school officials had not shown that the particulars of this case were destructive of legitimate school functions.

United States v. American Library Association (2003): Congress required public libraries to install filtering software on all public computer stations in libraries that receive federal funding. The American Library Association sued, claiming that the act required them to violate the Free Speech rights of their patrons. The Supreme Court ruled that the act did not violate the Constitution and thus that Congress could make certain requirements as a precondition for receiving federal funds.

Van Orden v. Perry (2005): Van Orden sued the state of Texas in federal court, claiming that a monument to the Ten Commandments on the grounds of the state capitol violated the Establishment Clause. The Supreme Court ruled that the Ten Commandments, though religious in origin, are part of American history and society and could therefore be included in public displays without violating the First Amendment.

Wallace v. Jaffree (1985): An Alabama law authorizing teachers to conduct prayers and other religious activities during the school day was found to violate the First Amendment. Religious services could serve no secular purpose, thus violating the *Lemon* Test (*Lemon v. Kurtzman*). Additionally, the law violated Alabama's responsibility to maintain neutrality towards religious groups.

Walz v. Tax Commission (1970): This case challenged tax exemptions for churches in New York. The plaintiff held that his own responsibility for paying taxes was essentially a subsidy for churches that did not have to pay property taxes and thus was a form of state aid to religious institutions. The Supreme Court held that the government could maintain a position of benevolent neutrality towards churches and religious institutions without violating the First Amendment and thus that tax exemptions were not unconstitutional.

West Virginia State Board of Education v. Barnette (1943): This case overturned the *Gobitis* decision, just three years old at the time, as the Supreme Court ruled that mandatory salutes to the flag were unconstitutional.

Westside Community Schools v. Mergens (1990): School officials denied permission for the formation of a Christian club in local schools. A group of students sued, claiming that their rights to equal access to public facilities had been violated. The Supreme Court held that since there were other non-curricular clubs recognized by the school, they could not deny another club on the basis of their religious content.

Widmar v. Vincent (1981): This case concerned access to university facilities at the University of Missouri at Kansas City. A Christian club that had been allowed to meet in previous years was sued when a new policy prompted school officials to deny permission for the club to have access to university facilities. The Supreme Court held that the Establishment Clause did not require school officials to deny access to school facilities on the basis of the religious nature of the club.

Wisconsin v. Yoder (1972): This case revolved around whether or not Amish families could absent their children from school facilities after a certain age on the basis of religious conviction. The Supreme Court held that public schooling was in direct conflict with the Amish way of life and that the state of Wisconsin could not therefore compel students to attend after the eighth grade.

Witters v. Washington Department Services for the Blind (1986): Witters, who suffered from a degenerative eye condition, sued to receive support from the state for his education to become a minister. Such aid would have been available to him if he had pursued a secular vocation, thus refusing him aid amounted to religious discrimination. The Supreme Court found that since the money was paid to him and not directly to the school it was not a violation of the Establishment Clause.

Zelman v. Simmons-Harris (2002): The Cleveland City School District's voucher plan offered publicly-financed aid for students to attend private, even religiously-sponsored, schools. A group of taxpayers sued, claiming that the voucher plan violated the Establishment Clause in that it provided public money for parochial education. The Supreme Court held that since the plan was part of the state's effort to provide an education for all children, and since the decision as to where a given child would attend school was not made by school officials, the plan did not violate the First Amendment.

Zobrest v. Catalina Foothills School District (1993): The parents of a deaf student attending a Catholic school sought to have the local school district provide an interpreter for their son even though he was enrolled in a private institution. When the school district refused, district and appeals courts both found that an interpreter would act in such a way as to promote the child's religious development and would therefore be a violation of the First Amendment. The Supreme Court ruled that the Establishment Clause did not prohibit the school district from providing an interpreter, since the decision to attend the private school was made by the family, not school or state officials.

About the Editors and Contributors

THE EDITORS

ANN W. DUNCAN is a Ph.D. Candidate in American Religious History at the University of Virginia. She received her M.A. in Religious Studies from the University of Virginia in 2005 and her B.A. from Duke University in 2000. Her research, publications, and conference presentations have focused on intersections of religion and politics, American Christianity in wartime, and, more recently, motherhood and American Christianity.

STEVEN L. JONES is Associate Professor of Sociology at Grove City College and is the former associate director of the Center on Religion and Democracy at the University of Virginia. He received his M.T.S. degree from Duke University and holds a Ph.D. from the University of Virginia. A former fellow of the Center for Children, Families, and the Law and the Institute for Advanced Studies in Culture, his main areas of academic interest are political sociology and family, state, and church conflicts. He is currently finishing a book on patriotism and church schooling in America.

THE CONTRIBUTORS

GORDON A. BABST, Ph.D., is Associate Professor of Political Science at Chapman University, where he teaches political philosophy and researches church-state issues in the context of liberal-democratic theory and practice. He is working on his second book, *Religious Rivals to American Freedoms*, which takes a critical look at political and legal deference to religion and religious belief.

LEE CANIPE holds an M.A. from the University of Virginia, a Master of Divinity from Duke University, and a Ph.D. from Baylor University. He is pastor of the Murfreesboro Baptist Church in Murfreesboro, North Carolina, and also teaches in the Department of Religion and Philosophy at Chowan University. His research interests include Baptist history and the intersections between Christian faith and American culture. His articles have appeared in *American Baptist Quarterly*, *Baptist History and Heritage*, *Baptist Quarterly* (UK), and the *Journal of Church and State*.

MICHAEL COULTER, Ph.D., is Professor of Political Science at Grove City College. He is a co-editor of the *Encyclopedia of Catholic Social Thought, Social Science, and Social Policy* (Scarecrow Press). He has contributed to, among others, *Perspectives on Political Science*, the *Journal of Markets and Morality*, the *Christian Scholar's Review*, the *Encyclopedia of American Religion and Politics*, and the *Encyclopedia of the Supreme Court*.

JASON R. EDWARDS received his Ph.D. in the History and Philosophy of Education from the University of Kentucky in 2003. He currently serves as Assistant Professor of History and Education at Grove City College. A Salvatori Fellow for the Intercollegiate Studies Institute, Edwards's research interests center on Agrarian philosophy in Western Civilization. He has published numerous entries for volumes on higher education and military history and is a regular contributor to *The Center for Vision and Values*.

MARK EDWARD GAMMON is Assistant Professor of Religion at Simpson College in Indianola, IA. He previously served as a research associate at the Institute for Communitarian Policy Studies at the George Washington University in Washington, D.C., where he worked on a number of public policy issues dealing with the relationship between individual rights and community responsibilities. He earned a Doctorate in Theological Ethics from Boston College.

J. DAVID HOLCOMB is Associate Professor of History and Political Science at the University of Mary Hardin-Baylor in Belton, Texas. He received the A.B. in History and Philosophy from William Jewell College and the M.A. and Ph.D. in Church-State Studies from Baylor University. He teaches courses in constitutional law, political theory, and church-state relations. His publications have appeared in the *Journal of Church and State*, *Baptist History and Heritage*, and the *Encyclopedia of American Religion and Politics*.

WILLIAM LESTER is Assistant Professor in the Department of Political Science and Public Administration at Jacksonville State University. He is a Civitas Scholar through The Center for Public Justice. His research interests include religion and politics, public organizational theory, ethics, and leadership studies.

Index

Abington Township v. Schempp. See School District of Abington Township, Pennsylvania v. Schempp
academic freedom, 19
access to facilities, 88, 187. *See also* Equal Access Act
accommodationist perspective, 75–76, 170–72
ACLU (American Civil Liberties Union), 24–25, 112–13, 134
"additional obligation," vii, 185
administrators: challenges for, 96–99; religious activities of, 88; requests to opt out and, 95–96; sources of conflict and confusion for, 92–94
adoption of children, 7, 11
Agassiz, Louis, 21
Agostini v. Felton, 137, 160, 179
Aguilar v. Felton, 160, 179
aid to religiously affiliated higher education: future of, 164, 173; *Locke v. Davey* and, 161–64; neutrality test, 160–61; overview of, 155; pervasively sectarian test, 155–60
America 2000 initiative, 36
American Center for Law and Justice, 113, 114
American Christians: political influence of, 118–19; pornography, children, and, 119–20; sexually explicit media and, 115–16, 122; sexual morality and, 116–18. *See also* conservative Christians
American Civil Liberties Union (ACLU), 24–25, 112–13, 134
American Episcopalian Church, 15 n.8
American identity, 48
American Library Association, 113, 186
American schooling debates, 20–22
Americans United for the Separation of Church and State, 131, 134
Amish, 95, 187
Aristotle, 18
Arizona School Tuition Organization Tax Credit, 144–45
Arkansas, 35
Ashcroft v. ACLU, 112–13
assignments: introducing religious viewpoint into, 89; opting out of, 94–96
Augustine of Hippo, 4–5
Augustine (saint), 116–17, 118

baccalaureate ceremonies at public schools, 92
Barnette case *(West Virginia State Board of Education v. Barnette),* 56–57, 78, 94–95, 187
Basic Educational Opportunity Grants, 182
Behe, Michael, 38
Bellamy, Francis, 49
Bethel School District No. 403 v. Fraser, 80–81, 180

Bible: Bryan and, 26–27; New Testament, 4, 117; Old Testament, family in, 2–3; study groups in public schools, 185
bigamy, 185
Bill of Rights, 30–31
Biological Science Curriculum Study, 30
Bird, Wendell, 37
Black, Hugo, 31, 58, 107, 134
Blackmun, Harry, 159
Blaine, James G., 129
Blaine Amendments, 129, 138, 152
blood ties, concern for, 6–7
Blum, Virgil, 130
Board of Education of Westside Community Schools v. Mergens, 83, 171, 180, 187
Board of Education v. Allen, 33, 180
Bob Jones University v. United States, 168–69, 180
Brennan, William J., 97–98, 106, 107–8
Breyer, Stephen, 161
broadcast decency standards, 110–11
Brown v. Board of Education, 180
Bryan, William Jennings, 19, 23, 25, 26–27, 28
Burger, Warren, 107
Bush, George H. W., 60
Bush, George W., 36, 63
Bush, Jeb, 141
Butler Act, 24, 26, 27–28, 32

Capitalism and Freedom (Friedman), 130
Cardozo, Benjamin, 107
Carlin, George, 110–11
Carnegie Foundation for the Advancement of Teaching, 153–54
Catholic Church, sexual ethics of, 117
Catholic League for Religious and Civil Rights, 130
Chesterton, G. K., 28, 41
Child Online Protection Act, 112–13
children: adoption of, 7, 11; American Christians, pornography, and, 119–20; legitimacy of, 11; protecting from obscenity, 110–13; rights of, 122–23
Children's Internet Protection Act, 113
Christian clubs at schools, 187
Christianity and family, 4–5. *See also* American Christians

Christmas display, 184
Church of Jesus Christ of Latter-day Saints, 185
Church of Jesus Christ of Latter-day Saints v. Amos, 165–66
citizenship training: dialogue in public schools and, 98; public schools and, 48; Supreme Court and, 53–54
A Civic Biology (Hunter), 22
Civil Rights Act, 154, 165
Clark, Tom, 170
clothing, religious, 92–94
Cold War, 29–30
College of William and Mary, 149, 151
colleges. *See* higher education institutions
Colorado Opportunity Contract Pilot Program, 142
Columbia Union College, 162–64
Committee for Public Education v. Nyquist, 130, 139, 180–81
common school model, 20, 128
Communications Decency Act, 111–12
communism and Pledge of Allegiance, 50–51, 52
communitarian interest and Pledge of Allegiance, 53–56
community standards of obscenity, 108–9
Comstock, Anthony, 105–6
Comstock Law, 105, 106
Concannon, John, 53
conservative Christians: Pledge of Allegiance and, 60–61; sexually explicit media and, 114. *See also* American Christians
Constitutional literacy, 97
construction of facilities, 186
Corporation of the Presiding Bishop v. Amos, 181
creationism: belief in, 40; fundamentalism and, 37; *Lemon* test and, 33; materialism and, 38; religion and, 33–34; scientific arguments of, 34–35
cultural diversity and Pledge of Allegiance, 64–65
cultural understandings of family, 12–13
Curti, Merle, 49–50

Darrow, Clarence, 24, 25, 26, 27, 28
Darwin, Charles, 20–22

Darwin on Trial (Johnson), 37–38
Davey, Joshua, 162
Dawkins, Richard, 40
Dayton, Tennessee, 24, 25
Dembski, William, 38
Democritus, 18
Dennett, Daniel, 40
deviance, sexual, 115
Dewey, John, 48
discrimination: in hiring, 165–68, 181; racial, 168–69
disestablishment, as incomplete, 123
disruptive behavior, definition of, 80
division of labor within family, 5–6
Dobson, James, 63, 113
Docherty, George M., 51
Dornan, Robert, 61
Douglas, William O., 107, 158
dress code, 93–94
Dukakis, Michael, 60

Education Amendments of 1972, 154
Edwards v. Aguillard, 36, 37, 181
EEOC v. Mississippi College, 167, 168
EEOC v. Southwestern Baptist Theological Seminary, 167–68
Eighteenth Amendment, 42 n.15
Eisenhower, Dwight D., 30, 53, 58
Elementary and Secondary Education Act, 154
Elk Grove Unified School District v. Newdow, 62–64, 181
employment, discrimination, and private institutions, 165–68
Engel v. Vitale, 31, 58, 78–79, 130, 181
Epperson, Susan, 32
Epperson v. Arkansas, 32–33, 181–82
Equal Access Act, 81–85, 171, 180
"equal time" legislation, 34, 35–36
equal treatment test, 160–61
Establishment Clause: ACLU and, 25; incorporation of, 30–31; *Lemon* test and, 33; Ohio and, 138, 139; of Wisconsin Constitution, 135; *Zelman v. Simmons-Harris* and, 140–41, 146
Everson v. Board of Education of Ewing Township: no-aid principle of, 129, 158; overview of, 182; precedent set by, 31; U.S. Department of Education guidelines and, 86
evolution: Biological Science Curriculum Study and, 30; impact of Darwin's arguments about, 20–21; legislation opposing teaching of, 22, 24, 29, 32; media and, 39–40; *Tennessee vs. John Scopes* and, 18, 25–29
excessive entanglements, 135, 155–60

facilities: construction of, 186; use of, 170–71
Falwell, Jerry, 160
family: contemporary American, 9–13; definitions of, 1–2; functions of, 6–9; historical overview of, 2–6; liberalism and, 13–14
Family Research Council, 113
"family values," 117–23
Federal Communications Commission v. Pacifica Foundation, 110–11
Federal Defense of Marriage Act, 11
Ferguson, Homer, 52
filtering software, 186
First Amendment: religious expression in public schools and, 77–81; violence and, 121. See also Establishment Clause
flag, salutes to, 184, 187. See also Pledge of Allegiance
Florida Opportunity Scholarship Program, 141–42
Fortas, Abraham, 84
Fourteenth Amendment, 30–31
Frankfurter, Felix, 54–55
Fraser, Matthew, 180
freedom of association, 88, 97–98
Freedom of Choice in Education (Blum), 130
freedom of speech: in classroom, 19; lewd language and, 180; in public schools, 79–81; restrictions on, 103–4; school assemblies and extracurricular events and, 90; war protest and, 186. See also obscenity
free exercise rights: in public schools, 96–98; Supreme Court and, 79–80
Freethinkers of America, 68 n.45
Friedman, Milton, 129–30

functions of family, 6–9
fundamentalism: creationism and, 37; in early twentieth century, 29; progressivism and, 23–25; religious, and functions of family, 8; scientific, 32, 33–37

Gay Rights Coalition of the Georgetown University Law Center, 169, 173
General Education Board, 153–54
Georgetown University, 169, 173
German educational approach, 153
G.I. Bill, 154
Ginsburg v. New York, 110
Goals 2000 initiative, 36–37
Gobitis, Lillian and William, 54
God, ambiguous definition of, 61–62
Goodwin, Alfred T., 62–63
government regulation of private institutions: employment and discrimination, 165–68; tax exemption and discrimination, 168–69
graduation exercises, student prayer at, 91–92
Grand Rapids School District v. Ball, 160, 182
Gray, Asa, 22
Great Awakening, 151
Greece, ancient, 3, 18–19
Grove City College v. Bell, 182

harm: concept of, 104; types of, 113–17
Harrison, Benjamin, 49
Hart, Luke, 51
Harvard, 151
Haynes, Stephen, 153
Hazelwood v. Kuhlmeier, 81
Hebrew Bible, family in, 2–3
Heins, Marjorie, 114–15
Heraclitus, 18
Herberg, Will, 58
Herschel, John, 21
Hicklin test *(Regina v. Hicklin)*, 104–5, 106, 110
Higginbotham, Paul, 133
Higher Education Facilities Act, 154, 157
higher education institutions: accommodation of religion in, 170–72; aid to religiously affiliated, 155–64, 173; controversies regarding, 149–51; government regulation of religiously affiliated, 165–69; in historical context, 151–54
Hill, Morton A., 113
hiring and religious discrimination, 165–68, 181
Hoover, J. Edgar, 66 n.13
human sexuality, religious constraints on, 6. *See also* sexual morality
Hunter, George W., *A Civic Biology*, 22
Hunt v. McNair, 163–64
Huxley, Thomas, 21–22

Illinois Educational Expenses Tax Credit, 144
immigration and Pledge of Allegiance, 49–50
incorporation of Establishment Clause, 31
Inherit the Wind (movie), 17, 41
instructional time, prayer during, 89
intellectual freedom, 19, 28
Intelligent Design, 37–39, 40
Internet and sexually explicit material, 109, 111
interracial relationships, 184
IRS section 501(c)(3), 168–69

Jackson, Janet, 111
Jackson, Robert H., 56–57
Jackson v. Benson, 134–35
Jacobellis v. Ohio, 106–7, 108, 182
Jefferson, Thomas, 152
Jehovah's Witnesses, 54, 56, 184
jewelry, religious, 92–94
Johnson, Phillip E., *Darwin on Trial*, 37–38
Jones, John E., III, 39
Joyce, James, *Ulysses*, 106

Kansas, 39
Kennedy, Anthony, 62, 140, 172
Keyishian v. Board of Regents, 97, 182
Kitzmiller et al. v. Dover Area School District, 39, 182–83
Knights of Columbus, 51
Kotterman v. Killian, 144

Lamb's Chapel v. Center Moriches School District, 77, 183
land grants, 152
Larsen, Edward, 29
Larson, Edward J., *Summer for the Gods,* 25
law, religion, and family, 10–12
Lee v. Weisman, 31–32, 62–63, 91–92, 183
legitimacy of children, 11
Lemon test: applications of, 180, 181, 184–85; employment and, 166; excessive entanglements and, 155–60; Milwaukee Parental Choice Program and, 134–35; Ohio Pilot Project Scholarship Program and, 137–38, 139; parts of, 33, 183
Lemon v. Kurtzman, 75, 156, 183. *See also Lemon* test
Leoles v. Landers, 53–54, 183
Leopold, Nathan, 28
Levine, Judith, 114–15
Liberty University, 160
libraries, filtering software at, 113, 186
Locke v. Davey, 161–62, 173, 183–84
Loeb, Richard, 28
Louisiana, 35–36
Loving v. Virginia, 184
loyalty oath, 182
Lynch v. Donnelly, 69 n.59, 184

macroevolution, 19–20
Maguire v. Marquette University, 166
Maine school voucher program, 143
marriage and religion, 10–11
Marsden, George, 152–53
materialism, 38, 39
McCollum v. BOE, 78, 184
McLean, Bill, 35
media: evolutionism and, 39–40; sexually explicit, 115–16, 122
Meek v. Pittenger, 156, 184
Mellen v. Bunting, 173
Mencken, H. L., 26, 27
microevolution, 41 n.3
Miller v. California, 107
Milwaukee Parental Choice Program (MPCP), 132–35
Minersville School District v. Gobitis, 54–56, 184, 187

Minnesota education tax credit, 143–44
Mitchell v. Helms, 160–61, 164, 184
moments of silence, 88–89
"The Monkey Trial," 18, 25–29
Monsma, Stephen, 155
Morality in Media, 113
Mormon Church, 14 n.1, 185
Morrill Act, 152
Motion Picture Association of America ratings system, 120–21
Motz, Diana Gribbon, 64
Mozert v. Hawkins City Board of Education, 95–96
Mueller v. Allen, 144–45, 184–85
Murray, John Courtney, 116

National Defense Education Act, 30
A Nation at Risk report, 36, 131
naturalism, distrust of, 38
natural law tradition, 116
natural selection, theory of, 21
neutrality perspective, 75
neutrality test in higher education, 160–61
Newdow, Michael, 62, 181
Newdow decision, 62–64, 181
New Testament, 4, 117
Nicholls v. Mayor of Lynn, 183
Nietzsche, Friedrich, 28
noninstructional time, prayer during, 87–88
non-preferentialist view, 76

Oakley, Ronald, 50
Oakman, Charles, 52
obscenity: community standards and, 108–9; legal history of, 104–8; protecting children from, 110–13; restrictions on, 103–4
O'Connor, Sandra Day, 112, 140, 161
Of Pandas and People textbook, 39
Ohio EdChoice program, 142–43
Ohio Pilot Project Scholarship Program, 136–41
Old Testament, family in, 2–3
opting out of assignments and activities, 79, 94–96
original sin, doctrine of, 117

origins, debate over: in ancient Greece, 18–19; Bryan and, 23–24; in 1980s, 35–36; in 1990s, 36; overview of, 17–18; scientific fundamentalists and, 32; status of, 39–41
Our Country (Strong), 49
Overton, William R., 35
Owens, Bill, 142

parens patriae, 110
parents, rights of, 122–23
Paris Adult Theatre I v. Slaton, 107
parochial schools, 179, 188
patriarchy, 10
Paul (saint), 4, 116, 118
Paul VI (pope), 117
Peay, Austin, 24
Pennsylvania education tax credit, 145
People for the American Way, 134
pervasively sectarian test, 155–60, 163–64
Pierce v. Society of Sisters, vii, 129, 185
Plato, 18, 19
Pledge of Allegiance: adding "under God" to, 51–53; American identity and, 48; communism and, 50–51, 52; conscientious objections to, 53–57; cultural diversity and, 64–65; expulsion for refusing to recite, 183; in historical context, 49–50; *Lee v. Weisman* and, 62–63; *Newdow* case and, 62–64, 181; quasi-theological dimension to, 57–61; *Sherman* verdict and, 61–62; as source of controversy, 47, 48–49, 65; states and, 64
political activism and family, 7–8
politicians, religious affiliation of, 10
polygamy, 14 n.1
pornography: cultivation of Christian character and, 119–20; exposure to, 114–15
PPRA (Protection of Pupil Rights Amendment), 94–96
prayer: *Engel v. Vitale and,* 31, 58, 78–79, 130; before football games, 185–86; Pledge of Allegiance and, 57–61; at public school events, 183; in public school system, 31, 58, 186; U.S. Department of Education guidelines regarding, 85–92
primary effect test, 134–35

Prime v. Loyola University of Chicago, 166
Princeton, 151
Prince v. Jacoby, 83, 185
progressivism: educational content and, 29; history of, 22–25; religious, 40–41; schools and, 20; secular, 29–33
protecting children from obscenity, 110–13
Protection of Pupil Rights Amendment (PPRA), 94–96
publications, religious, on campus, 171–72, 185
public schools: Equal Access Act and, 81–85; founding of, 20–22; freedom of speech in, 79–81; free exercise rights in, 97–98; minority viewpoints and, 73–74; prayer in, 31, 58, 183, 186; as quintessentially American experience, 73; religious expression in, 77–85, 92–94, 96–99; teaching of "truth" in, 28–29

Rabault, Louis, 51, 52
racial discrimination, 168–69
Radwan, Edmund, 51
ratings system, 120–21
Reagan, Ronald, 35, 131
Reed, Lowell, 113
Regina v. Hicklin, 104–5, 106, 110
Rehnquist, William, 63–64, 112, 140–41, 162
religion and higher education in historical context, 151–54
religious expression in public schools: challenges for administrators, 96–99; Equal access Act and, 81–85; First Amendment and, 77–81; sources of conflict and confusion, 92–94
religious progressivism, 40–41
Republican Platform and school choice, 132
Reynolds v. United States, 14 n.1, 185
Ridge, Thomas, 145
right to association, 88
Robertson, Pat, 63, 113
Rockefeller Foundation, 153–54
Roemer v. Maryland Public Works Board, 158–59, 163–64, 185
Rome, family in ancient, 3–4

Rosenberger v. University of Virginia, 171–73, 185
Roth, Samuel, 106
Roth v. United States, 105, 111
Russo v. Central School District No. 1, 59
Ryan, James, 139–40

same-sex parenthood, 7, 8–9
Santa Fe Independent School District v. Doe, 32, 90–91, 185–86
Scalia, Antonin, 140
scholarships for theology programs, 183–84
school choice debate, 127–28, 131, 145–46. *See also* school vouchers
School District of Abington Township, Pennsylvania v. Schempp: on academic study of religion, 170; *Lemon* test and, 33; mandatory requirements and, 58; opting out and, 79; overview of, 179; primary effect and, 31; religion of secularism and, 32; voucher movement and, 130
school vouchers: history of, 128–31; Milwaukee Parental Choice Program (MPCP), 132–35; Ohio Pilot Project Scholarship Program, 136–41; statewide programs, 141–43
science education, 30, 37
scientific approach to knowledge, 153
scientific fundamentalism, 32, 33–37
Scopes, John T., 25, 26, 28, 186
Scott, Henry, 105
Section 702 exemption, 165–66
secular progressivism, 29–33
"See You At The Pole" events, 88
separationist approach, 74–75
separation of church and state, viewpoints on, 74–76
Seventeenth Amendment, 42 n.17
sexual identity, 115
sexual morality, 6, 116–18, 119–20
sexual orientation, 169
Sherman, Rob, 61
Sherman verdict, 61–62
Shermer, Michael, 21
Simmons-Harris v. Goff, 136–37
single parenthood, 7, 8–9
Sixteenth Amendment, 42 n.16
social contract theory, 5

Social Gospel movement, 105, 114
Souter, David, 172
South Carolina College, 152
South Carolina Educational Facilities Act, 158
Soviet Union and secular progressivism, 29–30
Stalin, Josef, 50
Starr, Kenneth, 134
states: constitutional prohibitions of, 161–64; Fourteenth Amendment and, 30–31
state universities, growth toward, 153–54
Steinmetz, Donald, 134
Stevens, John Paul, 63, 90–91
Stewart, Potter, 107, 182
Stone, Harlan, 55
Strong, Josiah, *Our Country,* 49
student, religious expression by, 76
student publications, funding of, 171–72, 185
subsidiarity, principle of, 108
Summer for the Gods (Larson), 25
supernatural explanations of events, 38–39
Supreme Court: Communications Decency Act and, 112; consideration of case by, 140; higher education institutions and, 150, 155; neutrality perspective and, 75; obscenity and, 106–8, 111; Pledge of Allegiance cases and, 53–57; public school and religion cases brought before, 78–81; religious schools and, 129, 130; school choice and, 128, 140–41. *See also specific cases; specific justices*
symbolic religious expression, 93–94

tax credits for private school enrollment, 127, 128, 131, 143–45
tax exemption for religious institutions, 168–69
tax-exempt status, 180, 187
teachers: as arbiters of acceptable religious discussion, 89–90; religious activities of, 88
technology, recourse to, and functions of family, 8, 13
Ten Commandments monument, 186
Tennessee vs. John Scopes, 18, 25–29, 186
textbook publishers and evolution, 29

textbooks, loan of, 184
Thelin, John, 153
theology programs, scholarships for, 183–84, 187
Thomas, Clarence, 140
Thompson, Tommy, 133
Tiahrt Amendment, 94–96
Tilton v. Richardson, 157–58, 163–64, 186
Tinker v. Des Moines Independent Community School District, 79–80, 81, 84, 92–93, 186
Title VII exemptions, 165–68
Tocqueville, Alexis de, 65
transportation to and from school, 31, 182
true liberty, war for, 41
Tudor v. Board of Education of Rutherford, 78
tuitioning, 143
tuition tax credits, 127, 128, 131, 143–45

Ulysses (Joyce), 106
unanimity, strength of nation and, 57
United States Conference of Catholic Bishops, 140
United States v. American Library Association, 113, 186
universities. *See* higher education institutions
University of Missouri, 149–50, 170–71
University of North Carolina, 152
University of Virginia, 152, 171–72
U.S. Department of Education guidelines regarding public school prayer, 85–92

Van Orden v. Perry, 186
Vermont school voucher program, 143
violence, 120–23
voucher plans, 187–88. *See also* school vouchers

Wallace v. Jaffree, 31, 186
Walz v. Tax Commission, 168, 187
Warren, Earl, 32
wedding rings, 3
Weeks, Kent, 159–60
West Virginia State Board of Education v. Barnette, 56–57, 78, 94–95, 187
Wiccan movement, 65
Widmar v. Vincent, 82, 171, 187
Williams, Karen J., 64
Wills, Garry, 59, 60–61
Wisconsin v. Yoder, 95, 187
Witters v. Washington Department Services for the Blind, 160, 187
women: political activism for, 7–8; pornography and, 119–20; technology and, 13

Yale, 151

Zedong, Mao, 50
Zelman v. Simmons-Harris, 140–41, 146, 187–88
Zobrest v. Catalina Foothills School District, 137, 188
zoning questions and obscenity, 108–9
Zorach v. Clauson, 96

REFERENCE
ELIHU BURRITT LIBRARY
CENTRAL CONNECTICUT STATE UNIVERSITY
NEW BRITAIN, CONNECTICUT